For Christine

RADICAL
VICTORIANS

RADICAL VICTORIANS

THE WOMEN AND MEN WHO DARED TO THINK DIFFERENTLY

JAMES HOBSON

PEN & SWORD **HISTORY**

AN IMPRINT OF PEN & SWORD BOOKS LTD.
YORKSHIRE – PHILADELPHIA

First published in Great Britain in 2022 by
PEN AND SWORD HISTORY
An imprint of
Pen & Sword Books Ltd
Yorkshire – Philadelphia

ISBN 978 1 39900 826 6

Typeset in Times New Roman 11.5/14 by
SJmagic DESIGN SERVICES, India.
Printed and bound in the UK by CPI Group (UK) Ltd.

Pen & Sword Books Limited incorporates the imprints of Atlas, Archaeology,
Aviation, Discovery, Family History, Fiction, History, Maritime, Military, Military
Classics, Politics, Select, Transport, True Crime, Air World, Frontline Publishing,
Leo Cooper, Remember When, Seaforth Publishing, The Praetorian Press,
Wharncliffe Local History, Wharncliffe Transport, Wharncliffe True Crime and
White Owl.

For a complete list of Pen & Sword titles please contact
PEN & SWORD BOOKS LIMITED
47 Church Street, Barnsley, South Yorkshire, S70 2AS, England
E-mail: enquiries@pen-and-sword.co.uk
Website: www.pen-and-sword.co.uk

Or
PEN AND SWORD BOOKS
1950 Lawrence Rd, Havertown, PA 19083, USA
E-mail: Uspen-and-sword@casematepublishers.com
Website: www.penandswordbooks.com

Contents

Introduction

'The History of the Victorian Age will never be written:
we know too much about it'
Lytton Strachey *Eminent Victorians* (1918)

What was a 'Victorian radical'? Surely the long reign of Queen Victoria and the vague nature of the word 'radical' means that a book of this size cannot do justice to the subject?

With a working definition of radical as 'one who thought differently from the majority and therefore wished life to be different', there are indeed, too many Victorian radicals for a book of this size. So, a process of selection is necessary, and this is where the vast size of the Victorian era comes to our rescue. The book is about radical Victorians whose ideas were *not* much acted on during her sixty-three-year reign. These radicals changed the future; a future they (mostly) did not see themselves. They may have reached important milestones in their campaigns, but never lived to be totally vindicated and celebrated; some are waiting still; some perhaps do not even deserve to be celebrated.

So, there is no room in this book for Edwin Chadwick, a public health visionary, as his views had become mainstream by the death of Queen Victoria; factory reformers had chased young children from factories; Charles Bazalgette's sewers had been built. The Chartists of the 1830s could see history turning in their direction by 1900. Florence Nightingale died a national treasure, with the government hanging on to her every word despite being a pain in the side of the War Office in the 1850s. Charles Darwin the evolutionary biologist is absent from this book; Darwinism had triumphed by the time the old queen died, but some of his followers, with even more radical conclusions, do have a place in the book.

In other ways, our radicals are a mixed bag. Some of their ideas, like eugenics, repulse many people today. Atheism, socialism and republicanism are matters of opinion, but their relevance cannot be doubted. Spiritualism, in the meaning of actively seeking out communication with the dead rather than the concept of spirituality, is alive and well, if not very reputable. Some ideas, like cremation and birth control, have shifted into the area of practical personal preference, although there is a philosophy and ideology behind these subjects as well. As well as women's social and political rights, the book covers areas that attracted people of 'enhanced sensibility' – vivisection, vegetarianism and animal rights.

Some radicals struggled to produce newspapers that the ordinary citizens failed to read and held meetings that contained tens of fellow believers. They still managed to regularly fall out with each other, but their ideas became a part of mainstream economic, political and social discussion in the twentieth century. One or two have broken into the standard history books, but most are quite obscure. To use a cliché, they were ahead of their time, and on the whole this made their life very difficult. In order to be a Victorian radical, you needed resilience, bloody mindedness and, in the case of many of them, an inability to suffer fools gladly and total confidence in your own opinions. They are not, generally speaking, ideal desert island companions.

The good news is that there are women in this book as well, put there by the fact that they made strenuous efforts to improve women's rights, and by doing so put themselves outside mainstream opinion and condemned themselves to constant struggle. They were mostly clever women from privileged backgrounds whose fathers were principled, apathetic or dead enough to allow their daughters an education.

The book focuses on the intellectual elite who were organisers, propagandists and authors. With a few exceptions, there are more resolutions than riots, more chairing the subcommittee than manning the barricades, and very few people who were born poor. Taken as a group, they are very middle class indeed; the aristocracy was too entrenched in its privilege, and the poor too brutalised and disempowered to take an active part. They were the first metropolitan liberals, the progenitors of the chattering classes; it's a class that has never gone away.

Behind their socialism, spiritualism, vegetarianism, free press and free thought were the wider themes that this book covers; the dissolution of firm religious belief in one of history's most religious societies; the effects of industrial capitalism on the mind as well as the spirit; and the reaction against the dominance and hypocrisy of men.

The structure is simple – each one is a radical idea through the prism of one or two of its proponents. Most of them crossed over into other radical areas, and this has not been overlooked, but one radical idea has been given prominence. Other radical thinkers, not all of them less important, are mentioned *en passant*. Some of them appear in the book as background when they interact with other main characters; for the most part, their image as a bit player is an illusion caused by the need to put the emphasis on others; another book could have been written with a different name for each chapter. Perhaps it should be.

Chapter One

Vegetarianism
Anna Kingsford

In a freezing February in 1888, a vicar's wife lay dying at the tragically early age of forty-one. Her husband was the vicar at Atcham, Shrewsbury, but her deathbed scene unfolded at their rented flat at 15, Wynnstay Gardens, Kensington, a newly-built mansion block of apartments for the respectable middle classes. She had known she was dying since the previous November, but it was taking a very long time. Recuperation in the South of France and the Italian Riviera had not helped. She had suffered with her lungs all through her life; now they were killing her.

When the crisis came, she was attended by a Catholic priest and the last rites were administered. She was buried modestly at her husband's church in the presence of close friends, and her grave can still be seen today, placed prudently at a high point above the waterline of the nearby river, as directed in her will. In the lottery of Victorian mortality, she predeceased her mother Elizabeth Ann, who died three weeks later. These were the last days of Anna Kingsford, born Annie Bonus, in 1846. The death certificate revealed nothing; she was a wife of Algernon Godfrey Kingsford, a clerk in Holy Orders; she died of Pulmonary Phthisis – Tuberculosis – a scourge of the Victorian era.

This sounds dull and conventional. It was neither.

One of Anna's regrets was that her illness prevented her from writing her annual prayer of remembrance for her guinea pig Rufus; one of her main consolations was that Rufus's replacement, Piggy, had died on Boxing Day 1887 and had therefore gone to heaven ahead of her. Rufus had died on August 15, 1885, the assumption of the Blessed Mary, and this, to Kingsford, was not a coincidence. She died a Roman Catholic in theory but never in practice; she accepted the last rites merely for the experience. Her husband was a Church of England vicar. This was par for the course for Anna Kingsford; she defied classification. 'Medically speaking, I know that I am dying' was reputed to be some of her last words; this was a deliberate use of words; she was not dying in any way that she thought meaningful.

She was not obscure. The tragic news was recorded in the newspapers, and the second clue was the tone of these obituaries:

> Death of Doctor Anna Kingsford
> By the death of Mrs. Anna Kingsford, M.D. which has just taken place in London, after a consumptive illness of many months' duration...

Anna was the eighteenth British women to qualify as a doctor (1880), which was enough to make her significant at the time, though not quite significant enough for her profession to appear on the death certificate.

The obituaries continued:

> a remarkable figure in certain sections of metropolitan society is removed from the world.

'Remarkable' and 'certain sections' were euphemisms; it was shorthand for a woman with too many unconventional opinions; a middle class vicar's wife who ought to have known better and fifty years earlier would have not have been heard at all. The obituaries acknowledged her importance but mocked her as an outlier, a maverick and a deluded extremist. This conclusion has not shifted much in the century and a half since her death.

Apart from some recent revival of interest, she is a forgotten woman. This is undeserved. The reasons for her obscurity are many; she was a woman; she was a woman whose ideas did not prosper until a century after her death, so when her principles became popular she was given none of the credit. Some of her other ideas, the ones that were the most dear to her, are regarded today as unconventional and this means that she has not, like other radicals featured in this book, been able to claim the mantle of a prophet. The final reason for her obscurity is an egotistical man who thought he knew her better than she did herself. Kingsford *was* both rash and unpredictable; but at least she was self-aware and often surprised herself.

> It is quite true that I find myself much the most interesting person I know.
>
> It is because I am such a puzzle to myself and I want to be explained.

She was incapable of being controlled by the normal rules, defied classification and could not be pigeon-holed.

She reacted extremely to the traditional education offered to middle class girls. Her Brighton finishing school failed to turn her into a marriage-friendly material. Her main objection was the suppression of emotion and feeling. Learning Shakespeare became merely reading it aloud, bad enough for a girl who read veraciously, but worse when she was reprimanded for pretending to be the character. She troubled the authorities by asking religious questions that were not satisfactorily answered. She saw an unambitious education system designed merely to provide superficial knowledge of preselected subjects to avoid social embarrassment. An unchallenging education was the first stage in women's inferiority. The antidote to education was her own reading. Two years after her short two-year spell at school, her poems about love, loss and the nature of the soul were being reviewed by the *Athenaeum*.

She campaigned actively and fearlessly from the late 1860s and crammed a lot into her four decades. She was brave, forthright and charismatic, could hold an audience in the palm of her hand and was an accomplished writer of both fiction and non-fiction. She supported the women's campaign for property rights and the vote. She rejected the outward form of the Church of England as insufficient to her spiritual needs. She was an anti-vivisectionist as well as a proselytising vegetarian, which was the thing she was most remembered for at her death. She was, according to one paper 'addicted to vegetarianism'.[1]

Her radicalism was aided by the fact that her family were rich. Anna was allowed to follow her interests after the death of her father John Bonus in 1865. She had around £800 a year to live on, enough to do nothing with her life if she had chosen to. The first stage of this life of domesticity was marriage, and her mother rightly saw her as an excellent prospect. The family were rich, successful and prosperous and Anna was intelligent, strikingly beautiful and financially secure.

Her choice of husband was her first cousin Algernon 'Algie' Kingsford, a mild-mannered clerk who had recently entered Litchfield Theological

College – a poor man's route into the Church of England, much less prestigious than the traditional route via the ancient universities. Her mother was aghast at the prospect of a prospective husband who might as well have had 'curate forever' written on his forehead because of his lack of qualifications, connections, and family money. His father had committed suicide in 1852 by cutting his throat, and the stigma passed down the family.

The rich and respectable family reacted in the traditional way to such youthful flings, but without the traditional success. Her mother planned to send her to Switzerland with other girls for distraction and a boring elderly relative to ensure that distraction did not become bad behaviour. Kingsford was having none of it. She was able to exploit rigid Victorian rules about conduct before marriage by eloping with Algie unchaperoned for two weeks, thus making marriage inevitable. Algie and Anna married on the last day of 1867 in the parish church of comfortable, middle class St Leonard's-on-Sea, an event that was recorded three days later in the *Times*.

Many of our Victorian radicals had little good to say about marriage in the nineteenth century, so when they did form a relationship, it tended to be unconventional. This was certainly the case with Anna and Algie. For a start, she chose him and not the other way around, and the fact Algie promised never to impede her career was one of the main reasons that she married him. They agreed to have only one child, and Eadith Bonus Kingsford was born later the same year, named after the Anglo-Saxon queen and wife of Edward the Confessor, Edith of Wessex.

Their marriage was platonic from that point. According to her friend Florence Fenwick Miller, this was a lifestyle choice rather than a health issue. Her life was not going to be wasted on constant reproduction. Anna would be outspoken, independent, often selfish and a creator of events, not a follower of them. For the rest of their lives, they lived as brother and sister in a relationship where her values and opinions counted as much as his, and probably more so. This was the inversion of a traditional Victorian marriage.

She had started agitating before her marriage, and she did so through writing. In 1868, she supported women's suffrage in a pamphlet. She supported the campaign for a Married Women's Property Act, to allow women control of their property after marriage, despite the not needing such a law for herself. Her father had made special legal provisions to protect his daughter's inheritance of the kind only the rich could afford to make.

She was often self-centred and unthinking and caused embarrassment and pain. One event, minor for her but less so for others, was her flirtation with secularism, showing an interest in the Ladies Secular Club (1868) which counted Susannah Bradlaugh, wife of the infamous atheist Charles Bradlaugh, as one of its founding members. Bradlaugh was associated with the atheist rejection of religion – rather than mere freethought – and any association with him was a social death sentence.

While collecting names for the Ladies Secular Club, Kingsford passed on that of Emily Faithfull, a campaigner for women's employment, publisher and journalist, without asking Miss Faithfull whether she was a secularist or not. She wasn't; she had a horror of blasphemy. Her father was a vicar; she was politically a conservative and had been the queen's printer for nearly a decade. Kingsford could have found this out. Faithfull was so outraged that she sued the man who reported that she was an atheist. She gained forty shillings but more importantly, she was free from the slur of atheism. Unusually, despite clearly signing the founding document ('Mrs Ninon Kingsford Warrior Square') she later cried off claiming ill health, but it was probably family pressure. In any case, the whole incident was absurd as for much of her life; there was nobody less freethought and secular than Anna Kingsford.

In 1872, she used her privileged background to buy her way into a position of influence. She purchased *The Lady's Own Paper* with some of the £700 she had been left by her father. She changed the magazine overnight and without apology from 'a magazine of fashion, fiction, music, literature, drama and domestic economy' to a progressive journal.[2] The new masthead slogan 'A Journal of Taste, Progress and Thought' matched the content – temperance, women's rights, cruelty to animals and a sceptical view of male-dominated politics at Westminster.

One of the articles on vivisection was prefaced by Frances Power Cobbe and this sparked Kingsford's interest in the subject. Edition three contained a petition against vivisection and polite abuse about male MPs who objected to votes for women. There were only four editions in total. Established readers were lost before new ones could be gained, and Kingsford rejected advertisements that she disagreed with, like corsets or leather products. She was a life-long advocate of rational dress; 'girls are gravely mistaken if they believe that by deliberately abandoning the form of a human creature to assume that of an insect they are commending themselves to male admiration.'[3]

She was more successful as one of Britain's first women doctors, although she did not do it by obeying the rules. In 1873, she made the acquaintance of Florence Fenwick Miller, one of the few people impressed by the *Lady's Own Paper.* Miller was nineteen, from a comfortable middle class background and totally in agreement with Kingsford. Despite the age gap, it was Miller who was to become the mentor to her older friend.

Fenwick Miller's lower middle class mother had removed her from school at sixteen and kept her home to learn housework, housekeeping and while away her life with tea parties and social diversions. The daughter had other ideas, and in 1871 she persuaded her parents to allow her to join Sophia Jex-Blake's campaign to open Britain's medical schools to women and to seek matriculation at the University of Edinburgh. She passed her initial examinations with distinction. However, Edinburgh's powerful professors refused to allow women into their classes, so Miller studied medicine at the Ladies' Medical College, completed a clinical practice in midwifery, and set herself up in private practice from her mother's home – all before the age of twenty.

It was at this point that Fenwick Miller met Anna and Algie. They met for the first time at her mother's house, and Florence had gone to the effort of consulting a vegetarian friend about what would constitute a good meal; it was mushroom omelette and macaroni cheese, stewed apple with cream; one of the first consciously created vegetarian meals recorded in British history.

Fenwick Miller visited them in Shrewsbury in 1873, noticing the pleasing unorthodoxy of their marriage. This included religion. There were not many Church of England vicarages where the cleric's wife had a stature of the Madonna clad in blue robes and baby Jesus surrounded by candles in a permanent vigil.[4] She had converted to the 'roman religion', as the Victorian newspapers primly put it, in 1872. She had fallen out of faith with the established Christian church early in her life and had converted in order to exclude herself from helping her husband in his pastoral role and charitable role as a country vicar. She wished to avoid the daily grind of visiting the sick and attending church ('tracts, jellies, baby clothes and bazaars'); these were a distraction from her own intellectual endeavours; one of the qualifications for being a middle class radical Victorian woman was the refusal to live with boredom.

She was fascinated by some aspects of the Catholic faith; she claimed to have seen manifestations of the Virgin Mary and she adopted the name Mary Magdalen. She never actually practised her faith formally despite being confirmed by Cardinal Manning (1872); she fell out with the Pope on the subject of animal cruelty and the presence of a priest at her deathbed was contentious. She picked out the things she liked and never adhered to a dogma. An unpleasant interpretation would be that it looks like a 1960s, hippies 'pick 'n' mix' religion based on personal need, but in the 1870s it was innovative, contentious, brave and quite blasphemous.

Science was as much an interest as religion to the two women. Both were in agreement about vegetarianism and vivisection, but it was the younger woman who was more knowledgeable about physiology. It was these discussions that inspired Kingsford to study medicine in Paris, and she insisted that Fenwick Miller join her. She even enlisted the help of Charles Drysdale, Fenwick Miller's mentor and the brother of George Drysdale (Chapter Seven) but with no success.

Two years later, at the age of twenty-two, a radical men's working club invited Fenwick Miller to stand for election to the London School Board – a body responsible for the education of nearly half a million children. Fenwick Miller agreed and was elected to that post, which she held for nine years, and became one of many female radicals who took part in education and local government. Kingsford took a different route; she wanted to become a doctor, not for the usual humanitarian reasons, but to give more heft to her arguments. In the same way that she was a Catholic who rejected the Pope, she became a doctor who rejected science.

The medical bar in England was so complete that she had to do her studies at the Ecole de Médicine in Paris, following in the footsteps of Elizabeth Garrett, who had graduated from the same school four years earlier, in 1870. It was at this point she changed her name to Anna. Her intellectual efforts in the next six years were impressive, and the main obstacle was the question of vivisection, which was expected for training doctors, but not, luckily for Anna, specifically required in writing.

Vivisection was new and not common, except in French medical schools. It was the noise of dogs being experimented on that she heard first; the lecture rooms were next to the dissecting rooms. The response to her protests was contemptuous and unempathetic; 'Que voulez vous? C'est pour la science!' was the response of the arrogant old men who ran the institution. She hired private tutors to avoid the building. She was advised to keep quiet about the whole issue in case the rules were changed pre-emptively to stop her from qualifying; this, at least, she managed in the face of male provocation. She qualified in 1880. She opened a private practice in Park Lane; she did not register as a doctor, she did not need to in order to practise. It would be 1892 before women were allowed to join the British Medical Association. She is on the 1881 census, with a Swiss servant and her friend and constant companion Edward Maitland as visitor.

Kingsford was a radical woman doctor, embracing animal rights, vegetarianism and suffrage, living in an open and equal marriage, but is forgotten today because her name is an embarrassment to many. Late in her life she attended the Vegetarian Society's 'Great Meeting' at the Exeter Hall, London as guest of honour and said this:

> I always speak with the greatest delight and satisfaction in the presence of my friends and members of the Vegetarian Society. With them I am quite at my ease. I have no reservation, I have no dissatisfaction. This is not the case when I speak for my friends the Anti-Vivisectionists, the Anti-Vaccinationists, the Spiritualists, or the advocates of freedom for women … The vegetarian movement is the bottom and basis of all other movements towards Purity, Freedom, Justice, and Happiness.

She was a spiritualist and an anti-vaxxer. She was also a believer in eugenics – selective breeding to encourage the better part of society to reproduce. Her vegetarianism also seemed cranky and obsessive; she believed that not eating meat was the ultimate answer to all social problems. One key reason for her medical work was that it would add credibility to her campaign against meat-eating and cruelty to animals. In 1881, she republished her doctoral theses under the title *A Perfect Way in Diet*. All the ethical elements of vegetarianism, which had been removed at the insistence of her male examiners because it was unscientific, was put back in again. It was hardly surprising that Kingsford held such a low opinion of a medical profession that was only interested in the mundane materialist elements of life; her work was designed for a higher ambition, as the opening of her book testifies:

> By what habits and modes of life has humanity in the past reached its highest development?

The answer was vegetarianism, and the book had some strong arguments to make. Firstly, it regarded meat-eating as a modern phenomenon and that the solution was to return to a purer past. The subtitle was 'A Treaty Advocating the Return to the perfect Diet of Our Race'. The so-called Stone Age 'Paleo diet' is not new.

A Perfect Way was a diet book but went further. Eating meat affected the body and its functions, changing them for the worse; and it did the same for the mind. She condemned the slaughterhouse and animal transport because they demeaned and desensitised those who took part in them. You became a hypocrite because by eating meat you have deliberately ignored suffering and death; most people, even the most affluent, would have smelt and seen the butcher after a day's work – 'no flesh eater considers the slaughter house'.

Meat-eating was a visceral, murderous activity which led to male vices of cruelty and vice; men loved their meat, and women were demeaned by cooking and serving it. 'The super-eminence of man is the super eminence of pain'; and eating animals led to animal passions. Wasn't sex called 'carnal delights'? Meat stimulated the body and created other morally unacceptable appetites. *Kreophagy*, an ugly word for meat-eating that Kingsford seems to have invented, created genital stimulation that led to prostitution; it caused changes to the gastric system that encouraged alcoholism. To the argument that animals eat and prey on each other, and that it was 'nature', she argued that for most of the time 'nature was habit' and that man could improve himself by rising above such habits, and that flesh-eating was something that brought man down to the level of brutes. Being literally a strong and clever beast was not enough; there was more to life than physical gratification.

There were no upsides to meat-eating. Most of the strongest animals were herbivores; the fruit-eating gorilla could beat the kreaphagist lion in a fight; the mighty hippopotamus ate no meat. It was the same in great civilisations that were based on fruit, vegetables and grain, both in the past and those that existed now. The Roman gladiator lived on oatcakes and oil; Chilean copper miners ate figs, fruit and bread. Modern societies that were prosperous ate meat, just like the meat-eating and excess of the Roman Empire at its most corrupt. Meat was moral and bodily corruption. A spiritual person would not eat meat. Purity of diet was pointed out as the open door to intellectual, psychical, and spiritual development.[5]

Kingsford went further; not just believing that people had moral duties towards animals but also that they had souls and could go to heaven. Her Catholicism was shaken when she went to Rome and saw the casual cruelty to animals; horses and dogs kicked and stamped on by those who believed that animals had no spiritual value. Kingsford doubted the compassion of any god who did not allow the poor patient suffering animal into heaven when most humans were less deserving. This is why she expected to see her guinea pig in heaven and why she organized a petition to the Pope to change Catholic doctrine about animals having no souls, but this was met with such a lack of Vatican sympathy that she became quite discouraged. But her religious views had to change to accommodate her views on animal welfare, not vice-versa. Whether it was Charles Darwin or the RSPCA, Kingsford condemned unconditionally all those who refused to condemn kreophagy.

Kingsford believed in the health benefits of vegetarianism. Some of the claims are a little outrageous today, but they still echo a little. She became a vegetarian due to the recommendation of her brother John Bonus in 1870, as a way of curing her chronic lung weakness, and some Victorian vegetarians claimed meat-eating caused TB (a claim that carried some initial credence after 1882 when Robert Koch discovered that bovine and human TB were caused by the same organism). Some people claimed that vegetarians did not get cholera, yellow fever or smallpox. Kingsford herself claimed that eating vegetables was enough to cure TB. Cancer was correctly diagnosed as a disease caused by modern civilisation and what could be more a sign of a brutal civilisation gone wrong than meat-eating?

Global vegetarianism would obviate the need for doctors; it would also mean that vaccination, already dangerous in her eyes, would also become superfluous. Although she had joined the ranks of the traditional doctors, she did this to undermine their beliefs and instead promote the philosophy of health without medicine. It was individual choice that created health. The right food should be enough.

Kingsford was worried about population outstripping food supply, but her response was nether moral restraint or birth control, but 'better distribution of the soil'. She rejected the pious commonplace 'Where God sends mouths, he sends food'. An acre of wheat fed ten times more than an acre of sheep, she pointed out; sheep eat when the poor starve. She also rejected the use of fur, leather and ivory as mere human exploitation of animals for their own luxuries and caprices. She stood up for the silk worm by rejecting silk. On holiday, she walked the Swiss Alps in vegetarian shoes. She condemning the culling of seals a century before it was a commonplace view. 'The savage may need fur, the civilised man does not'. She also rejected tobacco, alcohol, fish and seafood, cannabis and opium, mineral salt, suet, vinegar, mouldy cheese, pickles, most spices and condiments, eggs, and pies made with raising agents.

Kingsford was *the* key figure in Victorian vegetarianism; when she died, the Vegetarian Society treated her as a secular saint.[6] Vegetarians were niche, noisy and moralising. The movement started in 1847, by the end of the nineteenth century organised vegetarianism was a tiny movement with 7,000 members and associates of the Vegetarian Society and its London-based rival. It attracted progressives from other areas too – such as Annie Besant, George Bernard Shaw, Isaac Pitman, with a preponderance of women. It caught on to a certain extent; by 1880, the famous Mrs Beaton's *Book of Household Management* had a selection of vegetarian recipes, which is not the same as a vegetarian diet and the personal consequences that went with it.

Lifestyle vegetarians were seen as odd and obsessive; it was still the same a generation later. George Orwell liked to characterise the vegetarian socialist as nudist, be-sandaled, fruit-juice drinking and sexually unorthodox. In Victorian times it had a strong whiff of moral purity, which arguably it still has; 'Purify your bodies, and eat no dead thing that has looked with living eyes upon the light of Heaven,' as Kingsford said in one of her religious tracts.

Her opposition to vivisection was borne from the same desire to keep awful human tendencies at bay and draw a line in the sand between the human/animal distinction that had been blurred by the work of Charles Darwin. Vivisection was just another case of male brutality and rampant materialism; men torturing or eating the most defenceless.

By 1881, she was operating on a parallel track – publishing her own thoughts on religion and also lecturing on the rational and scientific need for a vegetarian diet. Although vegetarians have forgotten Kingsford, Christian mystics and occultists have not. The infamous occultist Aleister Crowley had great regard for her; this has not helped her posthumous reputation. The Humanitarian League, formed in 1891 by the radical socialist Henry Salt, would have agreed with Kingsford at the time but have distanced themselves since:

> It would be a still greater injustice to the cause of humanitarianism were it to be associated with mystic doctrines and revelations with which, as an ethical principle, based on the simplest natural instinct, it has no essential connection.

What were these 'mystic doctrines and revelations' that had no connection with humanitarianism? From around 1876/1877 to a few years before her death, Anna had dreams (and inspirations while awake) which revealed cosmic truths about the world which she claimed had come from inside her, retrieved from her own memory. She called them 'illuminations', which would stop if she was on tour or exceptionally busy with work.

Anna Kingsford was a mystic and this mysticism and focus on the religious experience were the very centre of her radical thought. This was not a sudden development. As a child she claimed to have left notes on flowers for the fairies. At seventeen she wrote her first published novel – *Beatrice: A tale of the Early Christians*. Beatrice's brothers are persecuted by the Romans and she escapes to live a pure life, but she is martyred and murdered herself. 'Eve was also condemned to suffer many sorrows and greater bodily pain than her husband, beside being required to yield entire obedience to his will, a commandment by no means easy to observe,' she noted. Men, she also noted, were more selfish than women; the result of millennia of unchallenged supremacy.

The key event of her life was meeting Edward Maitland in 1874, and it was Algie who introduced them. It was her most important male relationship but it did her post-mortem reputation a lot of damage. Maitland was her constant platonic companion until her death and the self-appointed interpreter of her beliefs and her reputation after it.

From that point, Maitland dominates the interpretations of Kingsford; her friend Fenwick Miller knew Maitland, did not like him, did not like his influence on Kingsford and thought his spiritual beliefs bordered on insanity.

Maitland was destined for a career in the church but lost his faith, and indeed losing his faith in established religion was an absolute prerequisite for what he believed next. He claimed that he had been previously reincarnated as such people as Marcus Aurelius, Daniel and Saint John the Evangelist. Fenwick Miller was not impressed with him or his influence of Kingsford; he used to convince himself of his previous lives by sitting alone and constantly asking himself if he truly was a reincarnation, eventually convincing himself.

In 1877, Maitland wrote a work of mystic religion called *The Soul and How it Found Me*, which incorporated some of Anna's 'illuminations'. Maitland claimed to have received advice from the spirits about the perfectibility of man, which included a ban on woollen underwear and the need to purge yourself after eating lobster. The reviews were not kind; Kingsford appeared in some, represented as his hysterical side-kick. She successfully asked for the publication to be withdrawn.

Maitland reported that her first mystical dream was of a runaway train. Anna was on board with other passengers who were unaware that they were about to crash. Anna, with Maitland's help, uncoupled the engine, which sped away and the passengers were saved. Perhaps Kingsford had trains on her mind, as she used them often enough to shuttle between Paris and London; it was published posthumously and, as would prove a problem later, always interpreted by Maitland. In 1886, Thomas Hardy met both Maitland and Kingsford and called them 'very strange people'. He suspected Maitland's way of writing; she would jot down some sentences after her illuminations and he would copy them up. He thought it was very odd.

Though she heard voices and saw visions of the ascended Masters, Anna insisted that she was a prophet, not a medium. She had risen above the vulgarities of spiritualism and clairvoyance to the divine grace of 'straight-knowledge'. She had seen visions which proved that the Bible had been interpreted incorrectly. They were returning to the old uncorrupted version, not creating something new – all religions came from the same place – a divine truth, which was the opposite of the church.

In 1882, they published a book called *The Perfect Way in Finding Christ*. Maitland sent a copy to Mohandas Gandhi in South Africa. Gandhi knew of her work on vegetarianism and sold copies of *A Perfect Way in Diet* in South Africa. He read this new book carefully. It was a complex piece of work, but Gandhi summed it up perfectly: the book was 'a complete repudiation of current Christian belief'.[8]

For a brief period of time, both Kingsford and Maitland were members of the Theosophical Society. She was elected President of their London Lodge in January 1883 at her first meeting; she was already a well-known figure in Christian esoteric circles. The ever-present Maitland joined at the same time; trouble ensued from their very arrival. The Theosophical Society still exists, despite splits and factions that are probably inevitable in an organisation that puts a premium on personal investigation to ascertain religious truth and regarded mysticism as part of that.

One of the tenets of Theosophy was that the ancient, uncorrupted faith of all ancient wisdom was necessary; in 1881 she described what Theosophy meant to her in a lecture to 170 people at the Prince's Hall Piccadilly. It was the science of the divine, she said, and relations with the divine were centred not on exteriors but from within. All religions held truth and a study of them and their symbols would reveal it. The Church of England it was not.

By April 1884, she and Maitland had left to form a rival group, the Hermetic Society, which was a mystical Christian group which relied less on Eastern religion. The journalist W.T. Stead (Chapter Eleven) called it 'the newest thing in religion' thus showing more skill in creating snappy headlines than understanding complex subjects. Kingsford put him straight; 'the society aims to recover of what is really the *oldest* thing in religion ... so old as to have become forgotten and lost, namely its esoteric and spiritual, and therefore its true signification'.[9]

Like all human beings, Kingsford had her faults and inconsistencies. Despite her belief that vegetarianism was a panacea and drugs were an unnatural interference in the body, she still took ether to an addicted degree to alleviate her life-long asthma. Her maternal instincts were not strong, yet she was obsessed with her guinea pig. When going backwards and forwards during her medical degree she was happy to leave Eadith with a nanny or her mother but smuggled Rufus backwards and forwards in contravention of the law. When he died, he had already illegally crossed the border many times, and because he died in Boulogne, he was to make one more journey.

She did not go into medicine to save people; she did not like most people.

> I do not love men and women. I dislike them too much to care to do them any good. They seem to be my natural enemies. It is not for them that I am taking up medicine and science, not to cure their ailments, but for the animals and knowledge generally. I want to rescue the animals from cruelty and injustice, which for me are the worst, if not the only sins. [10]

When asked a tricky question – would she wear out her horse and make it suffer and die in a mad gallop to save her friend in danger? She said that she would not, because the horse was also her friend.

She was much more than an esoteric dreamer. In 1886, she published her collected letters of advice to women under the title of *Health, Beauty and the Toilet*. Yet there was an ideology behind it; she disapproved the advice given by male doctors – they produced short term fixes based on medicine rather than lifestyle. For obesity, she suggested early rising, long walks and less fat, no cakes between meals and refusing drugs from doctors. She celebrated beauty but expected women to organise it for themselves using her natural remedies based on science. The book sold well, and for decades afterwards her name appeared in pharmacy advertisements in newspapers 'as recommended by Anna Kingsford MD (Paris)'.

Thus was created the humanitarian who did not like humans, the trained scientist who did not like science, the woman who fought to be a doctor but who did not like doctors, and who thirsted after practical knowledge but who also became enmeshed in the supernatural. Her vegetarianism and her spiritualism overwhelmed the other causes. She never became very active in the Women's Suffrage Movement, and this was not merely because of her relatively early death. She showed no real interest in the birth control movement (see Chapter Seven) or Josephine Butler's campaign against the Contagious Diseases Act (Chapter Ten).

Her reputation took a nosedive after her death; this was the fault of Edward Maitland, even if it was not his deliberate intent. In 1898, he wrote *Anna Kingsford, Her Life, Letters, Diary and Work*. Maitland wanted the monopoly over Kingsford's history and legacy; he told her life story without consulting anybody and got family details wrong. He published excerpts from her diary, interpreted them and destroyed them so he would have the last word. He wanted his to be the final voice, and to be fair, this was probably Anna Kingsford's intention when she left him her papers in preference to Algie. It is very doubtful that she wanted him to be the final arbiter of her illuminations; she rarely even interpreted them herself.[11]

The book reviews were appalling, especially from those who knew her and did not recognise the portrayal. The *British Medical Journal* called it a 'perfect wilderness of nonsense'. The Catholic *Tablet* had more than one reason to condemn Anna. Generally, they believed she had ill-used their faith, and specifically, she used to visit their office to harangue one Reverend Clarke on the subject of vivisection. They took Maitland's 'facts' at face value:

> Perhaps happily we never expected for a moment what we learn from this biography that we were entertaining unawares a lady who was over a thousand years old and who had previously lived on the earth in such varied characters as those of Mary Magdalen, the Empress Faustino, Joan of Arc, and Anne Boleyn.

The *Tablet* later claimed that Kingsford had had a deathbed reconversion to Catholicism; Maitland, correctly on this occasion, refuted the claim.

There were more unsubstantiated claims by Maitland; she had offered herself up as a human sacrifice in December 1877; she had contemplated suicide; she had hunted foxes in her youth; she had been subject to a physic attack by a black magician called 'Monsieur O'.[12] The most infamous claim was that Kingsford had killed two vivisectors and was targeting another, the famous Louis Pasteur. Maitland reported that:

> She declared on 11/12/1886, after their deaths, that she had killed Paul Bert and Claude Bernard, as she would kill Louis Pasteur for their animal testing, with the strength of her will.

She had, according to Maitland, put curses on both men. It sounded more like the kind of thing Maitland would do. Although the word was not used, Maitland's critics accused him of what we might call 'projection'.

On 17 November 1886, she paid a visit to Louis Pasteur's laboratory in Paris to gain information for her campaign against his mistreatment of animals. Maitland does not explain why she failed to use the same long-distance killing ability that eliminated Bert and Bernard; 'hurl your whole spiritual being with all your might' was Maitland's quotation. Kingsford 'waded across Paris in the sleet and mud, and stood a long time in wet boots and clothes, and got back at last after about five hours, soaked to the skin'. She was caught in torrential rain which led to the weakness that killed her, so it is probably more accurate to say that Pasteur killed her more by long-distance than the other way round.

Her friend Florence Fenwick Miller was equally incandescent. She claimed that Kingsford was 'absolutely absent in this book'.[13]

> This unhappy book appeared last year. Aleck what a melancholy display it was. The famous 'revelations' are printed in quantities, and they are mere ravings, the wild stuff of hysterical dreams, in which it is not easy to recognize the woman who had written not only sanely, but with the most calm logic and brilliant insight upon so many important questions—diet, the position of women, vivisection—and who was also the holder of one of the best scientific degrees of the world, the M.D. of Paris.

She also accused Maitland of egotistical ravings:

> More singular still, however, was poor Maitland's display in that book of egotism and vanity, a large proportion of the work being about himself, and including pages of such twaddle as what was said to him about himself by 'trance mediums' at different stages of his career.

Kingsford was radical, a brave and active doer, a woman unhappy with so many aspects of Victorian life. She was in agony about a world mismanaged by men, where women's attributes of spirituality, self-restraint and sensibility seemed to be underused and underappreciated. Her reputation has wavered because of the nature of some of her beliefs, but also because of the deliberate, successful biases of Edward Maitland. In life she fought against the brittle egotism of men, and in death, she was one of its victims.

Chapter Two

Anti-Vivisection

Frances Power Cobbe

Anna Kingsford was not the leading Victorian anti-vivisectionist; that was, in the words of one historian, 'the Anglo-Irish spinster Frances Power Cobbe'.[1] Cobbe (1822–1904) was born at Newbridge House, Dublin, in a house built for her grandfather the Archbishop of Dublin in 1736 which still stands today. She was born into the Irish nobility; there were five bishops in the family history.[2] She was a member of the British ruling class at the very highest level.

She may have been born into fortunate circumstances, but most of the power and privilege were in the hands of the men of her family, as would be expected. It was made worse and more obvious by the family's particular circumstances. There were five children and she was the youngest by five years and the only girl, with the implication that her parents Charles and Frances Cobbe would have been happier to stop at the last boy – 'a girl was by no means welcome'.[3] Her father was distant and domineering and mother Frances was ill and distracted, both physically and mentally. Her memories of her mother were in a darkened room but, as her 1894 autobiography accepted she was 'well born' and fortunate with dutiful parents, a loving home and insulation from poverty.

The four older boys, Charles, Thomas, William and Henry took precedence, not because they were born first, but because they were male. Great pains were taken with their education and career. Frances was brought up by servants, and she seemed well down the pecking order; the ill mother, the four elder sons and the dual heritage children of Charles Cobbe's brother all seemed to precede her. Charles kept an extensive diary for thirty-four years and mentioned his daughter a mere twenty-five times, many of them functional entries such as 'went to Bath whence I brought my daughter'.

By 1830, she was often alone in the house. Charles, Henry and Thomas were away at Charterhouse and they all had a future planned out. Charles was off to Oxford; later there was Sandhurst, the East India Company and Church, commerce, engineering, a potential trip abroad to New Zealand and Australia. There was none of this for Frances, or Fanny as she was known, and she was acutely aware of it. The males had choices as well as opportunities; there was always the option of turning things down. Tom successfully resisted the church; other avenues were created for him. None of her brothers did particularly well at the professions that they were guided into or the privileged education that preceded it. After 1832, Charles Cobbe took advantage of the widening of the franchise to ensure that his male children had a vote by giving them enough property to qualify. No amount of wealth would allow Fanny to have the vote.

Frances Cobbe spent time in Dublin and in the West Country in her first ten years. She was comfortable but isolated. There was a full house of brothers and cousins at holidays, but these were people with other things to do, and they left her when the holidays ended. In her adult life she was gregarious and engaging but she was for much of her early life 'mentally lonely'. She was serious, intellectually curious and precocious, and a tomboy; when asked in the 1890s to talk about her favourite doll, she could not provide an example.[4]

Charles Cobbe reluctantly sent Frances away to Brighton in October 1836. In March 1835, her brothers Charles and Tom had set off for an adventure in Europe, but Frances was going to the South Coast to complete her education. The Great Western Railway was still four years away, so there was a painfully slow four-day journey by steam packet and post chaise (a privately hired vehicle, one step up from a public stagecoach) with overnight stops to help her ailing mother, who was making the journey just to check the new school. Charles was chaperoning.

It started well at the new school – she was ushered into a nice room with a single bed while her mother was there, but when she returned home another bed was added, but by then Fanny was on her own in the school, but not in the room itself.

What was the point of such a distant education when she had personal tuition at home, the run of some very comfortable houses, and the demonstrable ability to think for herself? To ensure her future as the wife of a landowner, Charles required social respectability

19

and new connections, the acquisition of the necessary graces and accomplishments, and the rough tomboy edges rubbed off and enough superficial knowledge in a few key areas to avoid social embarrassment. He did not want an independently-minded autodidact; the expensive Brighton school was to be the cure.

Frances hated her time at the school at 32 Brunswick Square, Brighton, a very high class establishment run by a Miss Runciman and Miss Roberts ('my future tyrants'). The starting fees were £120 a year when an apparently equivalent education could be bought for a quarter of that. It was a similar, but much more expensive education, as was endured by Anna Kingsford. There were twenty-two girls there, aged nine to nineteen; Frances was in the middle, aged fourteen. History and Geography were bi-weekly lectures and memory tests, Scripture was learnt by heart before breakfast and verb tenses were repeated on communal walks on the seafront. On one occasion she learnt by heart thirteen pages of Alexander Fraser Tytler, Lord Woodhouselee's *Universal History – From the Creation of the World to the Beginning of the Eighteenth Century*; this number of pages would be 3,500 words.[5]

She was taught to walk and sit correctly, dress for dinner and practise conversation that was polished but not intellectual or profound enough to scare men off. And then there were lessons; although this probably gives the wrong impression to the modern ear. Twenty-nine people were all in one double schoolroom where individual tuition was attempted; it was a cacophony, even before the four pianos were being used by four girls who could not play the piano. She hated this and hated having the course of her knowledge directed by people that she had no respect for. 'Lessons, thou tyrant of the mind' was her description of her one to one attention from nannies as a child, and this was worse. Independent thought was not on the curriculum.

Cobbe, like Kingsford, resisted the attempt to make her socially acceptable marriage material. Not only was this schooling seen as an interruption to her education; it was frivolous, pointless, routine and without intellectual stimulation. It provided the maximum of cost with the minimum of education. It produced polite ornaments. So it is unsurprising that Cobbe became an advocate of women's education, and similarly unsurprising that she insisted it should be about learning, not superficialities and allow women to make their own choices.

It was an expensive and high pressure education, a cut above the genteel middle class boarding schools and in a different league to the charity schools for the poor. It represented the best a girl could get in the 1830s. Every Saturday was 'Judgement Day'. Poor behaviour – that could be walking badly or not tying your shoe laces properly meant that you 'lost your card' and spent Saturday afternoon on a hard chair and between two even harder schoolmistresses. The reward for those who had not lost their card was to sit in silence writing letters home that the girls knew would be examined before they were sent. The only unaccompanied walks were within the confines of the school's garden.

In his visit in April of the next year, Charles Cobbe regretted that she had not changed. Her own choice was to stay at home and educate herself more rigorously and on her own terms, and she got her wish in December 1838, when her education was cut short and she was sent home to care for her ill mother and to prepare for the role of housekeeper; starting in her father's house as preparation for her future husband. Her return home was done in one very long day. On the way home Cobbe resolved to read novels and anything else she wanted for the rest of her life – history, algebra, geometry, Greek Literature – whatever she wanted.

Her housekeeper apprenticeship did not take up the whole day. There were servants to absorb the time-consuming work, and her job was to supervise. The brothers had careers, not all of them prospering despite the opportunities and chances they had been offered. She was being sacrificed, and she knew it, although she remained on good terms with her brothers. It was not personal, it was a system. She was being groomed for the life of a wife, with the additional indirect power of being the wife of a rich man rather than a poor one, but it was never going to be enough; 'and if, I had become in mature years, a Women's Rights Woman, it has not been because in my own person I have been made to feel a Women's Wrongs'.[6]

Life was not intolerable. Her father was no monster; he was a stern religionist and prone to bad temper, but he also had humanitarian feelings. At one point he financed housing improvements for his tenants by selling some of the family's fine paintings (in 1839 he accepted £1,500 for two paintings) but he was still an authoritarian nineteenth-century patriarch with a family to administer and tenants to look after.

She 'came out' in 1840, but her interest in finding a man was non-existent. She had no interest at all in dancing and idle chit-chat with men;

she had resisted learning this at school, so it was unsurprising that she refused to do it at home. She never made a relationship with any man in her life from a conscious choice. In an interview with *Strand* magazine late in her life (1893), she noted that from her own experience men found it impossible to treat women as equals, and from secondhand experience that her married friends seemed to have lots of diplomatic 'headaches' at crucial times. She was never interested in physical relations with men, seemed slightly repulsed by the prospect, and suggested that many married women secretly agreed with her.

Cobbe, like Kingsford, rejected marriage as it stood in the mid-nineteenth century. Rather than rearrange the institution with the help of a male ally like Kingsford did, she remained single. In her 1869 pamphlet on women's property rights *Criminals, Idiots, Women, & Minors*, she seemed to be emphatic on the subject. 'It is in the nature of things disgraceful and abominable that marriage should be made the aim of woman's life,' she said; but the key phrase here is 'made the aim'.

Cobbe's key question was: marriage for what purpose? She was being very radical indeed by suggesting that marriage should be about free choice, esteem and affection, or, as she summarised it, 'love' and therefore rejected almost every justification that the Victorians had for marriage; to maintain rank, preserve wealth and pass on both to the next generation. This is why education mattered; women needed to be a viable economic unit that could earn a living independently of a husband, not merely a play thing moulded for man and marriage through lack of an alternative. Making marriage optional would, paradoxically, strengthen it.

Cobbe looked forward to a new type of marriage for the twentieth century. It would continue, as part of God's plan, but more women would choose chastity while others would enter into a different kind of relationship. Men would no longer claim absolute authority from the barbaric notion that 'might was right'. The average woman may not be intellectually equal to the average man, but enlightened men would reject the sexual double standard that worked in their favour. Women would reject petty vanity and show men how to be more humanitarian. Marriage would help everybody improve themselves.

In *Criminals, Idiots, Women and Minors* (1869), she asserted that the root cause of male violence was the economic dependence of women which was, in turn, caused by poor education and low life expectations. She wanted marriage to work for those who freely entered into it, and believed that the roles of wife and mother were the most important. This did not, in her mind, imply inequality in marriage; given that men and women were different, then this was her role. Married women then needed money of their own, control of their own spaces and fewer domestic chores and freedom from the threat of violence from a physically stronger partner.

Her doubts about established religion stem from the same time as her doubts about patriarchy. Cracks were beginning to appear, and Cobbe was not the only educated Victorian to be influenced by them. German scholars created doubts about the chronology of the Old Testament; Geology contradicted the assertions of Genesis; the immortal soul struck some as unscientific and immortality was doubted. As an educated girl, she asked her father questions about the literal interpretation of the Bible. At eleven she remembered asking her father about the logic of the loaves and the fishes and then remonstrating with herself, 'I am doubting the Bible ... God forgive me' but the little rift had begun.[7] In 1843, she told her father that she could not accept the formal dogmas of the church and was now a Theist, and he was metaphorically speechless. He told her that Theism was just a word in the dictionary, not a faith.

In 1844, the new railway made it possible for Cobbe to maintain another female friendship – that of Harriet St Leger – an intellectual Anglo-Irish aristocrat like herself. St Leger had a constant companion, Dorothy Wilson, and a fondness for clothes usually worn by men – a grey riding habit, leather boots and a beaver hat – and Cobbe rejected as small-minded those who thought it was offensive. Cobbe always supported St Leger. This was the kind of life she wished for herself.

Her relationship with her father was failing; eventually, he sent her away to Ireland by a written note but this did not happen until 1848 when his wife died and her role as companion was redundant. 'I was the first heretic ever known amongst us'. When she returned from her stay in County Donegal in 1849 he was rather suspicious and uncommunicative; she was 'in a sort of moral Coventry, under a vague atmosphere of disapprobation wherein all I said was listened to cautiously as likely to conceal some poisonous heresy'.[8] It is clear that her father made her return to fulfil her female role, her unorthodox religious views notwithstanding.

Her father died in 1857. This was a danger point for the unmarried younger sister with both parents dead; she was about to become an appendage in the household that she had previously run. Her life, already eventless, would not change but would be under the sufferance of others. In order to escape this fate, she spent nearly a year travelling the Mediterranean and the Middle East, leaving the country in December 1857 after a final night in St Leonard's with Harriet St Leger and Dorothy Wilson. She travelled on a well-established route to Rome and then Alexandria, Cairo and the pyramids, then Palestine, Jerusalem, Damascus, Istanbul, Corfu, Trieste and home through Italy and Switzerland.

This grand tour, or versions of it, was well known, but Cobbe's approach to it was not. She did the journey unchaperoned; unlike Florence Nightingale a decade earlier, who was only on her own while asleep. Neither did she take a maid or a lady companion. She was always ready to travel alone if necessary, although she learned the knack of meeting strangers and travelling with them. She used her letters of introduction to make connections, meet expatriates and intellectuals and enjoyed being recognised as an author by strangers. She stayed in comfortable hotels at times but learnt to rough it in tents, and reacquainted herself with horse riding. She enjoyed the tourism but preferred people and ideas; this was the life she wanted in England too.

She shared the racism of her age. On her visit to Giza, she insisted on being shown the *inside* of the Great Pyramid of Giza by guides who, in her mind had already tried to exploit her and extort money. A trip inside the pyramid could only be done by a lot of unladylike creeping, crawling and climbing in a smelly darkness in which there was nothing to see even if it could be seen. At one point she felt vulnerable, stuck inside a pyramid with five Arab guides who wished to exploit her. When they demanded money, she issued a set of peremptory demands which they obeyed, despite outnumbering her. She put her success down to their inferior slave mentality when confronted with a member of a free race. Her racist and imperialist assumptions are a little chilling now, but they were the in-bred entitlement of a member of the ruling class who had learnt to give orders to her father's tenants.

The postponed search for a role continued when she returned home. She was 'looking out to see what use I could make of my life'. The first stage was to make a long term relationship with a person like herself – an advanced thinker, like the kind she had encountered on her extended Grand Tour. She was recommended by Harriet St Leger to

Mary Carpenter and it seemed a good match on paper. Carpenter was, it seemed, similar in religious views. Cobbe had read and approved her ideas on fighting juvenile delinquency with love and education rather than the workhouse and prison. In November 1858, Cobbe moved into the house next door to the Red Lodge School in Bristol, hoping for 'a happy life, busy all day long'. It was a school for girls under sixteen who had offended or were in danger of doing so; it was one of the first Reform Schools, designed as an alternative to prison or the workhouse.

Cobbe was certainly busy. Carpenter was even busier, and she had neither time nor the inclination to embark on the type of relationship that Cobbe wanted. They were clearly quite incompatible. The arrangement soured quite quickly, although mutual respect was always there.

Carpenter showed little interest in the normal small pleasures of life. Cobbe, who had no interest at all in fashion, complained that Carpenter showed no interest in clothes. Cobbe also noted that her companion had no interest in food either; ham and salt beef were on the menu most evenings. Cobbe was already overweight by this time, and could not stand for the monotony and scarcity. When she asked for vegetable additions to the diet to avoid gout, six radishes were added to the same menu. There were no luxuries and no talk but work. When her dog warmed himself in front of the fire, Carpenter denounced him as a 'self-indulgent'. You did not insult Cobbe's pets without consequence.

Carpenter was more religiously orthodox than Cobbe had been told. She had anti- Catholic opinions which rankled a little; she invoked the name of Jesus too much. This was never going to be a partnership of equals. For a start, it was unclear if Carpenter wanted a companion. Cobbe was paying for her board and lodging. Mary simply wanted another person to work as hard as her in her own preferred way of life.

Red Lodge School *was* hard work. It was a fine rural Tudor townhouse when it was built around 1580 but by this time was surrounded by slums and the victims of industrialisation who lived in them. There was fighting, drunkenness and conflict outside the building and truculent pupils inside. The girls at the school were a terrible handful; they were the victims of poor diet, poor parenting and poverty and they stole, vandalised and were defiant. Cobbe witnessed this and Carpenter, with twenty years of experience, still found it difficult.[9]

Carpenter and Cobbe had one thing in common which paradoxically may have been the cause of their relationships failing. Both were single women all their life, with no hint or record of marriage or sexual links with men. Just before Cobbe's arrival, Carpenter had adopted a five-year-old child, Rosanna. She was pleased at first – 'just think of me with a little girl of my own...without the trouble of marrying'.[10] Carpenter was relatively plain and awkward in manners, and apt to stray from acceptable female behaviour in an effort to get things done. This sounded like Cobbe too, but it was not enough to seal their relationship.

Cobbe moved into London-based journalism and campaigning after the failure in Bristol. From 1860, she moved to London and lived at Hereford Square, Kensington from 1862. At this point, she started making connections at the very top of society. From 1863 to 1896, Cobbe lived with Mary Lloyd, a Welsh sculptor, in a relationship that was recognised by their friends as a form of marriage. She called Mary 'husband', 'wife' and 'dear friend'. The census enumerators used 'friend' (1871), 'boarder' (1881) and 'visitor' (1891); the last two were untrue. The use of 'friend' is unusual. The census enumerators either used family connections (wife) or economic relations (servant); friend is not common. The census enumerator would have recorded these details based on what he was told by the two women.

They lived at Mary's house, 26 Hereford Square, Kensington between 1862 and 1884 and worked together in all the reformists' movements that interested them both. When the London National Society for Women's Suffrage was first formed in 1867, Miss Cobbe and Miss Lloyd were elected as members of the Executive Committee. Their interests were identical. Lloyd mortgaged her house in 1876 to provide funds for the Battersea Dogs Home. They moved to Hengwrt in Wales in April 1884 and were to all intents a married couple with an intense emotional relationship. They could just bear to be apart in Europe, but Cobbe turned down an invitation to go to the United States by Fanny Kemble – one of her many famous friends – because she could not bear to be parted from Mary. Whether it was a sexual relationship is not really the point; it was their alternative to heterosexual marriage.

From 1868 to 1875, she wrote opinion pieces for the London *Echo*. In a nutshell, Cobbe was an excellent journalist and agitator for the causes she believed in – women's suffrage and education, better treatment of the poor, and most of all, opposition to experiments on animals. She was, primarily, an agitator, a journalist and a mind changer. She possessed a comprehensive knowledge of every London newspaper and magazine, including the views of its readers and what type of article they would accept. She concentrated her writing and reform efforts on behalf of the unrepresented. Her particular focus was an abhorrence of violence, whether in the home, the laboratory or the American plantation; the victims being women and children, and the perpetrators being men, men who made the laws for their own convenience.

The 1857 Matrimonial Causes Act was an example of that power. It made divorce part of English law rather than needing separate and expensive legislation for each divorce; until that point, only three women had successfully obtained a divorce through that channel. Women's property was now protected, but the key difference was a man could obtain a divorce due to adultery alone, while the woman had to prove adultery aggravated by bigamy, incest, bestiality, sodomy, desertion, or extreme cruelty of the physical kind – mental cruelty was not recognised. Adultery in women was enough to condemn; it brought the legitimacy of children and the inheritance of property into question, but it was not enough in the case of men, who were both regarded both as superior and held to a lower moral standard at the same time.[11]

The new divorce laws shone a brighter light on the extent of male violence and poor behaviour as women sought divorces in the courts. In 1878, she had been reading the newspapers about domestic abuse. Cobbe was incandescent with rage but with a hint of condescension.

> Who imagined that the wives of English gentlemen might be called on to endure from their husbands violence and cruelty we are accustomed to picture exercised only in the lowest lanes and courts of our cities, where drunken ruffians, home from the gin palace, assail the miserable partners of vices with curses kicks and blows?[12]

The respectable classes were now washing their dirty linen in the law courts, but with one court in central London and high fees, divorce was still not in the hands of the poor. The poor needed an alternative when male violence was turned against them. In 1878, she produced the pamphlet *Wife Torture in England* and three months later the law was changed; both friend and enemies acknowledged her influence. The Act allowed women to apply to the magistrate for protection against a violent husband; it allowed women to live separately with her children under ten, and enforced alimony payments. It was a cut-price version of divorce, used 8,000 times in 1883. Her enemies called it 'divorce made easy' but it was neither; it was a lifeline for the defenceless poor woman.[13]

In a lifetime of radical activism, Cobbe is most well known for her opposition to vivisection – experiments on live animals for medical research. Her crusade against animal cruelty was rooted in the same horror of male brutality and license; like Kingsford's vegetarianism, it was a purity movement for men, in this case, arrogant doctors who claimed the legal right to inflict pain. The behaviour of doctors on cutting up animals was a pale reflection of the more intimate, domestic, forms of physical and sexual abuse, but rooted in the same animus. It is no coincidence that Cobbe campaigned for the more respectful treatment of women patients in hospital by male doctors. It was all part of the same phenomena – doctors as the new elite, untouchable and arrogant.

Vivisection became an issue in the 1870s, and opposition was heightened when the government's 1873 proposed vivisection law did not mention the use of anaesthetic. It was at this point that Cobbe wrote a letter to Kingsford at the *Lady's Own Magazine* and converted Anna Kingsford to the cause. Cobbe never reciprocated by supporting Kingsford's vegetarianism; Cobbe did not have the spiritual bent to regard meat-eating as cruelty, and she had a hunting, fishing and shooting background much different to Kingsford's middle class suburban upbringing.

Vivisection was not a major part of British scientific practice. In 1878, when they were first licensed, there were only 270 experiments the next year, but it increased quickly, as the opponents of vivisection feared. For many British doctors involved in vivisection, the only problem was that this was not enough, and they were being overtaken by the French. Cobbe's opposition to vivisection was rooted in a more general radical view about the asymmetrical relationship between men and women. Men, in all aspects of life, were brutal if they were not reigned in.

Many feminists and radical reformers found that anti-vivisection was an obvious next step. Here was male cruelty and baseness in its most fundamental form. Opponents such as Josephine Butler made comparisons with the vaginal examination of prostitutes under the Contagious Diseases Act. Medicine, like marriage, condoned male violence. It gave them immunity from their lowest nature. This is how

Cobbe and Kingsford viewed it. Animal rights were women's rights, and protesting about the treatment of animals was a way of protecting women from men, and men from themselves.

There was a mini outcry against vivisection in the 1870s, with some horrible examples in the newspapers:

> A physician attached to one of the best London hospitals took sixteen cats, and, having opened their sides while they were under the influence of chloroform, tied their bile ducts, and then left them to expire slowly from the consequences of the operation.[14]

The result of this national debate was the Cruelty to Animals Act 1876, criticized by anti-vivisectionists as "infamous but well-named". It required licensing, record keeping and painkilling drugs for the affected animal and insisted that the experiments had to be 'absolutely necessary for the due instruction of the persons [so they may go on to use the instruction] to save or prolong human life'. It required trust in the word of the scientists – male scientists interested in 'progress' above all else.

Cobbe was aghast. Torture had been banned in politics and religion yet the new priesthood of male doctors reserved the right to continue with it, and receive praise. They were the new priesthood, the new Spanish Inquisition, using the new rack and it was clear that the new law did more to protect them than it did the animals. They could not be trusted, by definition. Cobbe would have agreed with George Bernard Shaw 'whoever doesn't hesitate to vivisect will hardly hesitate to lie about it'.

Cobbe's propaganda campaign dominated her life. Her campaign against vivisection was in two parts – the formation of the Society for the Protection of Animals Liable to Vivisection and the use of no-holds-barred journalism. She wrote books condemning vivisectors like Magendie, Mantegazza, Bert and Bernard. She used graphic illustrations of restraint and experiment, and could not be charged with sensationalism because she used illustrations from their own books. In her pamphlet, *Light in Dark Places,* she reproduced a machine used by Bernard showing how a cut rabbit was burned to death in an oven 'soon it becomes impossible to count its panting as at last it falls into convulsions, and dies generally suddenly in uttering a cry'.

Cobbe also campaigned against the use of curare.

> Well, our Professor, like his dogs, will need to be starved for eighteen hours. Then we shall curarise him and establish artificial respiration, and when this is done we shall cut open his abdomen, squeeze out his gall-bladder, clamp his cystic-duct, dissect out his bile-duct, tie a tube in it, inject various things into his intestine, and carefully note the results. It will not take more than seven or eight hours, it appears, to do all that is needful.[15]

Curare rendered animals unable to struggle, but still feel pain. It allowed long painful operations and took efforts to make sure that they were breathing throughout. This was wicked male vanity and cruelty, and the painlessness was a lie. George Hoggan, a fellow anti-vivisectionist believed that male scientists repeated the same operation many times, not to investigate, but to improve their manual skills and further their career. Curare helped them linger at the laboratory table.

As with Kingsford's argument about the slaughter house and the butchers, she challenged the hypocrisy of those who salved their conscience by not thinking about the problem:

> Do not refuse to look at these pictures. If you cannot bear to look at them, what must the suffering be to the animals that undergo the cruelties that they represent?[16]

You cannot caress your pet dog one day and consent to vivisection the next. Cobbe lived this philosophy by treating her own dog Hajjin better than most people; he was Kingsford's guinea pig; the principle was similar.

Vivisection was science challenging God, prioritising the body over the soul, the practical over the moral. It was an obsession with the physical health of the body over the spiritual side. The evidence was everywhere that men liked inflicting pain and liked watching it inflicted. If *Homo sapiens* were related closely to animals, as popular interpretations of Darwin suggested, then vivisection was a terrible example of the moral descent that was possible. Cobbe invented her own word for all this – 'hygieology', just as Kingsford did for meat-eating.

30

Cobbe had influence. She knew the poet Robert Browning, and he shared her disgust with pigeon shooting. The novelist Wilkie Collins detested vivisections as much as he did; Tennyson signed his name to most of her public petitions and was vice president of the British Society for the Prevention of Vivisection. She had direct access to major politicians like Lord John Russell and John Bright and journalists like W.T Stead. She chatted to Gladstone over breakfast; she knew progressives such as the Fawcett's, Matthew Arnold, John Stuart Mill, Josephine Butler, and Elizabeth Garret. The radical Thomas Carlyle and the Catholic Cardinal Manning supported her, even when they did not like each other, as did Lewis Carroll, Tolstoy and Victor Hugo. Her work was admired in the USA by the first doctor Elizabeth Blackwell, by Grover Cleveland, Henry James and Mark Twain.

Cobbe was a member of the establishment, without the progressive's guilt about a privileged background. She was a paid-up member of the Conservative Party and was not involved in the radical movement for the wide-ranging debate. She was not a committee woman. She was used to getting her own way, and in both speech and writing was direct, persuasive, and offered no scope for disagreement. She knew and corresponded with Charles Darwin until he refused to condemn vivisection. She was, as the saying goes, unable to suffer fools gladly, or experts who disagreed with her; this included even falling out with others who wanted the vote. She was an early supporter in 1867 as a member of the London National Society for Women's Suffrage but fell out with Manchester members who, in her mind, wanted to turn the world topsy-turvy rather than merely reform marriage and society.

Her desire for equality for women was rooted in the belief that men and women were different. As she commented in her 1877 pamphlet 'Why Women Desire the Franchise', it was still possible for men and women to have different tasks in life and still both deserve the vote so they could make a better life for all. The male doctor cannot protect the interest of the dissected animal; the male voter cannot protect the interests of women. There was no such thing as indirect representation of a person's interests.

Cobbe's propaganda continued until her death. As late as 1892, she told the *Globe* newspaper that she had published one pamphlet a week since 1888; of that 320 she had personally written 173 and published and distributed them free at her own expense.[17] She was an absolutist on the subject of vivisection, demanding immediate and outright abolition. In 1898, she broke away from the British Society for the Prevention of Vivisection who were now advocating gradual reform and formed the British Association for the Abolition of Vivisection, who wanted it banned immediately. Bill after bill banning experiments had failed to get through parliament; this did not make Cobbe wish to compromise at all.

She lived for another eight unhappy years after the death of Mary Lloyd. Knowing that death was imminent, she made her will. She seemed to have the Victorian dread of premature burial, especially in the aftermath of a seizure or stroke when consciousness is lost for a long time and the person pronounced dead. This had, according to family tradition, happened to her own great-grandmother. She had been declared dead and was being prepared for her interment when she woke up, thrived and went on to have twenty-two children. Her will was clear on the precautions to be taken. In a note found by her bed, she ordered a doctor to:

> perform on my body the operation completely and thoroughly severing the arteries of the neck and windpipe (nearly severing the head altogether) so as to render any revival in the grave absolutely impossible.[18]

Cobbe had an earth-to-earth burial in a wicker coffin that allowed for rapid decomposition. Her instructions specifically forbade her coffin being carried by men into the graveyard, but in one of her own carriages 'driven by my coachman at his usual pace'. There was no mourning or funeral attire. The honorary secretary of the National Anti-Vivisection Society summed up her life:

> There are still to be found in our country women as well as men who are ready to jeopardise worldly prosperity and all things that make this life precious or even endurable, for what their consciences bid them hold even more priceless.[19]

Cobbe has not really been remembered, although she is still honoured by Cruelty Free International, the successor organisation to the BUAV.

She was never part of the radical Edwardian Women's Suffrage movement. The WSPU was six months old when she died, and Cobbe had been moving away from the struggle for the vote for the last twenty years of her life. She remained focused on animal welfare and anti-vivisection, a cause that was not to become fashionable and mainstream until the 1960s. She produced no prose or poetry or other works of the imagination, so does not have a literary reputation. She deserves to be remembered as a truly great journalist and propagandist for humanitarianism, and, by promoting humane attitudes, improving the life of Victorian women.

Chapter Three

Temperance and Teetotalism

Ann Jane Carlile

The arguments against alcohol are as old as alcohol itself and were far from novel in the Victorian age. In summary, alcohol is a poison and its use was against reason. It endangered the drinker, their health and wealth and that of his family, his earthly reputation and his immortal soul. So it was a surprise that anybody touched the stuff – but they did, of course.

The Victorian temperance movement is forever associated, some would say tainted, with its link to the religious revival of the Victorian period. It's not easy to actively like the Victorian campaigner against drink, unlike some of our Victorian radicals. Hidebound by religious enthusiasm and moralistic finger-wagging, they seem to have been waging war on one of life's pleasures. They talked down to people in the slums while drinking expensive wine in their own comfortable homes, and restricted their moral condemnation to the working classes. In short, they were killjoys, hypocrites and authoritarians.

Some of these accusations were true, but perhaps not true enough to condemn them out of hand. The obvious counter to the first is that there was little joy to kill when it came to British drinking habits. If the drinkers of our age went back to 1800, they would have no doubt that drinking was a social problem with terrible consequences for the poor. Drunkenness was hard-baked into society, almost a right of freeborn Englishmen, alongside rioting and cruelty to animals. Eighteenth century governments were unwilling to legislate against personal vices unless social order was threatened. It was also a great revenue earner, one that the state could not, and did not want to, live without. When the House of Commons abolished the temporary Income Tax that was designed to finance the Napoleonic War (1816), they relied even more on the Malt Tax to plug the gap.

By the 1820s, the tide was turning. There was certainly a generational reaction against alcohol in the early nineteenth century, starting with individuals like the cartoonist George Cruikshank. George Cruikshank had been a heavy drinker. His brother was an alcoholic and his father died of TB in 1811 but his son believed that alcohol had killed him – multiply this by a million personal experiences, and change was inevitable.

Our main temperance radical is Ann Jane Carlile (1775–1864). She was a temperance campaigner straight out of central casting. She deserves our special attention though because she was a woman. Women were present in the lower echelons of the movement in great numbers as there was no better channelling of female philanthropy, but Carlile became a prominent leader. She was also one of the first people to tour Britain and Ireland giving impassioned speeches against alcohol, doing this in a society where women were not allowed to speak from any kind of pulpit on any controversial subject.

She managed to avoid the common temperance mistake of merely preaching to the converted. Unlike some drink reformers, she saw nobody as irredeemable and nobody was too wretched to deserve her attention. Her motives were mixed, from our point of view. She genuinely wanted to help, but was also convinced that the drunkard was disbarred from going to heaven.

She wrote her own material and influenced the debate on anti-alcohol campaigns, often being well ahead of the curve in methods and marketing, and most famously co-founded (some would say founded) the Leeds Band of Hope in 1847, an organisation which still exists today.

She was firstly saving souls and secondly making life better for the poor on earth. Temperance campaigners like Carlile were radical in the sense that they focussed on the appalling living standards of the poor. It is true that they did not ask *why* they were poor, because they thought that they already knew the answer but they did want to help, and took action rather than look away.

Carlile was born Ann Hamil in 1775 at Roosky, near Newbliss, Co Monaghan. She became the wife of the Presbyterian minister Francis Carlile in 1800, aged twenty-five. They were married for eleven years and she gave birth to six daughters and a son. She was no cipher or shadow of her husband; she came from a hard-working Huguenot business family and had a shop (probably selling china or drapery) even during her husband's lifetime, making up for her husband's tiny stipend of £50. They had no manse like most people in his job and had two congregations to look after. He would have spent much of his time on the road; food for his horse was £20 a year. This was by no stretch of the imagination a luxurious or privileged background.

Tragically, the Rev Francis became sick in January 1811 and, on 1 February, died aged thirty-nine, leaving his wife and six children, with Ann pregnant with a seventh. She supported her family by going into business as a flax buyer like her father, and as the landlady of the properties that she had inherited.

Ann was the most religiously orthodox of our radicals. The baby girl that her husband did not live to see died in infancy. Two of her daughters Martha and Mary died young. She accepted this as God's will. She also accepted the will of God when her eldest child Francis fell from the top of a cliff at Powerscourt Waterfall in County Wicklow on 31 July 1827. He was eighteen years old and just about to go to college, and went alone to the beauty spot. It is still a place where people try to climb up the 121-metre precipice and around the dangerous rocks, and people still lose their lives as Francis did. He slipped and fell; this was witnessed by some passers-by who reported it to the authorities but nothing was done until the evening when his smashed-up body was found at the base. His address was found in a letter found in his pocket, and his mother informed. Characteristically, she turned her grief into practical action. She devoted the money which would have been his to supporting a religious mission in India.

The family had moved to Dublin in 1822, where Ann became involved in prison reform. She became a member of the Female Gaol Committee and visited all the gaols in Dublin; she knew and worked with the more famous penal reformer Elizabeth Fry. Unlike most of our radicals, Carlile was brave enough both to care for and confront the women she encountered at Dublin Newgate Prison. It was clear to her, like almost everybody else, that addiction to alcohol was the gateway drug to crime, prostitution and family breakdown. It was an uphill task. When Carlile started her crusade, people were not just indifferent to temperance, they were indifferent to religion, especially the poor.

The first charge against drink reformers was always hypocrisy. Firstly, much middle class concern was against men drinking in public places, and women and children being present but it was pointed out that the middle and upper classes had their wines and spirits delivered to their house or their elite club. For the working classes, to drink meant to congregate. There were no cheap, screw-top bottles of pasteurised beer until the 1890s; it was the bar or the take-out.[1] Around 1827, she dispensed with the accusation of hypocrisy. Carlile was visiting some female prisoners; with her usually bravery she asked the group of forty-two wretched women her standard question 'what brought you here?' The initial answer was crime but the root cause was whiskey. Carlile denounced whiskey but was told in no uncertain terms that she was attacking them. Various versions of the reply have been recorded; 'The whiskey brought us here, but you can afford to drink your wine and we cannot' or 'It's easy for the like of ye to speak against the drop of whiskey or the taste of beer when you can take your glass of wine whenever you are tired or faint.'[2]

If wine could be drunk by the middle classes without harm, or under the pretence that it was a medical supplement, then the condemnation of alcohol for the poor was hypocrisy. After this encounter, Ann Jane signed a teetotal pledge, and finally rejected the idea that a small amount of alcohol is good for the health, although she had trouble convincing others.[3]

The accusation that she was merely a finger-pointing moralist with no experience of the lived experience of the poor was challenged when Carlile started to preach temperance in some of the most drunken and desperate streets of Dublin. Carlile's campaign against alcohol started when in 1830 she formed a temperance society in Poolbeg Street, an area frequented by sailors. These were strong people, with no home ties, prone to anonymous wickedness in far-away ports that they would be leaving quite soon. This was the greatest challenge possible. Sailors were an ideal target group for the evangelical teetotal. Her 'Mariner's Total Abstinence Society' attacked the problem with some of the worst offenders and was also offered as 'striking proof that hardship and labour do not require stimulating liquors'. Many who were not sailors were ex-convicts, and all were welcome.[4] She was an early adopter as well as a pioneer – similar organisations were formed in Boston (1826) and New York (1829) – the fact that all were busy ports containing rootless sailors was not a coincidence.

There was always ambiguity in the aims of the movement. There were different strengths and flavours of anti-alcohol thought. It started in the 1820s with a crusade against spirits, mostly in Scotland and

Ireland, where beer was seen as a moderate alternative, and actively encouraged. Small teetotal societies started in the 1830s. Early anti-alcohol movements were not always the middle class lecturing the poor; afterwards, the movement was split, with different aims and different audiences.

Her experiences with the drunken sailors of Dublin seemed to have convinced Carlile that campaigning against hard liquor exclusively was not enough. It had to be total abstinence. Moderation was something that was open to interpretation. The religious middle classes and the labourers did not agree on what it meant. The inventor of the word 'teetotal' was Dicky Turner, one of the seven great Preston pioneers, who also came up with the accurate northern aphorism on the ambiguities involved in the movement by saying that 'moderation is botheration'.

In one of her three famous religious teetotal tracts, Carlile made it clear that the drunkard could not enter heaven; but the reasons why were not clear cut. The campaign against alcohol was Biblical but not particularly theological. There is no commandment that calls for temperance. Most of the beverages that plagued the poor did not exist in first century Palestine, and the message was ambiguous; wine both 'gladdens the heart' and 'biteth like a serpent, and stingeth like an adder'. What did Jesus produce as the Wedding at Cana? Was it wine or was it grape juice? It mattered and was fiercely discussed in theological circles because one of the answers implied a recommendation for alcohol and the other did not. Evidence was created by absence – there was no strong drink in the Garden of Eden. Adam, the first Teetotaller, drank water although Noah planted a vineyard and then got drunk. Carlile pointed out that Abraham did not drink and he lived to be 175. Teetotalism was literally as old as creation.

Temperance was radical in itself because it gave a voice to women. Carlile became a female lecturer, taking the podium and even the pulpit from men in her lecture tours of Britain. Carlile is prominent because of her gender. Women were common in the movement, as it provided a respectable activity for middle class women with a conscience and time on their hands but few travelled the country like Ann, and few helped to popularize the temperance methods of persuasion and propaganda like she did.

She regularly resisted discrimination from men, even those who agreed with what she had to say. Women on platforms, no matter how worthy the subject, were not welcome and often her speeches were read out for her.[5] She didn't enjoy speaking very much and this was accompanied with a reluctance of men of the cloth to see her make a speech (especially in Scotland, she noted). Her first visit to Scotland in 1840 was meant to be a holiday, and she was persuaded to speak much against her will. Many of the clergy she met in Scotland did not like what she had to say and denied her right to say it. Not only was teetotalism an extreme view, said one, but they were reminded of the words of Paul who would not suffer a woman to speak. When her biography was written in 1897, the introduction pointed out that she had led the way in women's engagement 'by resisting the criticism of press and pulpit'.[6]

Temperance campaigners were accused of authoritarianism. The authoritarian streak was also a limited accusation, even when it was true. When religious men and women went into wretched working class communities to preach abstinence and self-denial (the language was similar to that of controlling sexual activity), they were also being very brave and making a statement about the need to improve the conditions of the poor and a personal willingness to do something about it when they could have done nothing.

The propaganda weapon of choice was the temperance meeting, and it was far more sophisticated than just preachy finger-wagging. It was a battle for hearts and minds; people had to continue to be sober once the lecture was over. So the key elements were the lecture, the redemptive story with witnesses, and then the signing of the pledge.

At a meeting at the Birmingham Temperance Society in 1839, chaired by the chocolate entrepreneur John Cadbury, an agricultural labourer, John Mayou, told the standard 'redemption' story. He had been a drunk for fifteen years and:

> It had robbed him of every domestic comfort, and during his time had spent in the public house sufficient money to have rendered him independent of all labour. He had been four years teetotaller, and though he did not wish to boast of what it had done for him, yet he might with truth say, that it had enabled him to find his way to a place of worship regularly ever since, and to pay for a comfortable seat there; besides which, was at least hundred pounds better in pocket.

Temperance was a rational decision – the money saved proved it. It was also Mayou's way of becoming independent of the bosses, and he used his newly found economic power to buy a better seat in church. Diverting his money from alcohol and other vices earned him respectability, better health and the use of the new savings banks, rather than the pub 'the losing bank'. Temperance was about helping the poor, but helping them towards the respectability of the middle classes. Most temperance societies had an anti-tobacco sideline for the same reason. Tobacco had all the same moral hazards as alcohol, except for the unreliable behaviour and effect on moral judgement.

Carlile's methods were reminiscent of the evangelical Christians of the twentieth century. A large meeting at a lecture hall was followed by a call for individuals to publicly commit themselves to abstinence. She worked mostly, but not exclusively with women and children, and mostly with the poor working classes, although many of the already respectable classes would take the pledge as well. It was a data-driven exercise – the numbers would be counted. In 1851, on a return visit to Ireland, the Belfast Newsletter recorded that 11,000 people had signed up on her recent tour of England and Scotland.[7] Then, if possible, she would leave behind a temperance society to continue with the work.

The fact that the pledge had been made in front of their own community made surveillance quite easy. Signing the pledge was an inclusive rather than a shameful act. Agreeing to be sober forever was not an admission that you had an immediate alcohol problem, merely that you aspired to be a better person. Alcohol was bad even if it could be afforded. Respectable people, who could afford alcohol and who would not suffer if they continued, were motivated by the duty of example to sign the pledge.

The pledges varied in their level of commitment. The basic promise was not to drink alcohol themselves, but there was always ambiguity. What if the alcohol was 'medicinal'? This was a time when alcohol was seen as such by all classes, and even today you are most likely to be offered a large brandy if you have just been part of a serious accident. Most temperance crusaders wanted to break the magic spell of alcohol. What about polite hospitality? Did the pledge include buying drinks for others in pubs, or offering them to non-teetotallers? What about the ancient bottle of sherry reluctantly offered to guests in dry households for the hundred years after 1850? In 1839, there was a split in the movement on the 'give and receive' cause, where some campaigners wanted to promise to include not offering alcohol to guests

On the whole, Carlile offered the pledge without caveats, but was also well aware that the temperance societies had to be valued by those who took part. She was up against a formidable enemy – the public house, a place where warmth, bright lights, music, singing, simple games, newspapers and good company – some of the things that made a dull life of work more tolerable, and most people knew that a night in the pub was not an invitation to crime.

Carlile tended to be cast in the role of men's helper, the best women could hope for in any area of Victorian life. She was certainly at the mercy of men's decisions. On one of her tours of Scotland, she used her considerable experience of prisons to persuade some hardened criminals to take the pledge, thus avoiding transportation. One Glasgow clergyman was so impressed that he broke his rule about allowing women into the pulpit, proving that such a rule existed. In 1843, she helped with the temperance work of Rev Theobald Mathew; he too had taken the pledge in 1838, having come to the same conclusion that moderation was impossible. He would drink no more whiskey punches. He became president of the Cork Total Abstinence Society.

Mathew is much better known than Anne Carlile in their native Ireland. He was dubbed the 'The Apostle of Temperance'. There are statues in Dublin and his native Cork, and a bridge in Limerick that acknowledge his enormous contribution to sobriety in Ireland. He was a priest (and a capuchin monk) of the Roman Catholic Church, but this did not stop Carlile from collaborating with him on his temperance tours of Scotland and England. The pair had been corresponding by letter since the early 1840s, and the fact that Carlile was a Protestant Presbyterian made no difference at all; it was remarkably free of sectarianism apart from a few diehards on either side.

Mathew's English temperance meetings raised eyebrows in Protestant heartlands, with town halls being suddenly double booked and newspapers publishing snarky letters. Carlile worked with Theobald in London in 1843 with his entourage of priests helping him collect pledges from the poor Irish diaspora, in a ceremony that was suspiciously mass-like. It is estimated that 200,000 signed the pledge on the 1842–43 tour of Scotland and England. The strong link with the Irish sometimes fuelled stereotypes about the Irish, but everybody knew the problem was not restricted to them; intemperance is Ireland's Bane, England's Curse, and Scotland's Woe, was the common cry.

Carlile is rightly most famous for the foundation of the Band of Hope in Leeds in 1847. A temperance society had been formed there in 1830 with only moderate success. Alcohol was popular. It made life temporarily easier for the male workers of Leeds. Engels had said that beer was the quickest route out of Manchester, and the same applied to the Yorkshire textile towns. Most English temperance societies were small. Manchester claimed 10,000 and was an exception. Blackburn had 2,000 and even Preston of the famous Dicky Turner only had 3,500; another tactic was needed.

The rationale behind the Band of Hope was to focus on the children. Children's temperance was not new; most established societies had a juvenile department. This was not a new idea. 'We have a more hopeful soil in which the seeds of truth and sobriety may be cast' said the temperance campaigner Joseph Livesey; but Carlile was responsible for bringing it to the next level of dedicated and sophisticated campaigning.

The man who normally claimed the credit was Reverend Jabez Tunnicliffe. Tunnicliffe has been criticised in recent years for taking some of the limelight from Anne Carlile, but he did have his own established track record of temperance. In June 1846, Tunnicliffe was parading all the local non-conformist Sunday schools and feeding them buns, oranges, lemonade and a sermon.[9] The convivial tea party was a common method of persuasion; Carlile had used the same method with the rough sailors of Dublin, selecting St Patrick's Day evening rather than a Sunday morning.

Tunnicliffe was also well versed in moral persuasion by anecdote, another temperance technique. Tunnicliffe told a story about a man who called him on his death bed and admitted that it was alcohol that had ruined his constitution and brought on consumption by his intemperate habits. It was the first glass that had caused the problems, and he pleaded with the reverend to start the fight before the point of the first drink. Tunnicliffe thought that not much could be done with drunkards or moderate drinkers of the day and it would be far better to devote their entire energy to an organisation devoted solely to the young.

This 'first glass' idea was common; coincidentally in the same year, Cruikshank's *The Bottle* was published. This series of lithographs showed the descent of a family into moral degradation. In the first scene, the family is prosperous and harmonious, there is one bottle of spirits in the well-kept house, and the title is 'Just to Take a Drop'. The plan of the Band of Hope was to stop the first drop, so it was aimed at children and it was mightily successful in doing so. Proverbs 22:6 summed it up 'Train up a child in the way he should go and when he is old, he will not depart from it'.

The Leeds Band of Hope was a success from the beginning. Carlile spent a mere fourteen days in Leeds on her third visit to England visiting schools and focusing very much on women and children. This she was very good at, but it was what she had been doing for a lifetime. It was the achievement of three decades, not two weeks, using all she had learnt. Her work in Sunday schools made the Band of Hope an easy transition. A woman who could sell copies of *Tee Total World* in the Dublin Docks, or get hardened sailors to enjoy tea, cakes and lectures on St Patrick's Day was going to have no problems with ragged children. She was seventy-two at the time and was in her third decade crusading against alcohol; a remarkable feat of stamina.

Three hundred children attended the meeting of the first Band of Hope Union in South Parade Chapel, Leeds in 1847. Leeds had no Temperance Hall for them to meet in. On that day the children signed the famous pledge; 'I agree to abstain from all Intoxicating Liquors and from Tobacco in all its forms'.

The focus on children was not alarmist. If the family had a drinking problem, then they would be in serious danger by that age. Alcohol was easily available to all. Britain's first Christmas card (1843) showed a small child drinking alcohol and there was a child-size pub glass called a squib, priced at one halfpenny. It was not until 1886 that children under thirteen were banned from buying alcohol in public houses. Carlile's Band of Hope allowed six and seven-year-olds to sign the pledge, which was proof that the problem was real.

Children were never pushed into joining; they had to ask. It was the children who provided both the band and the hope. They had to get their parent's approval and a home visit was often made, allowing a temperance presence into the adult home. Recruitment would also take place at the person's home address, and Carlile was perfectly happy to go to the wretched hovels in the slums to proselytize in person if necessary.

Four thousand children joined the Leeds Band of Hope in 1847. Bands were set up in other locations, mostly London, Scotland and the Industrial North and Midlands later in the same year, and many existing children's temperance groups took advantage of the branding and some that had previously existed changed their name. Carlile managed not only to create a meeting where children signed the pledge but also a template for an organisation that could be scaled up all around the country with marketing and branding techniques designed specifically for the recruitment and retention of children.

Meetings would begin with a prayer and a hymn. There were short one hour activities rather than two-hour sermons; blackboards and colour lantern slides, songs and slogans, stories of celebrity teetotallers, speeches and recitations and pithy slogans to shame parents ('drink steals the children's food').[10] There were pageants, medals, discussions and debates (originally just boys, and girls later on when it decided it would not jeopardize their sex). Children were encouraged to sadly regret the use of alcohol rather than condemn their parents.

Shame and pity were the weapons of choice. The Band of Hope also seems to have either invented or popularised the expression 'beer money'. It was not meant as a compliment. Beer was regarded by too many as a food. Prime Minister Disraeli called it 'liquid bread' and the temperance movement needed to counter this. There was always a tension between amusement, instruction and improvement, but at least all three were being attempted for the children of the poor. The slogan summarized their four-point attack – 'Scripture, Reason, Science and Experience'.

The songs were maudlin and melodramatic to the modern ear and sensibilities; as in the 1864 song by Henry Clay *Come Home Father.*

> Father, dear father, come home with me now,
> The clock in the steeple strikes one;
> You said you were coming right home from the shop
> As soon as your day's work was done;
> Our fire has gone out, our house is all dark,
> And mother's been watching since tea,
> With poor brother Benny so sick in her arms

Father does not come home; and by 3 a.m., Benny is dead, his last words being a wish to kiss papa goodnight.

The membership card cost a penny and had to be brought to a meeting. Children had to be clean and tidy. Registers were taken, and two-thirds attendance attracted a seaside excursion or similar treat. The membership card included the pledge, part of the Lord's Prayer about temptation and the poetic and memorable 'pray, study, work, play', that was illustrated and something to be proud of.

On the day Carlile left Leeds for the last time, a women's committee under the charge of the Rev. Tunnicliffe was set up – exactly what would be expected. Tunnicliffe continued to devote his life to the poor. He had worked himself to death by 1865 and three thousand people lined the streets at his funeral. His local council recognised that he had contributed greatly to the most successful organisation that was grappling with the national vice.[11] He did claim the credit in a speech a year before his death in 1864. He may have written the pilot, but it was Carlile who wrote the series.

Carlile may not have been comfortable in the company of any other the radicals in this book, but her methods were similar, and the key was the printed word, pamphlets with such titles as 'Confessions of a Publican', 'The Miraculous Deliverance', 'Delirium Tremens' and 'Self Imposed Burdens.'[12]

Carlile's most famous personal contribution was 'The Reformed Family of Ballymena'. During her travels, an unfortunate family is referred to her and her response is to visit them immediately. She had a morning to kill before her stagecoach left. Mrs Carlile visited a desperate, tawdry house where both man and wife were in bed nursing a two-day hangover. Using the same robust questioning that she had developed in Dublin Newgate, she ascertained that they had just sold their cow to buy whiskey. Carlile would visit people in their homes, showing concern for their welfare and contempt for their proclivity to vice. When told by one broken-down drunk that cutting off his ardent spirits would lead to his death, Mrs Carlile told him that she had ministered to the inmates of prisons and nobody had died when their liquor were cut off. On this occasion in Ballymena, she had her pledge book ready. In an hour and forty minutes, she had converted the husband and the wife.

Could they be reformed by exhortation? She found out when she revisited them. A mere year later they were total abstainers, the father had been restored to health and the table was groaning with wholesome food.

> The cold, damp, sepulchral-looking room, destitute of furniture and with the appearance of nought but discomfort, now seemed warm and cheerful. There was now presented a good carpet, handsome furniture, books arranged on a table, among which was a family Bible, opened when I entered.

Carlile did not focus too much on adult males; partly from the scale of the task, but partly because she felt that alcohol was a vice from which children could be rescued, and that was the job of the female. She was not scared to remind mothers that their children were born with an immortal soul and that their parental guidance would decide whether they went to heaven or hell.[13] It is easy to see this as bullying or discrimination, but in a world where women had little power and working class women had even less, it was perhaps good advice for them to control what they could control. Sober men were liberation for women. Frances Power Cobbe asserted that drink was the cause of drunken assaults on women, which was condoned and caused by the asymmetrical power relationship between men and women. Another Victorian feminist and socialist, Ethel Snowden, claimed that women married to working class men who drank were the greatest sufferers from the drink habit. Drink, like meat eating or vivisection normalised male cruelty and violence, making temperance a purity movement, and a slightly more down to earth one than vegetarianism or anti-vivisection.

Carlile's friend Father Mathew found it difficult to operate in Belfast. This was a job that had to be done by a Protestant temperance campaigner. In 1853, Carlile started a two-year campaign against the Belfast beer houses with Arthur Hill Thornton, and was instrumental in closing down two hundred drinking establishments. This sounds like the work of a killjoy, but Carlile was actually assaulting a quite vicious unregulated market in drink. After the 1830 Beer Act, there was almost a free trade where anybody could sell beer for a two guinea licence, and this did not change until 1870. It was essentially a tax-free product, available everywhere and sold by anybody who wanted to. Beer Houses, as opposed to pubic houses, were outside the control of the magistrates; it was a legitimate target in the eyes of the temperance movement.

Carlile continued her *modus operandi* until her death. In 1860, her biography reported that God enjoined her to establish temperance in her home county of Monaghan. She travelled there, inspired them and left the administration into the hands of the local churches. In this case it was local Presbyterians who reported back that market day was much less drunken. It was so much easier to monitor drinking in rural Ireland than urban Scotland or England – and even the 'poor blind papists were too ashamed to be seen drinking'. Carlile did what she always did and ignored their sectarianism and thanked them for their work.

In the last years of her life came the realisation that not enough had been achieved by moral exhortation, and the temperance campaign was shifting in emphasis. In 1853, the United Kingdom Alliance was formed to promote the prohibition of alcohol by legislation rather than persuasion. People on their own were not moral enough. Both Father Mathew and Carlile supported it. Carlile already had a track record of suppressing licences but the United Kingdom Alliance wanted to go further. In 1863, one of its members, radical Liberal Sir William Lawson proposed a bill in parliament which would ban the trade from an area when two-thirds of its ratepayers voted to implement the 'Permissive Bill'.

This failed to be adopted. The power of the Brewers and Distillers was immense, and they were well represented in the Commons. Lord Randolph Churchill suggested that 'two thirds of the members of the present house of commons are inspired by a terror of the organisation of the alcoholic liquor trade, wholesale and retail'.

Some of the counter-arguments were still sound. 'You can't make people sober by act of parliament' was one. People would migrate from area to area in search of drink. Like prohibition in next century USA, many would brew their own in their tea kettle or wash house boiler, and it would be worse and totally unregulated. The rich could store bottles of wine in their house and drink away happily and only the honest, moderate drinker would suffer.

Carlile died in March 1864, still hoping for her Permissive Bill which would justify her decades of work. 'Let thy servant depart in peace. I feel assured that it will be the first great step towards the salvation of my country'. On this basis, she did not depart in peace, as much of the work had to be done, and most of the successes of temperance happened after her death.

Carlile tried to estimate her legacy. She counted 7,000 people who had taken the pledge in her lifetime. She was unable to subtract from that figure those who had reneged, and in any case, figures themselves do not tell the whole story. The Band of Hope was her major contribution, but most of the growth took place after her death. In 1901, there were 28,894 local societies, with a total membership of 3,536,000.[14]

Temperance and teetotalism deserve to be called progressive, not reactionary. Their proponents wanted life to be better and were prepared to take on the establishment and big business to do so. Because of the religious element, and the fact that they did not ask *why* people drank so much, temperance has been dismissed and people like Carlile were not regarded as social reformers. It may not have advocated reform but temperance was never far away from social issues such as child cruelty, infant mortality, domestic violence, cleaner drinking water, social housing and shorter working hours. Most temperance tracts, including Carlile's, were rarely more than a few paragraphs old when they boasted about the improved social conditions for women and children. Carlile was obviously being myopic when identifying alcohol as the root of all misery, but that did not make her much different to Cobbe's obsession with vivisection or Kingsford's monomania about vegetarianism.

Carlile did not know it, but events were turning her way. The established Church also started to show an interest. As Carlile said in her autobiography, 'The time will come when this matter must be taken up by the Church, and when your old grandmother will not be dubbed an enthusiast'. The alcohol-free Salvation Army was established by General William Booth in 1863; laws on alcohol grew stricter from 1872 and remained so for another one hundred years.

Temperance became part of a wider movement. Socialists like Keir Hardie (Chapter Thirteen), who asked why the poor were poor and realised it was not due to drink but low wages and unemployment, was also temperance through his own lived experience. He had experienced the evils of drink directly from the behaviour of his stepfather.

Temperance was a mass canvassing activity on the streets and in the churches, one that would have perished without the unacknowledged work of women – it was little like other progressive movements in that regard. Individual names do not come naturally to the forefront, but Carlile deserves to be remembered. Even if temperance is ignored, she blazed a trail for women in the church to speak for themselves.

On the centenary of the Band of Hope, the celebrations were most notable in Northern Ireland. It was 1947, and the National Health Service was being organised, and some politicians made a direct link to temperance. 'The founders of this movement were the pioneers of our social services,' said William Grant (Minister of Health and former shipwright and trade unionist), 'for they awakened the social conscience towards the intolerable living conditions of the workers.'[15]

In February 2015, the Minister for Arts, Heritage and the Gaeltacht, Heather Humphreys, unveiled an Ulster History Circle plaque in her honour at the Presbyterian Church in her home town of Bailieborough, celebrating Carlile's non-sectarian care for the poor in Ireland. She deserves to be called a radical Victorian.[16]

Chapter Four

Spiritualism

Florence Cook

If the late Victorian, Edwardian, and First World War eras in Britain witnessed the growth of science and an emphasis on reason, why did they also spawn and cultivate the seemingly illogical religious movement of spiritualism?

Spiritualism is very easily broken down into clichés and stereotypes, and it is not difficult to see why. There was always a performative element – the darkened room, the mixed eager and sceptical audience of believers and debunkers, the manifestations, the moving objects and the table rapping. Both then and now, it succumbs to ridicule easily, and the fact that it may be an active fraud does not take away from its importance in the Victorian era. Spiritualism was a very radical notion in the nineteenth century and very much deserves to be a part of Victorian radicalism, even if the truth of it will always be a matter of opinion.

Spiritualism was a lot more than knocking on tables to attract the spirits of the dead, although, to be fair, it did start that way. Arthur Conan Doyle, one of a long list of celebrity spiritualists, believed that the movement started in its modern form on 31 March 1848, when Charles Rosna, dead five years, told a huddled séance that he had been murdered by a man called Duesler and then buried ten foot deep in a cellar. This message was the work of two New York sisters, Kate and Margaret Fox, aged twelve and thirteen, who had been hearing rapping and noises for a while. The details were prised out of the spirit by a method that would become standard; closed questions with one rap for yes, two for no, and alphabetic rapping to find out more

The two Foxes were frauds. Forty years later, Margaret was to confess that they used an apple tied to a string to make bumping noises and cracked their toe joints to persuade people that they were in touch with spirits. They weren't allowed to recant of this teenage prank at the time, as their much older sister Leah took them on a tour of New England to accommodate an unfilled desire to talk to the dead. During their heyday in the North Eastern USA, the spirits told them that they would be communicating via other people as well. This opened up a gap in the market on the other side of the Atlantic.

This melodramatic spirit rapping may sound trite and contrived, but it spread quickly from New England to Britain in the early 1850s. It was a woman called Mrs Maria Hayden who brought spiritualism to Britain in 1852. She was proud that it had arrived in the USA first and had to be transplanted to the mother country through missionaries, and she was convinced that it would thrive in another free country where people had become more open-minded about religion, more unsure about the truth and hungry for reassurance.

Séances were a minor craze in the 1850s and 1860s. Queen Victoria attended one in the 1860s in which a thirteen-year-old boy made contact with her beloved Prince Albert. Charles Dickens attended them out of curiosity; Gladstone, the most orthodox of Christians, did the same. The nation was already well acquainted with ghosts, and the interest was already there; hence the consummate businessman's seasonal novella *A Christmas Carol* (1843) which features three ghosts who visit, chastise and eventually convert Ebenezer Scrooge into a decent human being.

Until the Victorian era, communication with the dead was a one-way street; they brought threats or bad news. Only evil people sought to conjure them up. The Bible forbade it, and Maria Hayden was correct in that it would only be popular in a country that was free to think what it liked about Christianity, which was just about the case in the Britain of the 1850s. Although it was mostly the upper 10,000 of society who flocked to séances, and many of them were doing it for the thrill, it was certainly part of a crisis of faith as well. Spiritualism was 'a parlour pastime for some and a religion for others'.[1]

Spiritualism was a challenge to traditional theology. Even some secularists were drawn to it. It created confusion in the Victorian mind about exactly what it meant to be dead; it questioned the nature of the afterlife and salvation. People who abandoned traditional religion were drawn to it. It had the major advantage of being a regular proof of the existence of an afterlife; a Victorian obsession. You didn't have to believe, it could be proved in front of you. It was also quite democratic. You did not need to have a degree in theology to ask after a dead friend or relative, and unlike the traditional pulpit, the religious gatekeeper was often a woman. It became a powerful women's movement which privileged females over males.

Many people were sceptical and most were suspicious of fraud. Dickens, who regarded his novella as a money-making piece of fiction rather than a new philosophy of life, took a materialistic and scientific view. It was his mind and body that was conjuring up the ghost:

> You may be an undigested bit of beef, a blot of mustard, a crumb of cheese, a fragment of underdone potato. There's more of gravy than of grave about you …!

Victorian scientists were mostly the implacable enemies of spiritualism, with a few exceptions for reasons that may not have been motivated by science, as can be seen later in this chapter.

There were famous spiritualists in this period, but the most famous national celebrity was Florence Cook (1856–1904). She was the daughter of a respectable lower middle class family in Hackney, and at first, her parents tried to control her over-active imagination.

> From my childhood I could see spirits and hear voices, and was addicted to sitting by myself talking to what I declared to be living people. As no one else could see or hear anything, my parents tried to make me believe it was all imagination, but I would not alter my belief.

By fourteen, tables were being mysteriously rapped and small objects moving autonomously around the room and her mother pointed her in the direction of one of the many spiritualist societies that had grown up during the spiritualism boom of the 1860s. She had in any case already received a spirit message in a séance which she noted down in mirror-writing advising her to do this. These societies often had the word 'investigation' somewhere in their name; in reality, they had mostly made up their mind. Their local society was the Dalston Association of Inquirers into Spiritualism, very close to their home, and under their guidance, Cook's mediumship skills grew in complexity. She met Thomas Blyton, editor of the Spiritualist and secretary of the association, and like every other man she met, exploited their interest in both spiritualism and herself as a spirited young woman.

Cook was intelligent and sensitive. She had already embarked on a career as a pupil teacher in a local school, the most prestigious occupation for the bright lower middle class girl before marriage. The school promptly sacked her when poltergeist activity started in her presence but this was a career with far more to offer. It could also be said that Cook started a new apprenticeship under Blyton and others. The repertoire of events that happened in her séances became wider and wider, and she reached the point of materialising spirits, starting with arms, legs and faces and eventually whole bodies.

More remarkable than the control over the dead was her ability to exploit live men. Unlike most spiritualists, Cook never charged for her services. In 1872, she had begun to receive financial support from the businessman and fellow spiritualist, Charles Blackburn that ensured she would be able to take séances without taking fees and avoiding the accusation that it was a money-making venture. Blackburn paid her an annual retainer and called her 'my medium' but he had no control whatsoever over what happened at séances. The fact that she did not charge money for entry meant that no ghost grabber could follow up with a charge of defrauding the public.

In one séance with her mentor Frank Herne, another man who mentored her and then she surpassed, a spirit's voice told the listeners that there was an obstruction in the gutter which was directing water into the house's foundations. On examination, this proved to be true. It had been raining, possibly coincidentally during the séance. This spirit, far from suffering in hell or even rattling his chains like Marley, was giving advice about house maintenance. The majority of Victorian spiritualists were female, and in the context of a séance they gave regular advice – not on house maintenance, but on marriage, diet and lifestyle and were prepared to countenance questions from the audience that would be scandalous in polite society. Communicating with the dead allowed all society's rules to be broken; spiritualism was a new democratic method of communication like the railway, the telegraph and the cheap unstamped newspaper, bringing new opportunities to all.

Cook developed her abilities and by 1873 was holding séances in her own modest Hackney home; she had learned from Herne and was moving on from him – a constant theme in her development. Another reason for the move, and a criticism that followed Cook constantly, was that her clothing was indelicately moved during the séance. Purists were upset by the number of times spirits seemed to lift up her dress and rearrange her clothing. The whole ethos of séance, darkness, closeness, random touching, while not exactly erotic, did break away from the way women were expected to behave. Like the ventriloquist with the rude puppet, she had somebody else to blame.

Cook's greatest creation was Katie King. In order to dispel doubts about the truth of her manifestations – one of the developments in her powers, originally encouraged by Frank Herne – Cook would lock herself inside a cabinet or sometimes hide behind a damask curtain. After half an hour, at least, of anxious anticipation (during which it could be argued that true believers would be ready to see anything), the spirit of King would appear, looking, even the believers said, much like Cook herself, although later differences did appear in the face. Katie claimed to be related to John King, a spirit that had earlier been materialised by Herne, who was exposed as a fraud in 1875 without damaging either Cook's career or Katie King's plausibility as a spirit. Katie was active, rude, and assertive; while Cook was locked in a cabinet.

Katie King was related to spirits who had appeared in North America. She had been a murderer who had died prematurely at twenty-two and had come back to earth to atone for her sins *and* to describe them in salacious detail. She was troubled and unhappy, but she was clearly not in Christian hell and her post-mortem attempt to get a pardon for her sins was religiously unorthodox. Katie King touched, flirted and even kissed sitters – behaviour that would have ruined a similar Victorian gentlewoman if the lights were up and no séance was taking place. Some grateful men noticed that Katie King wore no underclothes, and sometimes proposed marriage to total strangers with a ring.

Katie had been called to earth to witness the truth about spiritualism. Marley too, was able to roam the earth in chains despite being condemned; perhaps hell was in the head and not under the ground? Perhaps there is no death? Like other spirits manifested by thousands of other mediums, King was apparent empirical evidence for the reality of spirit life and the existence of an unseen world. This was by no means Christianity and was a threat to its teaching. It was also a flat rejection of science just like Cobbe's anti-vivisection campaign or Kingsford's vegetarianism.

Cook made enemies and attracted debunkers. Many spiritualists were exposed as frauds, mostly by somebody behaving badly at a séance by 'ghost-grabbing'. In December 1873, William Volckman grabbed one of

Cook's materialisations of Katie (who had just proved herself by spitting in the hands of the participants) and asserted that this was in fact, Cook. At this point, and arguably quite conveniently, all lights were extinguished. The spirit was rescued by the onlookers and put back into the cabinet and a few minutes later Cook appeared, still sealed up with tape.

The attempt had failed and other motivations were found. Volckman was a friend of a rival medium, a Mrs Agnes Guppy. In June 1871, in one of her first performances, a semi-naked Mrs Guppy had appeared at one of her séances and later Mr Volckman married Mrs Guppy when she became a widow. Cook's reputation was damaged. The real threat to her career was the doubt that she was genuine. Other mediums were debunked and exposed at regular intervals but people who wished to believe would never take that as conclusive. Newspapers would often bewail the fact that people still believed in spiritualism despite regular exposures of frauds but the will to believe was great. Katie King was a two-year phenomenon. She had often stated that she could not appear on this earth beyond the month of May 1874, and so, on the 21st she assembled her friends together to bid them all goodbye.

Florence Cook had it all – youth, beauty, charm, and a thriving business – total freedom of movement. She was set for life – as long as nothing interrupted the flow of money from her wealthy patron, Charles Blackburn. Cook's manipulation of men continued. In April 1874, Cook married Captain Edward Elgie Corner, the neighbour who had rushed to Katie's aid the previous December. Marriage normally meant the end of paid work. Even Charles Blackburn, who paid the bills and got no influence in return, expected her to give it up. She ignored both of them, which was brave but potentially dangerous, as will be seen.

She needed science, which in Victorian times meant needing men, and her power over men was as secure as that over the spirits. The man that mattered was Sir William Crookes, who was one of the people present at the tearful departure of Katie King. He was present at her last manifestation. Crookes was given a character reference by Katie and declared to be the best person to look after her. His reputation preceded him. He had discovered the element thallium in 1861, his work with cathode ray tubes led to the discovery of both x-rays and later, television. Crookes had completed a 'rigorous' scientific investigation of another medium, Daniel Home. Home claimed he could levitate and Crookes believed him. Cook needed that level of endorsement.

Cook had one advantage over Home; she was a young attractive female. To Crookes, with a clear lack of scientific detachment, she was 'dear Florrie'. Like Blackburn, he gushed and simpered about her loveliness and youth, and historians have speculated about the exact nature of their relationship. Cook was very young. She first appeared in the *Spiritualist* magazine on 15 July 1871 at fifteen and was still only eighteen at the height of her fame. When called on to help her reputation, Crooke seemed convinced that somebody so young and charming could not be a fraud. Crookes commented that it was his duty to help 'remove an unjust suspicion which is cast upon another' especially when this 'person is a woman – young, sensitive, innocent'. She was too innocent to be sinful; that was a strong card to play.

Despite his fame as a rational man of science, his argument was remarkably circular:

> Indeed, I do not believe that she could carry on a deception if she were to try ... and if she did she would be certainly found out very quickly, for such a line of action is altogether foreign to her nature.[2]

Crookes did everything he could to reduce the physical distance between himself and the teenage Cook. She and her mother moved into Crooke's house in Mornington Road and attempted to create a controlled scientific experiment. Cook wasn't allowed any time or resources to work on faking. Crooke noticed the intimate detail again.

> She brings nothing with her but a little hand-bag, not locked; during the day she is constantly in the presence of Mrs. Crookes, myself, or some other member of my family, and, not sleeping by herself, there is absolutely no opportunity for any preparation...'[3]

She was prepared to do her nightly séance with enough light to be photographed. Crookes lingered over the physical details of Florence and compared them to her manifestations. He photographed Cook in Katie's clothes to show that they were different. He looked very carefully at their faces and noticed that only Cook had pierced ears.[4]

Crookes became convinced when Katie asked him to lift Florence up from the sofa where she was unconscious. He saw them together; Katie would often take her hand, and he asked permission to hold hers – 'he felt he was in the presence of a lady'. It was at this time that she told Crookes that she was married. His wife was heavily pregnant with their tenth child and was confined to her room. Crookes would always know where his wife was; it was very convenient.

Cook was not going to be told what to do and that included her new husband, a ship's captain from Dalston who was conveniently away a lot. However, he became suspicious of Crookes and seemed to take it out on his wife. A mere three months after their marriage Cook was petitioning for a legal separation, citing extreme verbal abuse, threats and physical violence: 'He took an open razor and threatened to kill your petitioner … has daily used most blasphemous and disgusting language'. The legal separation never happened; they had two children quite quickly and lived apart for the rest of their lives.

In 1874, Crookes claimed that Cook was genuine, to the widespread scepticism of the scientific press. He never changed his mind, and this never damaged his reputation, even when fraud was discovered. He continued his dual-track as a scientist *and* believer in the esoteric other world. He became a Theosophist, briefly, in 1883 and would have rubbed shoulders with Anna Kingsford and Edward Maitland. In 1898, he had not changed his mind and said so in a speech to the British Association. He was knighted in 1897 and became President of the prestigious British Association for the Advancement of Science in 1898.

Despite the support of Crookes, Cook had passed her peak. Her next manifestations were a Frenchwoman called Marie, a singer and dancer, who often performed at séances; something, Cook's supporters pointed out, that Florence could not do herself. She was under assault again in 1880, when Sir George Sitwell, then a twenty-year-old Oxford student with a lifetime of eccentricity in front of him, ghost-grabbed Cook again. Sitwell attended a public séance and noticed that Marie's spirit robes covered corset stays (female semi-nudity remained a feature of the Cook's performance), so he reached out and grabbed hold of her. He held on tightly, he pulled aside Cook's curtain and found that the medium's chair was empty. He was not surprised to discover that he was holding onto Florence, clad only in her underwear. Unlike the Volckman ghost-grab of 1873, there was no five minutes darkened delay for the medium to get back into the box.

While Cook faded away, spiritualism flourished. It was an industry of newspapers, tracts and organisations, whose members were often part of other progressive causes. Spiritualism was a radical movement. It rejected material life and established religion, condemning both as mundane and incomplete. The Victorian age is often seen as fixedly religious; it was not. It was plagued with doubt and what spiritualism brought was certainty. Spiritualism created new churches. Emma Hardinge, a pioneer of women's rights, opened a Spiritualist Church in 1868 on London's King William Street. Spiritualists were looking for a better world. The *Spiritualist* Newspaper ('A Record of the Progress of the Science and Ethics of Spiritualism') of 5 June 1874 contained a plea from the Manchester Association of Spiritualists for believers to search for the reality of a future state of progressive existence for all. This description of what spiritualists think of themselves is modern, but has its roots in the nineteenth century:

> Spiritualism endeavours to find the cause of our social evils and to change man's material outlook into a spiritual one, for by thus transforming the individual, we can reform society as a whole.[5]

Many spiritualists became campaigners for votes for women, especially in the United States.

Cook had one more attempt to revive her career. In 1899, she was invited to Berlin to undertake a series of séances under test conditions by the Sphinx Society. She died of pneumonia in 20 Battersea Rise, Clapham, London in April 1904 at the age of only forty-eight. Her estranged husband lived another quarter of a century and was in a continuing relationship with Kate Cook, Florence's sister, who was also a medium and was present at the manifestations of Katie King. Crookes wrote a letter of condolence, stating that he still believed in her.

Was Florence Cook a radical, even if she might have been a fraud? Even if her communication with the dead is removed from the equation, it still remains remarkable how much extra latitude she was able to exemplify and to model for the Victorian woman. If spiritualism is put back into the mix, then she spearheaded a new, democratic movement that challenged the establishment, and was led by women.

Chapter Five

Cremation and Living with the Dead

Sir Henry Thompson & Isabelle Holmes

In the war of competing resources between the classes in Victorian Britain, there was one lingering question that was tackled with the greatest reluctance – what portion of the nation's resources should be allocated to the dead?

The eighteenth century solution was not fit for purpose. The parish graveyard was full, with the level of the ground swelling ever upward with every new corpse added to it. The parish church with its ancient lych-gate, timeless yew tree, cut grass and well-kept memories was a myth even at the time, and more so by the nineteenth century.

The overfull graveyard and the dangers of effluvia from bodies buried too close together and too close to the surface was a well-known problem. The authorities believed that by building new large suburban places of rest, and by closing the graveyards with the Act of 1850, sending the dead via the railway to suburban cemeteries, the problem would be solved. But it took radical thought to suggest that the dead were *still* taking up too much room, and cohabiting with their decomposing corpses was an unnecessary health hazard.

A few voices suggested that cremation was the answer. The Victorians mostly disagreed, and the reluctance spread a long way into the next century so cremation, or any change in the treatment of the dead, was a radical view in the nineteenth century. By 1901, there were only six crematoria in the United Kingdom, and only 427 cremations took place out of 551,585 deaths – less than one-tenth of 1%. By 1902, when its legality was firmly established, there had only ever been 4,409 cremations, 2,653 of which had taken place in one crematorium in Woking. Cremation represented barely 5% of interments even as late as the 1930s in the UK and was impermissible to Roman Catholics until 1963. Cremation overtook traditional burial as late as 1967.[1]

The turbulent and unorthodox life of Anna Kingsford has already been recounted; perhaps it is no surprise that, on her deathbed in 1888, she asked for her remains to be cremated. The first cremation of a human had been barely three years earlier and had not been established as completely legal when she requested it:

> It was her own wish that her body should be cremated, but after a period of unbending resolve to this effect, she yielded the long run to the objections which were brought forward with the view of showing, all things considered, its inexpediency as applicable to herself.[2]

It was not applicable to her because her husband was a Church of England vicar. The life of her husband would have been made intolerable if she had not changed her mind, because Algie, being a loyal partner in an equal relationship, would have agreed and taken the consequences.

Our radical thinker in the area of cremation is Sir Henry Thompson, a truly remarkable polymath. He became a qualified doctor later than normal for members of his social class. His father was opposed to it; 'all doctors become infidels' he was reputed to have said, and in this case, he was not far wrong. Thompson's first area of expertise was surgery, particularly the bladder, and in 1863 he saved the king of Belgium from a lifetime of suffering and insomnia by crushing his bladder stones without killing him with a subsequent infection, and adding £3,000 to his bank account, although it was fame that was always the doctor's motivation.

As well as being a surgeon, he was an artist whose work was displayed in the most prestigious galleries in Paris and London. He was a connoisseur and collector of Chinese porcelain and an astronomer who designed telescopes. He played the flute, wrote two novels – one of them a best-seller, bred animals, and was one of the first motor-car enthusiasts in Britain. He lived on a high intellectual and rational level, his opinion was sought on all medical subjects, and nobody had more confidence in his opinions than Thompson himself. His dinner parties were famous; eight courses, accompanied by eight wines, were served at eight o'clock to eight guests in addition to the host and the guest of honour. They would be accomplished people from different walks of life, and they would be expected to be both interesting and open-minded. These events were called Octaves, and equally inevitably, Thompson was an excellent cook, collecting recipes from all over the world.

He does not seem to belong to the turbulent, emotional world of the other Victorian progressives in this book but appearances can be deceptive. Rationality, scientific thought and reliance on data may seem boring to our twenty-first century eyes, but in the Victorian era, the consequences could be radical. Thompson was a utilitarian materialist who dealt with facts and figures, not feelings and traditions. He bred chickens as part of his interest in food, but he strove to make them as big as possible to provide food for the poor and was perplexed when others were breeding them for 'show' only. What, he thought, was the point of that?

Thompson had no time for the practices and dogma of the established church. In 1872, he took part in what was called the 'prayer gauge' controversy. He spent his life searching out the fixed, scientific laws of the universe, and could not accept that prayer to God would change them. In July of that year, Thompson created a sensation by an article in 'The Contemporary Review', in which he suggested that the efficacy of prayer in hospitals should be put to the test. Two hospital wards would be chosen, both with first-rate care, looking after patients with diseases whose mortality rates were known. Over five years, one ward would be prayed for and one not, and at the end of the period the mortality rates would be compared.[3]

This would be, said Thompson with his tongue in his cheek 'an occasion for demonstrating to the faithless an imperishable record of the real power of prayer'. He invited the cooperation of the clergy, but it was not forthcoming. Instead, he was abused by a religious establishment that still believed in the efficacy of prayer. Prayer was under attack. In 1853, the religious but also pragmatic Prime Minister Lord Palmerston refused a Scottish Presbyterian request for a day of prayer against cholera; it was a disease that spread and could be fought by scientific and physical laws, albeit ones created by God.

However, Thompson felt that the rationalist point of view was in retreat. In December 1871, it was believed that Edward, Victoria's unpopular elder son, was dying of cholera. A day of prayer was organised on Sunday 10 December, and after four days the prince had recovered. The nation was divided about whether these events were connected, but the religious establishment had no doubts. The miracle was followed by a service of thanks at St Paul's in February 1872, to which six scientists and twelve hundred clergy were invited. The clerical establishment was cock-a-hoop, and Thompson (and later Frances Galton, see Chapter Fifteen) were trying to bring them down a peg. This controversy raged on for decades afterwards. Thompson's experiment was not carried out; this took nearly a century. In 1965, there was a double-blind clinical trial on the effects of prayer on forty-eight patients with psychological or rheumatic disease. No link was found.[4]

So this data-driven, brilliant, ultra-rational scientist was the man who introduced cremation into Britain. In truth, it needed to be a figure like this – an establishment rebel, allowed to think new thoughts yet escape censure because of his social standing. In 1874, he became the first president of the British Cremation Society after a meeting in the same house, 35 Wimpole Street, as his famous dinner parties. This was their high-handed resolution:

> We disapprove the present custom of burying the dead, and desire to substitute some mode which shall rapidly resolve the body into its component elements by a process which cannot offend the living and render the remains perfectly innocuous.

Thompson made a cold rational decision in favour of cremation. He had seen the ovens working in Vienna in 1873. He was attracted by the simplicity of the process, examined the ashes it produced and declared it a solution to a public health emergency. It was a radical solution to the over-full graveyards caused by the large population, a saver of space and source of fertiliser. Thompson even suggested that disposal of ashes at sea would increase the fish population; this was a step too far for many people and proved so unhelpful and so counter-productive that anti-cremationists gave it publicity.

There was opposition, of course. It had been thirteen centuries since cremation had been common in Britain, and the rise of Christianity put an end to it. It was still associated with paganism and atheism; it was believed by many that a body would be needed for the resurrection.

The argument that cremation would make air pollution worse was an assertion that could be countered with scientific experiment. Thompson burnt animals of larger and larger size, including a horse, in an experimental Siemens incinerator. In an era that still was still convinced that bad air caused diseases, Thompson noted that cremation could take place without anything bad escaping into the atmosphere. The argument that these new private companies made money out of death and grief soon disappeared when people remembered the undertakers and burial clubs. Cremation aimed to be cheap, by streamlining the initial cost, eliminating the expense of ground rent and expensive monuments and encouraging simple mourning routine.

The main practical problem was the amount of land held by the Church in convenient places that they refused to hand over. The Bishop of Rochester banned the use of consecrated ground for a crematorium at the Great Northern Cemetery at New Southgate. Mammon was much more amenable; the new society leased land in Woking from a commercial internment company instead. Renting from a business created the impression that they were trying to make money; this was not the case (author Anthony Trollope, a founder member, did not need money). The furnace was in an open space originally and did not present a reassuring image, but it worked well. A horse was burnt with no ill effects using coal and wood in less than two hours.

So, by 1879 it was technically possible, but was it legal? There was certainly no law against it, but an attempt to make it formally legal failed in 1884. That the Church of England was opposed was enough. The Cremation Society was stuffed with lawyers and members of the establishment and went straight to the Home Secretary, who at one point threatened to close the Woking Crematorium and pass a law against it.

Those people who thought that cremation was a form of pagan worship had their worries magnified in 1883 when a Welshman William Price cremated his five-month-old child on a mountain top with petroleum. Price was a self-identifying druid. His costume was green trousers, white smock coat, and fox-skin head-covering. He was also a vegetarian, nudist and anti-vivisectionist who had a son with his housekeeper and called him Jesus Christ in a successful attempt to outrage the local churchgoers. However, he could not be written off as a crank because he was also a physician and a member of the British Medical Association.[5] The last thing Thompson wanted was the approval of druids, but it was the breakthrough they needed. The subsequent court case declared that cremation was not contrary to law as it did not cause a common law nuisance. Burial was a custom, not a legal requirement, but this was not a ringing endorsement. When Price died in 1893 he was cremated on a pyre of two tons of coal encased by cast-iron sheeting with an audience of 20,000, creating a memorable display but doing nothing for the reputation of cremation.[6]

Bishops and archbishops mostly opposed cremation; but the Bishop of Manchester came out in favour, knowing first-hand the problems of accommodating the dead in a fast-growing city. Many commentators agreed in principle to this essentially permissive reform; nobody was forced to do it. They just asked for people's religious feelings to be taken into account. The same newspaper, perhaps knowing Sir Henry Thompson's reputation, requested that 'materialist utilitarianism' should not alienate religious affections or feeling.[7] The same newspaper still had reservations about Thompson when he died. The *Standard* expressed regret that cremation 'has not found for its leading advocate a more discreet person than Sir Henry Thompson'.

The theological arguments were not that robust. If a body was needed, what about the Christian martyrs burned at the stake or ripped to pieces by lions at the Roman amphitheatre? The body decayed naturally – 'dust to dust', said The Book of Common Prayer and even more clearly – 'ashes to ashes', inspired by Ecclesiastes Verse 3 Chapter 20, 'All go to the same place; all come from dust, and to dust all return'.

Clearly, the spirit was everything and the body just a container. As the Bishop of Manchester put it, 'No intelligent faith can suppose that any Christian doctrine is affected by the manner in which this mortal body of ours crumbles into dust'. When it was widely debated in 1874, when Thompson was pushing the idea, there was even a joke syndicated in all newspapers. Cremation, thought Thompson, was 'a consume-ation devoutly to be wished', which is funny until it is recalled that Hamlet, who said this, was considering suicide.

The British Medical Journal came out in favour relatively early in the debate but believed that force of habit and cultural conservativism would limit its appeal. If a number of famous people were cremated it would catch on, and to a certain extent, it did. The Duke of Westminster, reputedly the richest man in Britain in the 1890s, was set to be the next Vice-chairman until his sudden death (and subsequent cremation at Woking) in 1899.

Progress in cremation was slowed by an alternative method which was less radical. Sir Francis Seymour Hayden's proposal of 'earth-to-earth burials', with a wicker or papier-mâché coffin that facilitated contact, suggested 'the sooner the earth and the body meet the better it is'. Close contact with the earth, and rapid decomposition, was often seen as a compromise.

The theological arguments fell away, but others took their place, and they were more difficult to shake off. Cremation could be used to hide murder; it was a poisoner's charter. Post-mortem exhumation often caught out a criminal who had been convicted of a subsequent murder by poison and was suspected of having 'previous'. Cremation would frustrate justice. Thompson pointed out that deaths caused by the putrefaction of overcrowded graveyards were a greater killer than occasional murder by poison, but when that did not cut through, he turned the argument on its head and argued that it was the actual availability of the body after death that made the system of registration and finding foul play so lax. He proposed a quick, fool proof test that the person was indeed dead, and the cause of death ascertained. In the 1890s, Thompson was still lobbying parliament to introduce a law that would improve the quality of the death certificate and oblige physicians to look for signs of decomposition before issuing any paperwork. Thompson was never ready to spare grieving relative's feelings. He courted more unpopularity when he suggested that cremation in cases of persons who have died of smallpox, scarlet fever, or diphtheria should be compulsory. He would never have prospered as the charming doctor of modern morning television.

Cremation was made difficult in order to silence the critics. The Cremation Society demanded an extensive paper trail before it would deal with you. You needed the written permission of the person and had to follow the same stringent rules that Thompson proposed for all deceased persons.

This emphasis on proof of death assuaged another Victorian worry – taphophobia – the fear of being buried alive, although cremationists pointed out that the long drawn out wakes of the poor and the elaborate funerals of the rich made the terrible event unlikely. One of our Victorian radicals, Frances Power Cobbe, took the same elaborate precautions as many other fearful Victorians.

Thompson became part of the new scientific priesthood with his own views vying with those of bishops, and not merely in the area of cremation. In the 1870s, he became a celebrity and was able to offer a rational opinion on all medical, social and dietary matters, and his blunt pragmatism was not always appreciated. Thompson had views on everything, and toured the country, to mostly eager and grateful audiences. The newspaper headline was usually 'Sir Henry Thompson on'; followed by a hot topic of the day.

His views on alcohol veered towards temperance. Alcohol was a luxury that added nothing to the living of a life. Even in moderation, it affected health, temper and mental powers, he told the Ladies' National Temperance convention in 1878.[8] Many temperance societies had allowed some consumption of alcohol for medical reasons, but Thompson told the ladies present that they were deluding themselves.

He believed that the root cause of drunkenness in the working classes was the lack of alternatives such as theatre, music, exercise, literature and sport. In 1874, he told the Students Total Abstinence Union that the answer to the problem was less moralising and more understanding.[9] Faced with blank, boring labour for half the day in crowded slum conditions with no better distraction, then drinking was inevitable. He praised, but did not name, a rector of Bethnal Green, who demanded the opening of museums and public places on a Sunday; this was Stuart Headlam (featured in Chapter Twelve).

He was neither a vegetarian nor an anti-vivisectionist, although it was one of his many opinions that people ate too much meat in a boring cooking regime that was dominated by boiling and basting. Who would proscribe for everybody else the diet which happens to suit the 'idiosyncrasies of their own digestive apparatus'?[10]

He opposed the 1876 Cruelty to Animals Act because it focused, for him, too much on the laboratory. What about the angler's wriggling worm, impaled on a hook and clearly dying in agony? What about the lobster, boiled to death just to achieve a particular flavour? What about the half-dead game bird lying in a thicket? Almost everybody was a vivisector – did the law apply to them, or just our eminent scientists?[12]

His views on religion were unorthodox, inevitably for a man who tried to take on the power of prayer and God's ability to intervene in the world. Towards the end of his life, he published an essay, 'The Unknown God', which established his deist beliefs of a creator that remained invisible to mortals. He rejected the form and rituals of both the Christian church and all other world religions. Like the rationalist he was, he rejected them due to lack of evidence that they worked.

Thompson was an early adopter of the combustion engine. He had no time for the new speed limits. 'He ridiculed the present absurd limit of twelve miles hour, and candidly admits that when the conditions are favourable he travels at the rate of fifteen miles'.[12] Henry Thompson died on 18 April 1904; two days before he had been driving his motor car, which he did almost daily. His body was cremated at Golders Green Crematorium, the first in London, which he had opened in 1902.

Isabella Holmes

Our next Victorian radical is Isabella Holmes. She represents the legion of middle class reformers who made a significant contribution to the life of the underprivileged. By the end of the nineteenth century it was clear that the living poor were losing out to both the dead and the living rich; the poor had no gardens and no clean air. Holmes was part of the movement to open up green spaces for the poor of London.

Isabella 'Bella' Holmes was born Isabella Gladstone in 1861, unrelated to the famous Prime Minister (although Isabella's half-sister Margaret married Britain's first Labour Prime Minister, Ramsay MacDonald).[13] Her background was comfortable, middle class and rational. Her father was a chemist and a fellow of the Royal Society. His own father had dissuaded him from becoming a minister and steered him towards science, but Isabella and her family were orthodox Christians.

In 1887, she married Basil Holmes and became part of the reforming Metropolitan Public Gardens Association. The connection between recreation for the poor and the dead was that the deceased were occupying large portions of the available land. Even before meeting her husband, Gladstone had done comprehensive data collection to ascertain that there were now unused and forgotten graveyards that could be turned into parks for the London poor and that many open spaces had been used for commercial development. Her investigations were printed in 1884 in the First Annual Report of the Metropolitan Public Gardens Association. From 1884, it was illegal to put new buildings on disused burial grounds. One advantage of Holmes's work was that she was able to identify old burial places that had been omitted from these Acts of Parliament.

Holmes did the paperwork. Her own status came from her husband, who was the secretary. The demographic profile was broadly similar to most 'reform' organisations of the time. It was mostly the middle and upper class intelligentsia – clergy, barristers and solicitors and unmarried middle-aged women, with a few aristocratic celebrity patrons. Whether it was feminism, temperance, socialism, birth control or any other cause, they drew their members from the leisured intellectual elite.

Isabella and Basil fitted into this category. In the 1890s, the family lived comfortably in Ealing, in a brick-built Victorian villa with maids and a cook. They had two daughters and two sons, with another son coming along in 1905. The family house had Ealing Common to one side and the tennis club on the other and they had all the green spaces they needed.

They were aware that the poor did not have such advantages, and campaigned for them. Parks were being built around the country for the middle class to promenade about, but there was nothing for the poor. Holmes had more than a patrician sympathy for the poor – she liked them. When exploring potential former graveyards – she spent twelve years in total in them – she met with resistance from those with a vested interest in keeping them undiscovered and had mud thrown at her more than once, but she found the poor she encountered cheerful and cooperative.

In the last chapter of her book *London's Burial Grounds* (1895) she recommended the work of Sir Henry Thompson and cremation in particular. Her whole book is not about cremation, but about the location and state of London's disused and forgotten graveyards. The book is a rational and dispassionate view of the disposal of the dead, with a bias in favour of the living that Thompson would have agreed with. The opening pages have a quotation from Wordsworth:

First learn to love one living man;
Then may'st thou think upon the dead

In the last paragraph of her book, she advocated cremation as a rational way forward. She shared the same materialist view as Henry Thompson. The needs of the living had to triumph over the needs of everything else. Removing graveyards created healthy spaces in growing urban areas, improved joy and national efficiency and prevented contagion for everybody. Graveyards were expensive, and the money better used elsewhere. In this, she had the support of the London County Council, who supported her publication, but she still did not always have the support of the general public. As she said herself:

> It has, to a certain extent, happened hitherto that those who have been cremated have been more or less associated (I hope I may not be misunderstood here) with the advanced school—those that consider themselves "enlightened," Radicals, or Socialists, or persons of little or no professed religious views.

She was correct. Cremation remained the eccentric or radical option. Jack London, who, like Holmes, had seen some terrible London graveyards, recommended cremation for others and was cremated himself. In 1911, her younger sister Margaret, the wife of Labour MP Ramsay MacDonald, was cremated at the recently opened Golders Green site.

Cremation was not a radical option to Holmes; it was common sense. She had come to a dispassionate conclusion based on the collection of data and was not going to allow emotion or tradition to get in the way. Where to bury the dead was another problem like disease, public health and slum housing – to be solved dispassionately.

Holmes spend the rest of her life in public service in what we might think is a minor way. She was a co-opted member of Ealing Council's Library Committee, on and off, for the period 1902 to 1914. She became, in the words of the Middlesex County Times, the 'lady member' of the committee consisting entirely of male councillors.

She was initially elected in January 1900 from the fourteen strong, all male committee.

Mrs Isabella Holmes	9 votes
Miss Morgan-Browne	3 votes
Mrs Owen Visgar	1 vote

One councillor withheld his vote because he had no preference. He gave the very strong impression that a choice of three women was hardly worth an intellectual exertion.

Holmes was described as:

> a member of the Council of the National Union of Women
> Workers, and also a member of the local Technical Education
> Committee. She had been resident in Ealing for thirteen
> years, and was the daughter of a known scientist.[15]

Her work with the parks of Ealing and the Cemeteries of London was also acknowledged. She was bookish, intellectual and had a famous father, so her victory was understandable, but what about the unsuccessful candidates?

Miss Morgan-Browne had a moderately famous father *and* mother. Like the Holmes, the Morgan-Brownes occupied a substantial Victorian villa where they held soirées for the progressive middle classes of West London. They were, if anything, more connected with the radical Victorian era than the Holmes. Laura Morgan-Browne was a key London suffrage activist, on nodding terms with nationally famous radicals like Elizabeth Wolstenholme-Elmy, author of suffragist and women's rights pamphlets and reputedly the first person to suggest making and selling suffragette pins.

Hubert Morgan-Browne was a barrister who argued for Indian Home Rule in the 1890s and fancied himself as a future MP of the Radical liberal type. He never made it that far up the greasy pole, but was a member of the London School board for Westminster, where he was in the same Liberal Left group as Stewart Headlam. He was the author of *Sporting and Athletic Records*, published in 1897, a form of early *Guinness Book of Records*. Both husband and wife were known to George Bernard Shaw, who in turn knew Headlam.

Miss Morgan-Browne was described in the newspapers as a lecturer, a member of the Sanitary Institute who was familiar with books, having been a member of a book club. Little else is known about her, but she was clearly part of the same web of radical and high achieving women that – in this case – were hidden in a minor election for a lay member of local government.

These were mostly middle class radicals. Mrs Morgan-Browne was by 1900 the chairman of the Ealing Women's Association but had arrived in Ealing in 1898 and starting a series of drawing-room soirees. The first was in December 1898 at their villa at 9 Blakesley Avenue, where the reform-minded women of West London questioned the socialist, trade unionist and Leeds parish councillor Isabelle Ford about the working conditions of shop girls, followed by tea and a charity sale of Armenian embroideries in aid of refugees.[16]

Three weeks before the overwhelming defeat of her daughter, Mrs Morgan-Browne's association had already submitted a resolution from her organisation offering deep thanks for the fact that three women had been nominated for the obscure library position. A meeting held a few weeks earlier had as its main topic the 'emigration of educated women' – clearly they did not think the world ended in West London or thought that there were enough opportunities in Ealing.

What about the one vote cast for Mrs Owen Visgar? She was fifty-nine, married to the local surgeon Harman Visgar and also lived in spacious suburban comfort in the Avenue, Ealing. Mrs Owen Visgar was a natural history author and a member of the writers' club, said the newspaper report. This was true, but only the beginning of her talent. She both edited and authored many books on nature under the ambiguous name 'J. A. Owen'. She was a key campaigner for the RSPB with a remarkable knowledge of birds. When she died, the RSPB commented that she 'must have inspired thousands of people with a new enthusiasm for the observation and study of the wild life of the country'. *Nature* magazine was laudatory, but with a sting in the tail.

> Readers of natural history works at the end of the last century were somewhat mystified as to the authorship of a number of books published under the pen-name of "A Son of the Marshes," with the editorship of "J. A. Owen." The latter was the name under which Mrs. Jean A. Owen Visger preferred to be known, whose death at Ealing on July 30, in her eighty-first year, we much regret to have to record. Mrs. Visger was a woman of considerable attainments, with a good deal of masculinity in her character, both mental and physical. She had an absorbing interest in anything appertaining to Nature, and her mind was a storehouse of material acquired during her long life.

So even a minor provincial election for a mundane local government post shows a web of radical and achieving men and women who would never feature in any book on their own but are indispensable to the demand for improvement. They may not all have been extreme radicals, but they were all progressive and talented and have been forgotten because there were so many of them.

So what of the successful candidate Mrs Basil Holmes, as she was invariably called? She was placed on the books committee rather than finance. Her main contribution to the first meeting was to oppose the closure of the library on Boxing Day as it would create a poor precedent for other holidays when the workers would expect a day off. Perhaps Mrs Morgan-Browne, whose parents held regular villa soirées about workers' rights and who hobnobbed with socialists, would have voted for a holiday, which is perhaps why she was defeated?

Less than six months later, for reasons unknown, her co-option was ended and a man put in her place. She was back soon after, and out by June 1902, but she was back by 1904. The sequence of events is unclear, but what is clear is that she was opposed by councillors who thought the feminist revolution in Ealing had gone too far. It's not as if she had controversial views; she preferred the library to stock *The Lady* rather than the *Gentlewomen* as it was cheaper. She suggested the *Rock*, a moderately militant church newspaper, but the committee said no.

The final attempt to remove her was in 1904 when an anonymous person asked the Town Clerk to find out whether a non-ratepayer like Holmes could even be co-opted. It turned out that she could, but once again it highlighted the inferior position of women like her and thousands of others around the country who persevered on the fringes of local government and voluntary bodies. She did not need to be socially progressive to be a radical; in 1904 she approved of the banning of Bernard Shaw's works. Later in her life she was involved in war work, helped British prisoners of war and supported a charity for befriending servants. Without the thousands of Bella Holmes, the radical reform movements would have been no more than talking shops.

Isabella and Basil seemed to have led a long and active life. They were both alive and well in 1937 when they celebrated their fiftieth wedding anniversary and afterwards she flew off with her daughter to holiday in Switzerland. She died aged eighty-eight, in June 1949, largely forgotten. Her brief obituary is headlined 'Woman leaves £19,398' and I have not been able to find out if she was cremated. Active middle class women like her were common by the end of the Second World War, but she started the trend before the First World War. She was a conservative and a Christian who never tried to transform the world, but she was a radical simply because she absolutely insisted that her voice be heard.

Chapter Six

Women's Legal Equality

Elizabeth Wolstenholme-Elmy & Richard Pankhurst

When we look back on the struggle for women's legal equality, the right to vote comes to mind, but the more pressing problem for many women was the unequal Victorian marriage. Marriage took away all legal rights and gave them to the husband. This inequality rankled just as much, and in practice more so, as it was a daily reminder of women's legal inequality. Our previous radical women approached the problem of marriage differently; Kingsford married an ally, Cobbe opted to live with a woman and Cook lived on her own, after failing to gain a legal separation from her husband.

Our next Victorian radical took rejection of marriage to the next stage. She rejected the whole notion and resolved not to take part in the institution at all. Like Kingsford, she married an ally, and they cohabited in Congleton, Cheshire, from about 1869. When they were forced into marriage in 1874 she became Elizabeth Wolstenholme-Elmy and became part of the tradition of joint naming that is common in modern marriage but blazed a trail in the Victorian era.

Both Elizabeth and her partner Ben rejected Christian marriage; they rejected each word separately and the whole concept, as they were not Christians. Elizabeth and Ben were both freethinkers. They would have read Drysdale (see Chapter Seven), known the work of Edward Truelove (Chapter Eight), believed that Christianity was a self-perpetuating and unnecessary restriction on human freedom and that Christian marriage was incapable of reform. They were libertarians for believing that people should be free to make their own judgements. Her relationship with Ben Elmy was her business and nobody else's – or so she thought.

Both were advocates of free love, shocking to even their most radical friends and even more surprising when it is defined; it does not mean the infamous sexual promiscuity of the radical 1960s. It meant merely that the state or church should not regulate personal relationships, and that marriage should be freely entered into, and freely dissolved, in a partnership of equals. When Elizabeth became pregnant in 1874, they expected their radical status quo to continue.

It was their radical allies, not so radical on the subject of marriage, who forced them to conform. Their friends knew that they had been cohabiting since the start of the decade, which was acceptable, but the birth of a child demanded a reversion to traditional rules. Cohabitation in Congleton was containable and people could look the other way; a baby was a different matter. When they realised she was pregnant, Ben and Elizabeth invented and performed a secular ceremony of their own, making solemn vows to one another before witnesses in a way that would feel modern to us today.

Elizabeth was five months pregnant when they married on 12 October 1874 at Kensington Registry Office; she was forty and Ben was thirty-six. Such events were rare at the time. Most people who opted for civil marriage after the law changed in 1837 did so to avoid contact with the state church; it was usually followed by a parallel event in a Catholic or non-conformist church. It was understandable that two secularists would want to avoid a church blessing but they also deeply resented the interference of the state in their relationship. They resented the calling of banns in church, and the alternative of a marriage organised by clerks who also administered the Poor Law. They could not see much difference between a large established church that told people what to do and helped those who cooperated with it, and a state bureaucracy that did the same thing.

Elizabeth refused to make the traditional promise of obedience. She also refused to wear a wedding ring or to give up her surname, settling on a new composite surname with her husband. Other radical women were doing the same thing; Florence Fenwick Miller married in 1877 but did not change her name. Elizabeth would have certainly noticed that the vows were far more binding on the women and that marriage widened the life opportunities for the man and narrowed them for a woman. According to her marriage paperwork, she had no occupation, which was untrue. Marriage was meant to nullify her achievements and merge her identity with that of a man. She knew of course that Ben did not want this; this may well have been some comfort.

She had succumbed to the pressure not to damage the reputation of the movement; it did not do her much good. She was already marked down as an extremist; it did not help that she was a paid employee of the women's movement at the mercy of richer ladies of more leisure and not quite their social equal. These famous feminists who took against Wolstenholme-Elmy were no fans of traditional patriarchal marriage. They were in favour of the institution, and against the Wolstenholme-Elmy's serial unorthodoxy, but they wanted an improvement of women's rights within the institution. Frances Power Cobbe, for example, was one of those for whom the Wolstenholme-Elmy solution was worse than the disease.

Other feminists ganged up against her; Millicent Fawcett asked her to retire from the suffrage movement and Lydia Becker voted for her removal from the Married Women's Property Committee in Manchester (the motion failed). Fawcett believed that only anarchists believed in divorce. Josephine Butler, who was inspired by Elizabeth to lead the fight against the Contagious Diseases Act, broke with them over their attitude to marriage. Josephine Butler called them 'such people as the Elmys', both dismissing them and rejecting their new joint surname.

There was no question of marriage stopping her work. Rather like the marriage of Anna and Algie Kingsford, the marriage produced one child, Frank, relatively quickly and then it became a free marriage of equals. Even then it took until 1880 for them to be forgiven. During that period Elizabeth did however continue her Secretary's role with the Married Women's Property Committee, working 'underground' and unacknowledged.

Elizabeth's whole life was spent campaigning around the idea that women's relationships with men were uneven and unfair; 'she was at the heart of almost every Victorian feminist campaign ranging from the demand for better education, the right to vote and the rights of prostitutes to the sensitive issue of marital rape'.[1] Her guiding principle, according to her biographer, was justice – the self-evident truth that women should be equal to men as human beings.[2]

Elizabeth Wolstenholme had been born in Eccles on 1 December 1833 into a comfortable family; comfortable and well connected enough to survive when tragedy struck. Both parents died before she was twelve and she was then in the care of her maternal grandfather, Richard Clarke, a wealthy mill owner who had done well for himself but was only one generation away from the artisan class – his father had been a handloom weaver. Her own formal education ended after only two years when Clarke decided that she had learnt everything she needed to know. This also applied to her brother Joseph but he needed (and received) an education that allowed him to become a professor of mathematics at the University of Cambridge.

At about the same time that she was denied a higher education of her own, she came to her lifelong conclusion about marriage. She placed her commitment to feminism from the moment when, acting as a bridesmaid aged seventeen, she fully realised what marriage meant for women – a 'lifelong sentence of pauperism and dependence' with no control over their actions or autonomy over their own bodies.[3] As both Kingsford and Cobbe realised, dependence on a man and the institution of marriage was the result of women having no marketable skills. Marriage was a property arrangement at best and a sex bargain at worst.

In 1850, she decided to become a teacher – a traditional dead-end job for the unmarried lower-middle class woman and not one that carried much esteem or respect, for men or women. For two years before that, she had been a governess in Bedfordshire, an even more desperate and lonely occupation. In 1853, she used the proceeds of an inheritance to buy a girls' boarding school in Worsley, Lancashire. Like Kingsford and Cobbe, she was able to strike out when she received an inheritance; you could not really be an effective radical unless you were at least halfway up the social scale yourself. If you were female it helped to be unmarried because your legal rights were far superior to married women, as Elizabeth became painfully aware.

She moved the school to Congleton in 1867, a town with which she is most associated. She shared Cobbe's and Kingsford's view of women's education, without their added bitter experience of the Brighton finishing school. She taught the accomplishments, but she also taught mathematics and science. While living in Congleton she met Ben Elmy, a Suffolk-born secularist, socialist, feminist and owner of three crepe mills in Stockport. She knew about the treatment of working class women in mills and factories. Ben Elmy had caused consternation when he paid the women's wages to the women themselves, rejecting the idea of a male-dominated family wage.

There were of one mind. He was never very popular with Elizabeth's radical colleagues; even after they had forgiven her for her marriage. He never forgave them for interfering. Claims of adultery and cruelty followed him around, but it seemed to be malicious gossip. It certainly was not evident in Elizabeth's lifetime attitude to him, and she was bereft when he died in 1908. Fearsome women like Elizabeth, who sometimes did not even suffer her friends gladly, would not have accepted an unsatisfactory or cruel marriage for a moment.

She went to Liverpool in May 1866 to see the work of Josephine Butler. She was like Butler in very few ways but they agreed that the problems of prostitution and poverty needed to be talked about if they were going to be solved. Like Kingsford, Cobbe and Carlile, Elmy was not afraid to talk in public about the subjects that men only whispered about among themselves.

In 1869, she first worked with Josephine Butler and contributed to her book *Women's Work and Women's Culture*. Her essay poured scorn on the idea that 'the first object of instruction should be to fit a man to earn his own livelihood'. Education should be wider than that but for girls, it did not even achieve that. Education for the poor trained them for obedience, and education for the middle classes was designed for marriage; another form of obedience. A useful education for women would bring freedom; it did not necessarily have to be identical to that of men.

She gave up her school in 1871 and gave up Christianity at the same time. It would have been impossible to be a headmistress and a non-believer. Her focus turned away from education into many other directions. Elizabeth was part of the movement fighting for legal equality for women. She had become the paid secretary of the Married Women's Property Committee in 1868.

She worked for the best part of fifty years in the fight for women's legal equality. She was a journalist, lecturer and most of all, a lobbyist inside the parliamentary system. Her interests were wide-ranging. She was involved in the women's suffrage movement as early as 1866, but this was not her only priority. She did not rely on the vote to improve everything else, as she proved in her own occupation – a paid lobbyist and parliamentary agent for the Vigilance Association from 1872, which lobbied for women's equality in all areas of civil and legal life.

Around the time of her arranged marriage, her main campaign was the Married Women's Property Act. The Married Women's Property Committee was set up by Bessie Raynor Parks with the aim of changing the law to guarantee women's financial autonomy after marriage. There was success in the form of the Matrimonial Causes Act 1857 which enabled legally separated wives to keep their earnings, but then conservatives argued that now that injured wives were provided for, it was not necessary to provide for those who remained happily married – their definition of happily married being not separated from their husbands. Elizabeth knew how men treated their wives through her experience of women in her husband's textile mills.

She was involved in the fight alongside Butler with the Contagious Diseases Act (see Chapter Ten) playing a subordinate role, not because of her own unpopularity but the recognition that Butler was better qualified and connected. Elizabeth and Ben had also supported the brief flourishing of republicanism in 1874; they invited the notorious atheists Annie Besant and Charles Bradlaugh to speak at Congleton in June 1875. The subjects were *Republicanism* and the *Value of Christianity*. The speakers were booed and when they tried the same thing a year later they were stoned and a mob surrounded their house into the early hours.

Elizabeth was an active member of the Pankhurst-led Women's Franchise League, which wanted to extend the vote to wives but formed her own organisation, the Women's Emancipation Union in 1891. Their programme extended further than suffrage to equality in all areas. Women were to be equal in all areas of civil life and men needed to respond to this demand by behaving better. The immediate spark for the WEU was the 1891 High Court ruling that prevented a husband from imprisoning his wife in order to pursue his conjugal rights. Wolstenholme-Elmy, like Kingsford and Cobbe, was concerned by the brutality of men and the legal system which allowed it and was brave enough to speak up against what she saw as conjugal rape. The illegality of rape within marriage was only explicitly formalised in 2003.

Elizabeth survived until 1918 and was part of the Suffragette movement, but she was living in straitened circumstances. She was now poor; she had been living on charity and a 'grateful fund' set up in 1888 after the failure of her husband's business. She became a member when the Pankhursts formed the Women and Social Political Union in 1903 but she looked out of place in the new militant organisation. She was a lobbyist, journalist and influencer in an organisation of active, campaigning militants. It was never very comfortable.

On a good day, the Pankhursts represented her as the brains of the organisation, which was fair. Her fifty years of advocacy for woman ushered the way for the Pankhursts and their movement. On the other hand, she was old and grey and unable to take an active part in processions, and they fell out. She was often portrayed as a shrivelled up Jenny Wren figure with an unfaithful husband. They owed her a lot, especially Cristobel. The need for 'male purity' had been an important but often now forgotten part of the WSPU campaign. When Cristobel Pankhurst noted that women would not be free until men behaved themselves, that was the influence of Wolstenholme-Elmy.

In 1913 she joined the Women's Tax Resistance League who campaigned to hold back taxes on earned income in a way that echoed the 'no taxation without representation' of the American Independence struggle in the 1770s. Essentially, she wanted full citizenship and autonomy for women in all areas of life, which included but did not stop at the vote.

She left the WSPU executive when the violent phase started in 1912. She was a lifelong pacifist, a cause to which she held true even throughout the jingoism of the 1899–1902 Anglo-Boer War. She was never going to join the imprisonment and force-feeding pantheon and did not count as a heroine when the new militant tactics preferred deeds to words.

Elizabeth Wolstenholme-Elmy died aged eighty-four, in a nursing home in Manchester on 12 March 1918. She had fallen down the stairs and injured her head. She was cremated according to the service of the Society of Friends, although she was not a member.[4] Although a little mentally confused at the end of her life, she lived long enough – by six days – to know that women would be given the vote. She had worked for fifty years for women's equality; she was known to write 300 pieces of correspondence in one day. She never voted in a national election herself.

There are fifty-five people named on the plinth below the statue of Millicent Fawcett in Parliament which was unveiled in Parliament Square, Westminster in April 2018. Wolstenholme-Elmy's name is on the plinth, as justice would demand, but this should be the first part of a new campaign to give her the significance she deserved.

The next campaigner for women's rights is a Pankhurst, but not the most famous one. Richard Pankhurst (1834-1898) shares Wolstenholme-Elmy's relative obscurity, but for slightly different reasons. He died early, failed to live up to his initial potential as a radical reformer who should have broken into the political establishment, and was outshone by his wife Emmeline and his daughters Sylvia, Cristobel and Adela.

In 1865, he joined the Manchester National Society for Women's Suffrage which had been set up by Wolstenholme-Elmy. Manchester was the base of both of them, and the home of English radicalism for most of the Victorian era. A remarkable 300 of the 1,499 signatures on the first petition came from there. In January 1867, the society became the National Society for Women's Suffrage led by Lydia Becker and Pankhurst provided free legal advice to the organisation. He qualified in law in 1858, despite being barred from the traditional universities by his nonconformist background. He had gained his education at Owens College in Manchester, and in 1858 he went back to work as an unpaid lecturer there, showing his commitment to working class education.

He had some initial success. The 1867 Reform Bill had given the vote in national General Elections to large numbers of men who met a ratepayer threshold. Rates were also paid by single and widowed women, but there was no plan to enfranchise them, so women were falling even further behind. Pankhurst was able to use his legal background to produce some good propaganda for the suffrage cause.

One of the first elections after the new franchise was in Manchester in a by-election of November 1867. The owner of a crockery shop at 25 Ludlow Street, Chorlton was added to the franchise as somebody who met the property qualification. However; it was a clerical error – the owner was Lily Maxwell, a sixty-eight-year-old widow. She did not notice it herself – this was no surprise as she would have known that women did not have the vote – but a political activist spotted this mistake and planned to use it to make political capital.

The Manchester Society for Women's Suffrage had just been founded. This was an excellent test case, and Lily Maxwell was persuaded to use her vote:

> A report in The Daily News noted the 'record and acceptance of a vote by a lady, at the Chorlton Town Hall'. Accompanied by [Lydia] Becker, Maxwell was 'escorted from the committee room by a large number of persons, and were much cheered as they passed to and from the poll.'[5]

Her preferred candidate did not need her vote. Jacob Bright was in favour of women's suffrage and won by 1,700 votes. He was very much in favour of Lily as well:

> This woman is a hard-working, honest person who pays her rates as you do. If any woman should possess the vote, it is precisely one such as she.

Her vote was later rescinded, but it encouraged the registration of women in the 1868 General Election. Journalist Peter Kellner believed there were 10,000 women on the register, and it seems clear that some of them voted successfully, while most of them were removed by the local revising barristers before they could do so.[6]

A test case was put forward, with Pankhurst as junior barrister. He went on to argue that the reference to 'men' in the 1867 Act meant 'everybody'. Their evidence was this; the first, modest Parliamentary Reform Act of 1832 had used the word 'male persons' (and therefore legally disenfranchised women for the first time), so the use of 'man' in the 1867 Act had a different meaning. In 1850, parliament had passed the Interpretation Act that stated that 'the masculine gender shall be deemed and taken to include females unless the contrary is expressly provided'. Unfortunately, during the debate on the 1867 Act, an amendment proposed by John Stuart Mill to substitute the word 'person' for man was lost by 196 votes to 75, thus taking away much of their argument.

They failed, but some success came later. Pankhurst drafted the 1869 Municipal Franchise Act, which gave unmarried women ratepayers the right to vote for local councillors. Pankhurst also wrote the initial draft of the Married Women's Property Act, passed in 1870, that allowed married women to be legal owners of their earned and inherited property.

He would have seen the fourteen-year-old Emmeline Goulden for the first time in 1872, when her radical mother allowed her to attend a women's suffrage meeting in Manchester led by Lydia Becker and made more substantial contact in 1878 at a peace rally to protest about the behaviour of the Turks in the Balkans (the 'Bulgarian Atrocities') and prevent British intervention against Russia on their behalf.

They married in December 1879; it was a happy marriage but an odd arrangement, as relationships between Victorian radicals tended to be. He was forty-five and very much on the verge of being a lifelong bachelor. He still lived at home comfortably and filled his life with a multitude of good causes. 'What is life without enthusiasm,' he once said, an odd expression from a middle-aged man that shows a little naivety. He was either sexually inexperienced or even virginal when he married. His household was disappearing – his father Henry Pankhurst, an auctioneer had died in 1873 and his mother Margaret Marsden earlier in 1879, hence a wedding that was subdued. The bride wore brown and the age gap was twenty-four years. He had wooed her not with romance and flowers, but talk of peace, equality and justice.

The couple had five children, including Cristobel, Sylvia and Adela and two boys, Francis and Henry, who died prematurely. It was never a conventional marriage. They never seemed to practise the birth control that was becoming common amongst middle class families. Richard did not control the family finances on his own (which thanks to his own efforts he was no longer legally entitled to do) but this was because he was incompetent.

Emmeline had originally suggested a free union in the approximate style of the Wolstenholme-Elmys, and although it was never agreed upon formally, the union was very free. Richard believed in compulsory education through state schools, but Emmeline had relatively conservative views on schools in general, believing that they stifled creativity. She won the argument. Both agreed that there was to be no religion or prayers in the house, but with the Bible being available to read and critiqued like any other book.

Richard never really made a success of his political career, despite the major advantages he possessed. His habit of working for nothing in the aid of worthy causes was both a great personal recommendation and personal misfortune. He was not a practical man, and although he was ambitious – being a High Court Judge or a Liberal Party MP were realistic targets for a man with such a profile – he did not like the law that much and was not greedy enough just to make a substantial living from it. His real passion was politics. He was too principled (or too stubborn) to trim and modify his principles even if it would have helped him achieve his ambitions.

Apart from working for nothing and creating regular embarrassment for his family, Richard was always slightly too radical for most of the radical establishment at the time. He was less and less comfortable in the Liberal Party. He stood in Manchester in July 1883 as an independent on a platform of adult suffrage, secular education, abolition of the Lords, the nationalisation of land, and disestablishment of the Church of England. His nomination papers were signed by members of the Manchester Working Men's Societies but by no prominent Liberals. Always an internationalist and pacifist, he proposed a United States of Europe. His defeat was inevitable; the Conservative candidate gained 75% of the vote on a 30% swing due to active opposition of the Liberals.[7]

He was well known in Manchester in progressive circles as 'The Doctor' or the Learned Doctor – unmistakable in court or in a lecture with his pointed (and highly unfashionable) red beard, high pitched voice, and (some said) 'small piggy eyes' but he was far too radical to win an election in Manchester despite his home city being, until the 1880s, the most radical part of the country.

The Pankhursts moved to London in 1885. It was part of a plan devised by Emmeline to get Richard elected to the Commons. He was selected as the Liberal and Radical candidate for Rotherhithe in the General Election of 1885. It looked to be a reasonable prospect. It was a new, single-member constituency and the Third Reform Bill (1884) had added two and a half million new voters nationally, many of whom would be sympathetic to the Liberals.

Richard failed to trim his views and presented the same radical programme as he had in 1883 in Manchester. Pankhurst demanded 'no privileged legislation, no heredity legislation'. He referred to the Lords as 'a huge collection of Barnum elephants'.[8] His programme was similar to that of Joseph Chamberlain – 'radical Joe' – so he seemed to be swimming with the tide in the Liberal Party, but this did not help him in Rotherhithe, which was not traditional Liberal country. It was never radical enough to appreciate Pankhurst, and to be fair, nobody of his politics was able to win the seat until the Liberal landslide of 1906.

The Conservatives found his weak spot – his failure to be consistent on the subject of religion, and put around the rumour that he was an atheist. They didn't just whisper it in dark places but produced thirty thousand leaflets, posters and placards which appeared overnight in Rotherhithe. It contained a contested quotation from the 1883 election campaign speech in which he seemed to deny the existence of God.

The Conservatives also created a checklist of questions to ask Pankhurst; as well as asking him if he believed in God, and whether he was chairman of the Republican club (he was), he was asked if he believed in the sanctity of an oath. This seems an odd line of attack, but it has to be seen in the context of Bradlaugh, the atheist MP, who had refused to take the religious oath of allegiance to the monarch in 1880. Pankhurst was successfully labelled as anti-God and anti-monarch, labels that stuck easily because he was unsure about both.

Pankhurst started proceedings against the newspaper that had provided the quotation for the placards and the Conservative candidate Charles Hamilton but did not do the obvious thing and deny that he was an atheist. A politician determined to win at all costs would have had no scruples here; for a start, he was not an atheist but an agnostic. He wished to assert his right not to talk about it because to him it was a matter of conscience not a public matter. He was more interested in a free universal education system that would allow individuals to make up their own mind.

If he had explained his view that the subject of God, the soul and immortality was unknown and unknowable, then that would still have seemed like atheism to the voters of Rotherhithe. His pragmatic wife suggested a simple flat denial and some strategic attendances at church. This would not have been too much of a wrench as Pankhurst had been a regular Baptist in his youth.

He also lost the Irish vote in 1885 despite still supporting Home Rule and land reform; the Irish Nationalist Charles Parnell had instructed Irish voters to oppose all government candidates, so he was positively disadvantaged by his position. He took it philosophically, but his wife did not. You always have your head in the clouds, sighed his wife, correctly.[9]

In the same General Election, Pankhurst took some time to support the Radical candidate for North Camberwell, who was an educational reformer and strong supporter of women's rights. What made this situation unusual was the candidate was Helen Taylor, daughter of John Stuart Mill and Harriet Taylor, who was of course incapable in law to stand as a candidate. Suspecting (correctly) that the returning officer would not accept her nomination, she nevertheless campaigned enthusiastically on a programme of universal suffrage, Irish Home Rule, free universal education, progressive income tax (a punitive 95% tax rate for those earning over £100,000), and the banning of war unless approved by parliament.[10]

Not even the women's suffrage movement supported her. Pankhurst broke off his own campaigning to support Taylor, and the support was reciprocated, giving the electors of Rotherhithe another reason to be suspicious; just as with the atheist row, his practical wife was distressed when Helen Taylor wore trousers during the meeting: 'Mrs Pankhurst was distressed that her husband should be seen walking with the lady in this garb, and feared that his gallantry in doing so ... would cost him many votes.'

Pankhurst lost with 46% of the vote to Conservative Hamilton in a two-horse race. He was never elected to parliament. Later in life, as he veered ever leftward, he was known as the 'Red Doctor' for a new reason, and could easily have been a Labour MP if he had survived into the early nineteenth century.

He genuinely believed that he had lost the election due to the atheist slur, and he pursued the newspaper and the Conservative candidate through the courts.[11] By 1887, it had been settled in favour at great cost and expense after a setback in May 1886 when Justice Graham gave an initial verdict for Hamilton, the same Graham who had been an unsuccessful Conservative in the same election and had been recently promoted to judge. Pankhurst was angry, as was his friend William Stead at the *Pall Mall Gazette*, but it was his wife who took action, writing to the judge in contemptuous terms, she said:

> It is regretted that there should be found on the English bench a judge who will lend his aid to a disreputable section of the Tory party in doing their dirty work; but for what other reason were you ever placed where you are?

She finished the letter with 'your obedient servant'.

By the time of his defeat in 1885, he was part of the metropolitan radical elite. There were regular soirees at the Pankhurst's house at 8 Russell Square after 1888; the new house was furnished and improved by Emmeline – another thing the impractical Richard did not do. They knew Annie Besant, William Morris, Tom Mann, John Burns, Helen Taylor and Florence Fenwick Miller. It was an open house for visiting foreign revolutionaries and anarchists and a political education for the young Pankhurst daughters.

Richard joined the Fabians but took very little active part – they were too gradualist for his taste. He never joined the Marxist Social Democrat Federation (see Chapter Thirteen) not because he disagreed; he had read

Anna Bonus Kingsford

THE

PERFECT WAY IN DIET

A TREATISE ADVOCATING A RETURN TO
THE NATURAL AND ANCIENT
FOOD OF OUR RACE

BY

ANNA KINGSFORD
DOCTOR OF MEDICINE OF THE FACULTY OF PARIS

LONDON
KEGAN PAUL, TRENCH, & CO., 1 PATERNOSTER SQUARE
1881

Kingsford on the morality of meat-eating

Frances Power Cobbe in later life
(Wellcome, London)

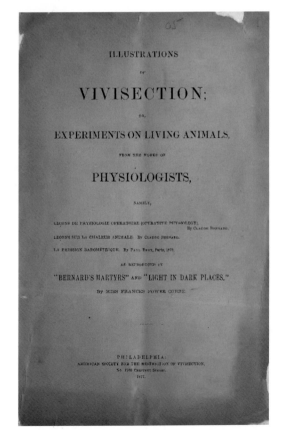

ILLUSTRATIONS

OF

VIVISECTION;

OR,

EXPERIMENTS ON LIVING ANIMALS,

FROM THE WORKS OF

PHYSIOLOGISTS,

NAMELY,

LEÇONS DE PHYSIOLOGIE OPERATOIRE (OPERATIVE PHYSIOLOGY).
By CLAUDE BERNARD.
LEÇONS SUR LA CHALEUR ANIMALE. By CLAUDE BERNARD.
LA PRESSION BAROMÉTRIQUE. By PAUL BERT, Paris, 1878.

AS REPRODUCED IN

"BERNARD'S MARTYRS" AND "LIGHT IN DARK PLACES."

By MISS FRANCES POWER COBBE.

PHILADELPHIA:
AMERICAN SOCIETY FOR THE RESTRICTION OF VIVISECTION,
No. 1705 Chestnut Street.
1877.

Cobbe on the morality of
vivisection

Jabez Burns and Anne Jane Carlile

The Childish Tee-Total Movement (Wellcome, London)

The original spiritualists –
Margaret, Catherine and
Leah Fox

William Conrad Crookes

Sir Henry Thompson

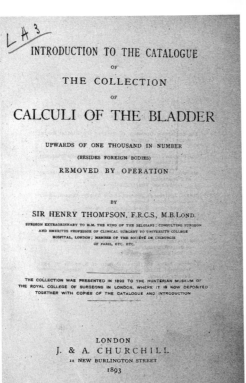

INTRODUCTION TO THE CATALOGUE

OF

THE COLLECTION

OF

CALCULI OF THE BLADDER

UPWARDS OF ONE THOUSAND IN NUMBER

(BESIDES FOREIGN BODIES)

REMOVED BY OPERATION

BY

SIR HENRY THOMPSON, F.R.C.S., M.B. LOND.

SURGEON EXTRAORDINARY TO H.M. THE KING OF THE BELGIANS; CONSULTING SURGEON
AND EMERITUS PROFESSOR OF CLINICAL SURGERY TO UNIVERSITY COLLEGE
HOSPITAL, LONDON; MEMBER OF THE SOCIÉTÉ DE CHIRURGIE
OF PARIS, ETC. ETC.

THE COLLECTION WAS PRESENTED IN 1892 TO THE HUNTERIAN MUSEUM OF
THE ROYAL COLLEGE OF SURGEONS IN LONDON, WHERE IT IS NOW DEPOSITED
TOGETHER WITH COPIES OF THE CATALOGUE AND INTRODUCTION

LONDON

J. & A. CHURCHILL

11 NEW BURLINGTON STREET

1893

Thompson's medical expertise allowed
him to have his opinions on cremation

Left: Richard Marsden Pankhurst – 'The Red Doctor'

Below: Elizabeth Wolstenholme – Elmy with Emmeline Pankhurst, 1908

Charles Bradlaugh

BRADLAUGH AT TWENTY.

A PLEA FOR ATHEISM.

BY C. BRADLAUGH.

GILLESPIE says that "an Atheist propagandist seems a non-descript monster created by nature in a moment of madness." Despite this opinion, it is as the propagandist of Atheism that I pen the following lines, in the hope that I may succeed in removing some few of the many prejudices which have been created against not only the actual holders of Atheistic opinions, but also against those wrongfully suspected of entertaining such ideas. Men who have been famous for depth of thought, for excellent wit, or great genius, have been recklessly assailed as Atheists, by those who lacked the high qualifications against which the spleen of the calumniators was directed. Thus, not only has Voltaire been without ground accused of Atheism, but Bacon, Locke, and Bishop Berkeley himself, have, amongst others, been denounced by thoughtless or unscrupulous pietists as inclining to Atheism, the ground for the accusation being that they manifested an inclination to improve human thought.

It is too often the fashion with persons of pious reputation to speak in unmeasured language of Atheism as favouring immorality, and of Atheists as men whose conduct is necessarily vicious, and who have adopted atheistic views as a desperate defiance against a Deity justly offended by the badness of their lives. Such persons urge that amongst the proximate causes of Atheism are vicious training, immoral and profligate companions, licentious living, and the like. Dr. John Pye Smith, in his "Instructions on Christian Theology," goes so far as to declare that "nearly all the Atheists upon record have been men of extremely debauched and vile conduct." Such language from the Christian advocate is not surprising, but there are others who, professing great desire for the spread of Freethought,

The Power of the Written Word

Josephine Butler Centenary
Poster 1928

William Thomas Stead

Annie Besant (Wellcome, London)

WHY I AM A SOCIALIST.

By ANNIE BESANT.

"A Socialist! you don't mean to say you are a Socialist!"
Such is the exclamation with which anyone who adopts the
much-hated name of Socialist is sure to be greeted in "polite
society". A Socialist is supposed to go about with his pocket
full of bombs and his mind full of assassinations; he is a kind
of wild beast, to be hunted down with soldiers if he lives
under Bismarck, with sneers, abuse, and petty persecutions if
he lives under Victoria. The very wildness of the epithets
launched at him, however, shows how much there is of fear in
the hatred with which he is regarded; and his opponents, by
confining themselves to mere abuse, confess that they find
themselves unable to cope with him intellectually. Prejudice
and passion, not reasoned arguments, are the weapons relied
on for his destruction. Once let the working classes understand
what Socialism really is, and the present system is doomed;
it is therefore of vital necessity that they shall be prevented
from calmly studying its proposals, and shall be so deafened
with the clamor against it that they shall be unable to hear
the "still small voice" of reason. I do not challenge the
effectiveness of the policy—for a time. It has been the policy
of the governing classes against every movement that has been
aimed against their privileges; Radicalism has been served in
exactly similar fashion, and now that Radicalism has grown
so strong that it can no longer be silenced by clamor, it is the
turn of Socialism to pass through a like probation. There is
always an ugly duckling in Society's brood; how else should be
maintained the succession of swans?

With a not inconsiderable number of persons the prejudice
against the name of Socialist is held to be a valid reason for
not adopting it, and it is thought wiser to advocate the *thing*

Besant was a socialist and birth
controller until c.1890

Left: Henry Mayers Hyndman,
founder of the Social
Democratic Federation

Below: The Bryant and May
strikers, with two members
of the SDF, Annie Besant and
Herbert Burrows (Wellcome,
London)

STRIKE COMMITTEE OF THE MATCHMAKERS UNION.

John Burns in 1889 during his
revolutionary phase

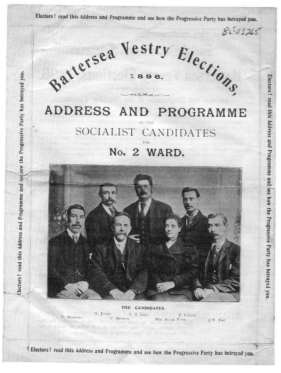

SDF local government candidates
in Battersea

George Butler, husband and
ally of Josephine Butler

Hypatia Bradlaugh Bonner,
daughter and ally of Charles
Bradlaugh

James Keir Hardie

THE LABOUR PIONEER.   JANUARY, 1906

GENERAL ELECTION, 1906.

Central Labour Representation Committee Manifesto.

To the ELECTORS of MERTHYR.

This Election is to decide whether or not Labour is to be fairly represented in Parliament.

The House of Commons is supposed to be the People's House, and yet the People are not there.

Landlords, employers, lawyers, brewers, and financiers are there in force. Why not Labour?

IS THERE NO NEED?

The Trade Unions ask the same liberty that capital enjoys. They are refused.

The Aged Poor are neglected.

The slums remain; overcrowding continues, whilst the land goes to waste.

Shopkeepers and Traders are overburdened with rates and taxation, whilst the increasing land values, which should relieve the ratepayers, go to people who have not earned them.

Wars are fought to make the rich richer, but the underfed school children of the poor are still neglected.

Chinese Labour is defended because it enriches the mineowners.

The unemployed ask for work; the Government gave them a worthless Act, and now, when you are beginning to understand the cause of your poverty, the red herring of Protection is drawn across your path.

Protection, as experience shows, is no remedy for poverty and unemployment. It serves to withdraw your attention from the land, housing, old age, and other social problems.

LABOUR ELECTORS.

You have it in your power to see that Parliament carries out your wishes.

The Labour Representation Executive appeals to you to forget all the political differences which have kept you apart in the past, and

VOTE SOLIDLY FOR

HARDIE

SIGNED ON BEHALF OF ONE MILLION WORKMEN—

A. HENDERSON, M.P. (Ironfounders), Chairman.   W. HYDSON (Railway Servants).
J. R. CLYNES, Vice-Chairman.   BEN TURNER (Weavers).
J. J. STEPHENSON (Engineers), Treasurer.   W. H. WILSON (Textile Trades).
J. N. BELL (N.A.U. of Labour).   J. KEIR HARDIE, M.P. (Independent Labour Party).
JAMES CONLEY, J.P. (Boilermakers).   JAMES PARKER (Independent Labour Party).
PETE CURRAN (Gasworkers).   EDWARD R. PEASE (Fabian Society).
J. HODGE (Steel Smelters).   J. RAMSAY MACDONALD, Secretary.

Hardie's Election Poster 1906

Charles Dilke

SIR CHARLES DILKE.
M.P. for the Forest of Dean.

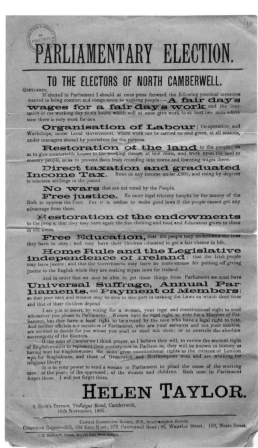

PARLIAMENTARY ELECTION.

TO THE ELECTORS OF NORTH CAMBERWELL.

GENTLEMEN,

If elected to Parliament I should at once press forward the following practical measures wanted to bring comfort and competence to working people :— **A fair day's wages for a fair day's work** and the limitation of the working day to six hours, which will at once give work to at least two men where now there is only work for one.

Organisation of Labour Co-operation, and Workshops, under Local Government, where work can be carried on and given, at all seasons, under managers elected by yourselves for the purpose.

Restoration of the land to the people; so as to give comfortable houses to the working classes, at low rents, and work upon the land to country people, so as to prevent them from crowding into towns and lowering wages there.

Direct taxation and graduated Income Tax. None on any income under £300, and rising by degrees to nineteen shillings in the pound.

No wars that are not voted by the People.

Free justice. No more legal trickery bought by the money of the Rich to oppress the Poor. For it is useless to make good laws if the people cannot get any advantage from them.

Restoration of the endowments to the people, that they may have again the free clothing and food and Education given to them in old times.

Free Education, that the people may understand the laws they have to obey; and may have their children educated to get a fair chance in life.

Home Rule and the Legislative independence of Ireland; that the Irish people may have justice; and that the Government may have no more excuse for putting off giving justice to the English while they are making unjust laws for Ireland.

And in order that we may be able to get these things from Parliament we must have **Universal Suffrage, Annual Parliaments, and Payment of Members;** so that poor men and women may be able to take part in making the Laws on which their lives and that of their children depend.

I ask you to assert, by voting for a woman, your legal and constitutional right to send whomever you please to Parliament. Women have no legal right to vote for a Member of Parliament, but they have a legal right to be elected by the men who have a legal right to vote. And neither officials nor members of Parliament, who are your servants and not your masters, are entitled to decide for you whom you shall or shall not elect; or to override the absolute sovereignty of the Electors.

If the men of Camberwell think proper, as I believe they will, to revive the ancient right of Englishwomen to represent their countrymen in Parliament, they will be known in history as having won for Englishwomen the same great constitutional rights as the citizens of London won for Englishmen, and those of Greenwich and Northampton won and are winning for religious liberty.

It is in your power to send a woman to Parliament to plead the cause of the working men; of the poor; of the oppressed; of the women and children. Rich men in Parliament forget these. I will not forget them.

HELEN TAYLOR.

8, Scott's Terrace, Trafalgar Road, Camberwell,
16th November, 1885.

Central Committee Rooms, 208, Southampton Street
Committee Rooms—355, Old Kent Road; 272 Camberwell Road; 95, Waterloo Street; 163, Neate Street.

J. H. BARLOW, Printer, 355, Old Kent Road, London.

Helen Taylor's radical manifesto, 1885

HALFPENNY DINNERS FOR POOR CHILDREN IN EAST LONDON.
SEE PAGE 221.

Above: The solution to hunger – charity (Wellcome, London)

Right: Another solution to hunger – state intervention (Wellcome, London)

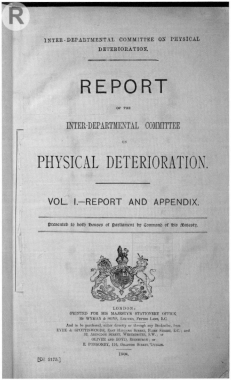

INTER-DEPARTMENTAL COMMITTEE ON PHYSICAL DETERIORATION.

REPORT

OF THE

INTER-DEPARTMENTAL COMMITTEE

ON

PHYSICAL DETERIORATION.

VOL. I.—REPORT AND APPENDIX.

Presented to both Houses of Parliament by Command of His Majesty.

LONDON:
PRINTED FOR HIS MAJESTY'S STATIONERY OFFICE,
BY WYMAN & SONS, LIMITED, FETTER LANE, E.C.

And to be purchased, either directly or through any Bookseller, from
EYRE & SPOTTISWOODE, EAST HARDING STREET, FLEET STREET, E.C.; and
32, ABINGDON STREET, WESTMINSTER, S.W.; or
OLIVER AND BOYD, EDINBURGH; or
E. PONSONBY, 116, GRAFTON STREET, DUBLIN.

1904.

[Cd. 2175.]

Francis Galton (Wellcome, London)

The many branches of Eugenics
(Wellcome, London)

Capital and had a library of books on class struggle, but because he did not appreciate their constant factional fallings out and expulsions. Pankhurst played a part in the match girls strike with Besant. Both attended the Trafalgar Square demonstration on 13 November 1887 – 'Bloody Sunday', and Richard played a prominent part in the funeral of Alfred Linnell, who was killed by the police during a demonstration against police violence

In 1889, the Women's Franchise League was set up, with the Pankhursts, Butlers and Florence Fenwick Miller as prominent members and Wolstenholme-Elmy as the first treasurer. It operated from their house in Russell Square. The immediate motivation was Pankhurst's refusal to support a private member's bill that would extend the female franchise but not enfranchise married women. Their aim was to secure the vote for *all* female taxpayers in local government elections – married or single. The right to vote, like the right of the slave to be free, was indivisible. They called their opponents the 'Spinster Suffrage Party' and accused them of lack of ambition.

The WFL could not cope with pressure from outside to make compromises and only lasted a few years, but its other beliefs – internationalism, trade unionism, opposition to imperialism and racism, and abolition of the House of Lords brought it very close to socialism. In 1894, having moved back to Lorne House, Victoria Park, Manchester, both Pankhursts joined the Independent Labour Party. Richard died a socialist; Emmeline, as will be seen, did not.

In 1898, when Emmeline and her daughter were travelling through Switzerland, Richard fell ill with stomach ulcers. They returned at once, but it was too late. Emmeline read that Richard had died while on the train from London to Manchester. He died a hero of the Labour movement and a socialist. His obituary in the socialist *Clarion* called him 'a sharp thorn in their comfortable cushion'.[12]

Two thousand people lined or attended what was essentially a non-religious ceremony at Brooklands cemetery. His daughter Sylvia said in her eulogy:

> Our father, vilified and boycotted, yet beloved by a multitude
> of people in many walks of life was the standard bearer
> for every forlorn hope, every unpopular yet worthy cause
> then conceived for the uplifting of oppressed and suffering
> humanity.

On his tombstone, his wife chose the epitaph 'Faithful and true, and my loving comrade,' modified from a Walt Whitman poem describing the grave of a soldier.

Life for Emmeline was now tough. She was a poor single parent, having been left a mere £500 in her husband's will. She moved to a smaller home and began working as a registrar for births and deaths. Her campaign for the vote was well known; Emmeline was hailed as a leader of the women's rights movement and was selected as a prospective Conservative candidate for Whitechapel and St George's, Stepney. She died before she could face the electorate, on 14 June 1928. What would Richard have thought about his wife dying as a member of the Conservative Party? He would have been happy that the world he had fought for was coming into existence, and his wife could make her own choice.

Chapter Seven

Birth Control
George Drysdale & Annie Besant

Is there a human right to sexual satisfaction? It's a radical view now, so imagine how radical it would have been in the 1850s! The traditional view at the time is well known. The rationale for sexual intercourse was procreation, and lawful sex took place within marriage for that purpose. Sex was not an end in itself, and sex outside these parameters was sinful and immoral. This notion survived the whole of the nineteenth century and the majority of the twentieth in some parts of the world and remains a common moral stance to this day.

It took a radical vision to oppose these ideas, and that radical was Dr George Drysdale (1824–1904). He accepted the necessity of effective birth control. He went further; sex was a good thing in itself that should be enjoyed safely without worrying about disease or religious conscience.

He was not the first to advocate birth control in the nineteenth century. The radicals Francis Place and Richard Carlile both suggested a form of vaginal sponge or douche as a way of reducing the chances of pregnancy; Carlile was interested in a woman's right to control her body, while Place had a more practical concern about the health of poor women worn down by constant pregnancy. In 1826, Carlile had published *What is Love?* This attacked Christian marriage and recommended that men and women enter into free unions, based only on love and sexual attraction, which could be dissolved at will – tellingly the book's subtitle implied a particular audience – '*Every Woman's Book*'.

Carlile turned theory into practice by leaving his wife Jane to enter into just such a 'moral union' (1832) with the freethinking feminist Eliza Sharples, who was later to be an important influence on Charles Bradlaugh; although Bradlaugh never accepted her view on marriage, he came to accept her views on birth control.

Dr George Drysdale went further than Place or Carlile, and he has been called the 'forgotten prophet of the sexual revolution'.[1] He deserves this title for two reasons; he was a prophet because he suggested that people would be happier if sex was divorced from morality, and this was a deeply unpopular opinion; forgotten because his views were indeed a hundred years ahead of his time and this was long enough to get none of the credit.

There was a population panic at the beginning of the nineteenth century, to the extent that even laissez-faire governments, who hated state intervention, made the gargantuan effort of compiling two population head counts in 1801 and 1811. In 1750 it was seven million and it had more than doubled a century later to eighteen million. It was clearly rising faster than at any time in history, and overpopulation became an urgent issue.

One man who would dominate the debate in the nineteenth century was the Reverend Thomas Malthus. Malthus believed that food supply could not keep up with a rising population and that this crisis would be solved either by starvation or natural causes like war, plague and famine. However, the answer was still not birth control – it was abstinence, self-control and postponed marriage – 'moral restraint'.

Drysdale celebrated birth control and was contemptuous of moral restraint. In the 1850s, he was an obscure medical student who wished to take a stand against 'the Puritanism, which has of late years increased among us, and given a sombre and painful character to all love.'[2] This sexual repression was not the Victorian myths about table legs being covered up and lesbianism not being illegal because Queen Victoria did not know what it was; he objected to the increasingly judgemental attitudes he encountered.

He published a book, *Physical, Sexual and Natural Religion,* in 1854 (later given the more anodyne title *The Elements of Social Science*). As the title suggests, Drysdale could not construct his theory without rejecting the prevailing Judeo-Christian attitude towards sex. The book by 'A Graduate (later a Doctor) of Medicine', in which the anonymous author (he did not want to upset his mother) argued for a new religion of reverence for the human body, condemned abstinence as unhealthy and misery-making, called for an unfettered right to intercourse among the unmarried and recommended regular use of contraception to guard against pregnancy. It was only fair; it 'put the two sexes almost on a par in sexual freedom', allowing a woman 'to indulge her sexual desires'.[3]

There were only five pages on contraception in his book (these were often excerpted and republished elsewhere). He disapproved of *coitus interruptus* as physically and mentally damaging and therefore completely counter to the real purpose of sex, and the condom as birth control. Drysdale approved of two – essentially female – methods of birth control. One was the use of a sponge and a douche in pure water after sex, and the other was the rhythm method, although Drysdale miscalculated the sterile period and recommended sex eight days after menstruation, which is a fertile period. He was not the only person who made this mistake.

He was opposed to the use of condoms, not just because it was associated with preventing disease more than preventing conception, but because the thick rubber took the feeling away. He opposed masturbation – a prevailing view – not because it led to moral or physical disease but because it was another consequence of enforced abstinence. He wanted an 'honourable provision for love'. Women were sexual creatures as much as men, and deserved the same satisfaction, even if this was unmarried love or even same-sex relations. Women suffered without sex too; they pined away with what was called the 'green sickness' which made them pale and hysterical. Sex, like eating or drinking, was simply a necessity. He quoted William Blake's aphorism, 'He who desires but acts not, breeds pestilence', the writer appreciated that thwarted desire could poison both body and mind.

Drysdale did not like prostitution *per se*, viewing it as one of the consequences of a system based on abstinence before marriage and rigid monogamy within in, but he quite admired sex workers. As things stood, they were sexual martyrs; 'Instead of contempt, these poor neglected girls deserve the warmest thanks of society, for the heroic mode in which they have borne the misery and the burden of our shame'. Drysdale called out the Victorian attitude as hypocritical. Critics said that following his plan would destroy all sense of the individual's moral restraint – and Drysdale would have agreed with them.

There were two broad views of prostitutes at this time – they were hard-headed sex workers who had chosen the career, enjoyed the advantages and therefore must take the consequences – or they were unfortunates soiled by sinfulness. Some people believed that they could be redeemed; others believed their situation was hopeless. Drysdale thought neither; 'they are much what society has made them, and society uses them, enjoys them and even loves them; yet denies them, spurns them, damns and crushes them'. The best that the establishment could do was to deem prostitution as a necessary evil (see Josephine Butler in Chapter Ten); Drysdale believed that it was evil that it was necessary. He rejected as a social constructs both the idea of purity and the notion that women needed to be purer than men. Like Josephine Butler a few decades later, he opposed regulating prostitution using the state intervention common in France and Belgium.

His enemies accused him of producing 'the Bible of the Brothel', discouraging morality and being the initiator of what the Victorians called 'free love'. It is hardly a surprise that he never put his name to the book. The book was not an easy read. It was a six hundred page treatise on marriage, sex education and population, but its dedication 'For the poor and suffering' summed up its aims. It was published by the radical publisher Edward Truelove (see Chapter Eight) and by 1904 had sold about 80,000 copies and been translated into ten languages. Truelove was allied to the freethought movement; Elizabeth and Ben Wolstenholme-Elmy would have known about it. Anna Kingsford read it and recommended it to others in her youth – this book, she contended, 'contained that which is more precious than gold- plain honest truth'.[5]

Drysdale did not want to put his name on the book but his authorship was reasonably well known amongst radical circles. One man who did not get the secrecy memo was Thomas Riley who operated in the Woolshops area of Halifax. In 1877, in the midst of other prosecutions of birth control publishers, he advertised more than once in the *Halifax Guardian* – 'The Elements of Social Science by Dr Drysdale – the next book selected for the next prosecution'.[6] Without the small but determined owners of secularist bookshops around the country, the radical voice would never have been heard.

One radical publisher, Edward Truelove was also selling the book in 1877, hiding Drysdale's identity but making the claim for the book clear:

The Elements of Social Science

AN EXPOSITION of the true cause and the only sure of three social evils – poverty, prostitution and celibacy.

The pioneer sex researcher Havelock Ellis reported that while teaching in outback New South Wales in the late 1870s he read 'the notorious Elements of Social Science ... which I had somehow heard of and that it had an influence in stimulating the course of my thought away from Christianity'.

Drysdale was an unlikely proponent of free love and intercourse unfettered by fear. He seems to have been a depressive and celibate for much of his life, which may have helped him to come to the conclusions he did. He was born in Edinburgh in 1824, the son of Sir William Drysdale. The photographer pioneer Robert Adamson started with studies of the elite of Scotland and the Drysdales were in that number. In the early 1840s, George was featured in two early calotypes, a photographic process only invented in 1841; he is, therefore, one of the world's first photographed humans. One calotype shows George with his brother Charles, both looking smart, wistful and reflective.[7] A later one shows Charles as a young academic, with a heavy book and pen in hand at his desk.[8]

Charles Drysdale also studied medicine and was a radical in the same way as George. He didn't marry either, as he was opposed to it for the same reasons as his brother – it was 'legal prostitution', but he was in a relationship with Alice Vickory.[9] They had a son, who was born in Paris in July 1874 where Vickory was studying medicine at the same time as Anna Kingsford, and it was this Drysdale who became the first president of the Malthusian League in 1877. They were normally called Neo-Malthusians, accepting the parson's premise about population but substituting a new solution.

If you believed that sex was a joy that Christianity had poisoned, then you were a freethinker, and in the 1860s and 1870s, the only outlet for your beliefs was the secularist media. Drysdale was a friend of leading atheist Charles Bradlaugh and wrote for his newspaper, *National Reformer*. Drysdale and later people like him seem as far away as possible from the Reverend Malthus, but he accepted the basic premise that the population would become out of control without action; they just disagreed about the action to be taken. Malthus saw self-restraint as a moral good, a precursor for receiving the grace of God, but Drysdale did not believe in either. He wished for a little less religiosity everywhere, and the bedroom was no exception.

It was through secularism that Drysdale met Bradlaugh and the remarkable Annie Besant (née Wood). She was a secularist, atheist, socialist, women's right campaigner, trade unionist, Irish nationalist and anti-colonialist. This chapter focuses on her birth control work, and her place in history would be assured had she only achieved that.

She was born into the secure upper middle classes, made less secure by the early death of her father when she was five. Her mother Emily worked against the odds to achieve a public school and university education for Annie's brother; in the meantime, Annie received quite a progressive education at boarding school, one that she valued a lot throughout her life. Despite this carefree education, like most middle class women of the time, her life was channelled towards marriage without anybody telling her what marriage entailed. Most Victorian women were given little clue about the physical aspect and Besant was different only in the fact that she was given none at all. She seems not to have thought about sex until her wedding night. Despite being bookish, she had not even read romances, so she could glean no clues there. Her interests were religion and helping people, and she admired the ideal clergyman as a shining example of both; then, unfortunately, she met one in the flesh.

Annie was introduced to the young Cambridge theology student Frank Besant at Easter 1866 in a London mission where both were helping the poor. Three months later and with improved weather, there was a week of organised walks, rides and drives and Frank asked her to marry him 'taking my consent for granted as I had allowed him full companionship'. She did not know the rules to this game; she was merely being polite, and the idea that marriage was a logical conclusion to a week's summer holiday never occurred to her. Her initial reaction was to refuse, but Frank, ever the romantic, had to rush for a train and swore her to secrecy, so the decision was delayed.

She tried more than once to say no, but she liked the idea more than she doubted the person.

> My dislike of the thought of marriage faded before the idea
> of becoming the wife of a priest working ever in the Church
> and among the poor. I had no outlet for my growing desire
> for usefulness in a happy and peaceful home [10]

Annie wanted to be useful on her own terms and also wanted to be married; but these two contradicted each other. Once she had accepted she was more or less obliged not to change her mind. They married and went to live in Sibsey, Lincolnshire.

The Reverend Besant has a poor reputation; to a certain extent he deserved it, but Annie was by her own admission totally unsuitable for marriage as it existed at the time. She was proud, dreamy, imaginative and completely impracticable, with a certain faculty for seeing visions and dreaming dreams and had no wish to change, even if a man told her to. She had never bought herself a pair of gloves or handled money except her own for spending and she couldn't handle the servants. She was a little like Anna Kingsford, except Anna found her Algie and ignored the pressure from her mother. She had received a formidably good education but she had not learned to obey.

She was a nineteen-year-old girl-wife. The first night of marriage was traumatic. Later when she became a campaigner for birth control she had no time for the notion that bringing up girls in perfect innocence was anything but a dangerous idea that did more than anything to put marriages in danger – 'No mother should let her daughter, blindfold slip her neck under the marriage yolk'.

It wasn't just the prim middle classes that went into marriage with no sexual knowledge. It was the same for the working classes from the surviving autobiographies that have been investigated.[11] From these accounts, it is clear that many people entered the marriage bed with no knowledge of the basics. Menstruation was taboo; both girls and boys did not know where babies came from until they were born; and despite living in one or two room houses, people were never totally naked. Besant's lack of knowledge was understandable, predictable and respectable, but not very useful for the life she wanted to lead.

She had two children, Arthur and Mabel, in the space of nineteen months. She was ill after the birth of her daughter and wished to have no more children. This led to more rows with her husband. Besant did not have the agreement that Kingsford had with her husband; sex within marriage was a man's conjugal right. It was traumatic; in the summer of 1871, looking for an escape from her marriage, she contemplated suicide, using the remains of chloroform that had been used to quieten her sick child.

She was wracked with religious doubt; this problem was not caused by her husband. In a moment of piety at the time she met Frank, she decided to retell the last days of Jesus by combining details in the four gospels. She realised that the stories were different and mismatched. She was expecting certainty but:

> I saw with a shock of horror that my harmony was a discord
> and a doubt of the veracity of the story sprang up like a
> serpent hissing in my face.[12]

She managed to fight this off, but a mixture of her own reading and her husband's behaviour made it return.

She was troubled with many questions, the same as many educated Victorians – the historical accuracy of the Bible and therefore its infallibility; the doctrine of eternal punishment and the nature of the Trinity. Her faith began to waver in 1871. She was ordered to conform outwardly by going to communion and the arguments with her husband continued. Sometimes the words turned into physical violence. Her objections were profound; she could not understand how a God could condone such misery as she had encountered; Genesis 3:16 was clear – 'unto the woman he said, I will greatly multiply thy sorrow and thy conception; in sorrow thou shalt bring forth children' and she wrote a doubting anonymous essay ('the wife of a beneficed clergyman') titled *On the Deity of Jesus of Nazareth*.

She was consorting with some dangerous people, when not stuck with her husband in Lincolnshire. Her religious pamphlets were published by the freethought publisher Charles Scott of Ramsgate, who knew Kingsford, Maitland and Bradlaugh. In 1872, she met and was mentored by Charles Voysey, then a controversial Church of England vicar who essentially believed there was a God but rejected everything else. She read widely, including Theodore Parker and Francis Power Cobbe. When she approached more established theologians like Edward Pusey, she was told to pray more and read less.

It was religion that was to break her marriage, but there were other areas of dispute with Frank. She would not play the wife's role – she was interested in Irish nationalism and the state of the Irish peasantry – she was three-quarters Irish herself. She kept company with radical lawyers like Mr Roberts, who was a friend of the radical chartist Earnest Jones and worried about the poor labourers in her husband's parish, living three generations in one slum hut. Her later interest in birth control and the population question started here; a woman's lack of control caused poverty for the poor, and terror for the vicar's wife for whom sex was unwelcome and dangerous.

She soon realised that philanthropy was not enough. Frank Besant initially shared her humanitarian concerns, but later it turned out that Frank was more interested in doling out charity from a position of privilege rather than changing society. When typhoid fever broke out in Sibsey, she nursed people back to health with the aid of the church but looked to public health and diet improvements to help the poor rather than a God who brought misery of the already suffering yet spared the affluent. She became interested in Trade Unionism, supporting Joseph Arch who was organising the poor labourers in East Anglia. When Frank helped out with the blacklisting of Trade Unionist's families and their families starved, Annie opposed it. She wanted justice, not charity.

She started writing for publication, and her main success was stories for the *Family Herald* magazine. When her first cheque for thirty shillings arrived, she was thankful for the chance to contribute to their meagre joint income, but she was told that the money was not hers to surrender. Her income belonged by law to her husband, something that she had not really thought about. Marriage made her think quickly and radicalised her from being by her own admission a spoilt, immature girl to a hardened rebel.

The crisis point came with Holy Communion in her husband's church. Frank insisted on this onward sign of conformity. She could cope with a service that was organised by and for humans, but when it came to the part where God was imminent, she walked out. Her husband's congregation were worried and afterwards, she received concerned enquiries about her health; they did not consider that she could have a contrary opinion to her husband.

In the summer of 1873, she was told by her husband that she must conform or leave. She was still ill from the birth of her second child and she had problems with her heart caused by the stress of marriage. A separation would have ruined her reputation, endangered her possession of the children and led to a life of lonely poverty. She decided to leave him; it was a brave decision. Her brother offered her a home if she gave up the dangerous friends she had made and settled into a few decades of lonely spinsterhood before death. She declined that too.

The relationship was over, but the marriage was not. She was able to get a separation only and was forever burdened with the surname of the man who had tormented her; and that torment was to continue later. She moved to Norwood, South London in 1874 with Mabel but with no firm plans on what to do next. She moved there to be close to Charles Scott, the freethought publisher, recently removed from Ramsgate and spent her time researching in the British Library. The Scotts would feed her and she had a maid to look after Mabel. In the summer of 1874, she bought the 19 July edition of the *National Reformer* from Edward Truelove and he recommended one of Bradlaugh's lectures at the Hall of Science. She read her heretical newspaper on the train, much to the shock and annoyance of the buttoned-up man next to her. She enjoyed the reaction.[13]

She met Bradlaugh for the first time on 2 August and they became friends very quickly. Despite her reading and authorship, she did not know who Bradlaugh was, and when she invited him to her modest house for tea, he asked her to reconsider as he was one of the most hated men in London and this would do absolutely nothing for her reputation. When she started to write for the *National Reformer* she used the nom de plume *Atlas* due to the fact that many freethinkers had reservations about Bradlaugh. In 1876, she broke her anonymity when she did her first public lecture; not on religion but on the poor political and economic status of women, a subject that she had learnt about through rapid and traumatic personal experience.

Besant became a national figure in 1877 when she and Bradlaugh republished an established American book, coyly entitled *The Fruits of Philosophy*. The content had been circulating since the first British edition in 1834 and had sold 42,000 copies in forty-three years. It was a handbook on contraception and the dangers of population increase. Its other titles were *The Private Companion of Young Married People* and *A Treatise on the Population Question*. Its author, Charles Knowlton, had clearly influenced Drysdale, who would be aware of the book as it was sold in radical booksellers like that of Edward Truelove.

This was Besant's first campaign for birth control; two years earlier, at a fractious lecture/debate at Leicester in June 1875, she was accused by a hostile member of the crowd of being the author of Drysdale's book, *The Elements of Social Science*. She not only denied authorship but claimed to know neither book nor author. In 1889, she made the same claim – that she had not come across the book until 1875 – at a libel trial, where an East London cleric had declared her immoral.

She also expressed her view that it was – 'physiologically mischievous and morally detestable'.[14] In 1875, she had to consult an earlier review by Bradlaugh, who had ignored the purely scientific part, probably out of ignorance, praised the part on population and birth control and totally rejected Drysdale's conclusion on free love. She tended to share his conclusions.

Something must have changed by 1877; it was George Drysdale himself who provided the medical commentary to *The Fruits of Philosophy*, modifying some of Knowlton's information about the physiology of reproduction. Both Besant and Bradlaugh were happy with Drysdale's science but were less happy with some of his conclusions about sexual morality, but clearly, his role here was acceptable to them.

The book itself was flawed, and Besant was more interested in the principle of freedom to publish on the subject of birth control. The books had been left alone for decades but in 1876, a local Suppression of Vice Society had successfully prosecuted Henry Cook, a Bristol boot-stitcher with a side hustle in obscenity, for producing Charles Knowlton's book. Cook had added some graphic pictures and upped the price to create the belief that it was a hardcore publication.

When it came to peddling 'offensive' material, Cook had form. In July 1875, he was fined £2 with costs for distributing material deemed offensive by the 1857 Obscene Publications Act. He wasn't selling them under the table in a plain brown wrapper, but handing them out and haranguing passengers at Weston-super-Mare railway station. These were described as 'medical illustrations that were deemed shamefully indecent and unfit for circulation'. If he was peddling pornography then he was doing it the hard way – to an audience of middle class commuters on their way to work. His *modus operandi* was more suited to somebody proselytising for birth control. His motives remain unclear as he failed to turn up for his trial.

In January 1877, he was sentenced to two years in prison for selling his 'spiced up' version of the Knowlton pamphlet; then the authority's anger fell on the owner of the copyright, Charles Watts, who was a friend of Bradlaugh and a recent associate of Besant. Watts wouldn't fight the prosecution, much to the disgust of Besant, but Watts was probably correct. It caused a rift in the freethought movement; some of its long-established members were ambivalent to birth control and rather resentful of the rise of Besant as a comrade and companion of their leader and felt the book was not worth struggling for.

Besant and Bradlaugh did not fall into this controversy by accident. From the very beginning, it was a planned confrontation with the authorities. Besant argued that they should republish the book and see what the consequences would be. They were not so much martyrs for free speech, but deliberate actors who attempted to goad the authorities into prosecuting them. They formed their own company, the Freethought Publishing Company of Stone Cutter Street, East London. They made it obvious that they were printing it, and did so for sixpence (there was a tendency for the authorities to look the other way if such books were too expensive for the poor to buy them). They omitted the 'obscene' pictures which had already been condemned in the Cook case as Besant wanted the test case to be about the original version. Some of their supporters believed that this was not an issue worth going to prison over, but it was more about the freedom of the press than one specific issue. Besant and Bradlaugh even offered to resign from the National Secular Society because of the members' reluctance to support them.

Besant was worried that all secular and freethought publishing would be extirpated by using the 'obscenity' gambit. Their introduction to the book makes this clear:

> The pamphlet which we now present to the public is one which
> has been lately prosecuted under Lord Campbell's Act and
> which we republish in order to test the right of publication.

Lord Chief Justice Campbell was the man behind the 1857 Obscenity Act; its key phrase was to make illegal anything that tended to 'deprave and corrupt'. They also pointed out that they did not necessarily agree with all of it, that some of it was factually wrong (hence George Drysdale's role) and it was published merely to allow free discussion. It could be defended morally. Would a book that tried to make sex easier and pregnancy harder be obscene?

> We took a little shop, printed the pamphlet, and sent notice
> to the police that we would commence the sale at a certain
> day and hour, and ourselves sell the pamphlet so that no one
> else might be endangered by our action.[15]

No arrests took place on the first day, Saturday 24 March. They reminded the authorities about what they were doing and what time they would be available to be detained. They were duly arrested and released without bail. The subsequent trial made Besant and Bradlaugh famous. Perhaps more importantly, birth control was talked about everywhere, including in distant Lincolnshire – SIBSEY VICAR'S WIFE ACHIEVES FAME – said one local newspaper.

Besant and Bradlaugh conducted their own defence, and Besant became the first woman to publically advocate birth control. She did so at very great length and in as much detail as would be tolerated; she was exploiting her national stage. Besant argued sex helped men and women stay healthy, and birth control could help tackle poverty. 'This is a dirty, filthy book, and the test of it is that ... no decently educated English husband would allow his wife to have it,' said the Solicitor-General, in an echo of the Lady Chatterley trial nearly a century later. Besant insisted that the so-called filthy parts be read out loud; the magistrate then asked for the women to leave the court while this was happening; it was pointed out that they were the witnesses. Like the other female radicals – Cobbe, Carlile, Kingsford and Wolstenholme-Elmy – she spoke out on subjects on which respectable women were meant to be silent.

Most people, including the officials, were satisfied with their sincerity – the jury in the verdict said as much, but it was still technically a guilty one. They were both found guilty after a four-day trial and sentenced to six months in prison and a £200 fine. However, they appealed the conviction, and the case wound up winning on a technical point, citing the fact that the verdict was vague and not drawn up correctly. Their trial was a massive piece of publicity for the book. They did not do time in prison and achieved their aim of protecting free speech and publicising the book. It was a success.

The book became famous; selling 185,000 copies in three and a half years and 350,000 in total. The Vice Society tried to prosecute individuals, but it seems that it was hawked on the street after the trial, including fake versions. Besant kept on selling it until they were privately assured that there would be no more prosecutions – then, having served its purpose, it was withdrawn, and Besant wrote a better book to replace it, *The Law of Population*. *The Times* accused Besant of writing 'an indecent, lewd, filthy, bawdy and obscene book'.[16] This did not stop 175,000 copies being sold by the time it was withdrawn in 1891.

Besant's family life was destroyed by the trial, although the process had started earlier. In August 1875, her daughter Mabel was more or less kidnapped by Frank on a family visit; Annie had to threaten him with *habeas corpus*. Her husband had started proceedings before the trial on the grounds that she was an atheist; Besant became so infamous that she lost custody of her children, now deemed an unfit mother – 'unfit' defined as having the wrong opinions. Her promotion of sex for pleasure, birth control and atheism condemned her. She did gain some rights of access, but the visits upset her daughter so much that she decided not to contact her children until they were mature enough to understand and judge for themselves. Eleven years later, both children chose to return to her.

Bradlaugh thought it would damage his chance of getting into parliament as the MP for Northampton. Besant thought it would damage her reputation as a woman and suitability as a mother. As it turned out, Bradlaugh was worrying unnecessarily but Besant was not; and the difference in their concerns speaks volumes for the different rights and expectations of Victorian men and women. Atheism was not a bar for Bradlaugh; atheism destroyed Besant's family – 'It was Christianity that robbed me of my child'.

Besant and Bradlaugh were Neo-Malthusians, like Drysdale and Truelove. They differed from Malthus only in identifying new checks on the population. It was no longer war, disease and famine, as they pointed out in their introduction to *The Fruits of Philosophy*:

> The checks now exercised are semi-starvation and preventable disease; the enormous mortality among the infants of the poor is one of the checks which now keep down the population. The checks that ought to control population are scientific, and it is these which we advocate.

Industrialisation created wealth but distributed it badly, creating poverty, slums and overpopulation. Religion stood in the way of the positive checks against overpopulation and poverty. Human progress would be impossible until the population problem was solved. These were the views of the new Malthusians.

The Malthusian League started in 1878, founded by Charles Drysdale and Alice Vickory, his lifelong companion. Bradlaugh had been considering such an organisation for a decade, but the foundation can be traced to a meeting of the London Dialectical Society on July 10 1877, when Annie Besant suggested the formation of a committee to defend the birth controllers from the Suppression of Vice Society, who were thought (correctly) to be behind the prosecutions.

Neo-Malthusians, in their earnestness, thought they were advocating happiness, in the form of early marriage (thus avoiding prostitution, disease and lonely celibacy) and small families (eliminating poverty and fear of pregnancy). Most of Victorian Britain did not see it that way. The established church opposed them; so did most of the medical profession and many scientists. Trade Unionists and socialists were never keen; they fully expected smaller families to be followed almost immediately by lower wages, as it was relations between capital and labour that caused poverty rather than relations between men and women. Socialist leader Keir Hardie made the point: *How long would wages remain at the same rate if the capitalist knew that there were fewer mouths to feed?*[17]

The League was always on the defensive. They were never very well off, and their membership was never more than about one thousand, heavily weighted towards progressive elements in London. Their main aim was to make their ideas acceptable, encourage publication and discussion, and fight against the laws which still put them in danger of prosecution for obscenity.

Their popularity was limited by the fact that they seemed to be targeting the poor. When Besant suggested that they should 'stamp with disapproval every married couple who selfishly overcrowd their home, to the injury of the community of which they are a part', she meant the rich as well as the poor, but everybody knew which of the two could not afford large families.

Then there was the problem of those deemed unfit parents who should not be allowed to breed at all, said some Malthusians. The birth controllers came close to the views of the eugenicists who were more unpopular than the Malthusians at the end of the century. Those followers of men such as Francis Galton (Chapter Fifteen) wanted to restrict the reproductive capacity of unfit populations, including people with hereditary diseases, mental illness, and exhibiting what was considered immoral behaviour. Birth control was a method to do this, hence the confusion, but the Eugenicists were suggesting state organised compulsion to restrict births while incentivising the fittest individuals to have large families through selective marriages with other fit individuals. That was the main difference. Malthusianism was about population, while Eugenics was focused on racial purity.

Malthusians like Besant were accused of forcing birth control onto the poor. They certainly encouraged doctors to identify married couples who were not fit to have children and to forcefully introduce them to birth control. Besant saw the situation the other way around; contraception was already available to the middle classes and she wanted it extended to the poor, where it had begun with Place and Carlile.

After 1878 Annie Besant reported that she received thousands of letters from women, 'many the wives of poor clergymen and country curates'. She may of course have been referring to her own experience but her main aim was to share knowledge – an exercise in democracy, but much of her work was only benefitting the middle classes. Middle class family size began to fall in the 1850s; overall birth rate fell from 1876 and, by the end of the century, the middle class were having fewer children than the working classes. Despite the efforts of Carlile and Place, the middle class got to contraception first or perhaps more accurately, to birth control, of which artificial barriers to conception were just one part. The doctors and the clergy, the most vociferous opponents of birth control, saw their family size fall by the 1890s while it remained unchanged for a working class occupation like cotton spinners.[18]

By 1890, Besant had a lifetime of achievement under her belt. She then did something remarkable. She had a massive change of heart; rejecting much of what she had previously believed in. Her atheism and interest in secular issues were waning; in an 1889 libel trial against an East End vicar who was trying to sabotage her election to the London School Board, she reported that she was no longer an atheist but a pantheist. In 1890, she met the Theosophist founder Helena Blavatsky and adopted the same esoteric religion made famous by the recently deceased Anna Kingsford. In 1891, she withdrew her own pamphlet on contraception and forbade its reprint.

The materialism and atheism were gone, but she was still a radical. Besant first went to India in 1893 and devoted the rest of her life to women's education and Home Rule; from 1909 India was her base. She was interned by the British Government during the First World War for promoting independence from Britain. She still supported the militant suffragettes in Britain and attended the famous victory celebration on 5 July 1928 at the Cecil Hotel, where 250 people recreated the breakfasts given to women released from Holloway two decades earlier. She gave an impromptu speech on India.

> An unexpected pleasure was the presence of Dr Annie Besant, looking like a priestess in her white, gold-embroidered robe, who spoke proudly of the fact that Indian men had enfranchised their sisters and now gave them high official positions.[20]

She was now the 'grand dame of India', and an Indian nationalist praised by Gandhi. She was also the leader of World Theosophy, which most of the British obituaries had difficulty understanding. She had recently announced the arrival of a new world messiah and believed that she would be reincarnated. She was cremated on a sandalwood pyre at sunrise on the day after her death in 1933.

When she died, only the Labour and radical feminist media remembered her earlier work. Many of the battles had been forgotten because they had most been won. With the rights of Trade Unions, women and nonbelievers mostly settled, she was lauded for the fight for free speech and the fight for the right to assemble. Her long, long life and her legacy were not able to be summarized adequately – that, paradoxically, was her legacy.

Chapter Eight

Freedom of the Press

Edward Truelove

Are sedition, blasphemy and obscenity bad things? They are strong, striking words and perhaps the first thought of the reasonable person is that they ought to be held back by law, and that was the case in the nineteenth century.

There were laws against sedition; they were powerful because they were broad. It protected the monarchy, the church, the government, the judiciary and the established church from hatred and contempt, and forbade the espousal of violent methods of change. Blasphemy was even vaguer – it protected the established Christian religions from ridicule. The mid-century laws against obscenity proscribed anything that, in the now notorious phrase, tended to 'deprave and corrupt'.

Some of our Victorian radicals started to question these assumptions. Why did sedition laws favour the establishment and the status quo? Why did blasphemy laws privilege one set of religious sensibilities over all the others in the world? And what was 'obscene' about birth control and other medical information that saved lives and reduced suffering?

Our radical thinker who asked these heretical questions was Edward Truelove. Truelove spent a lifetime and all of his money fighting these laws, and unsurprisingly, his paths crossed with many of the people in this book; Holyoake, Besant, and the Drysdale brothers, and very often he was their voice, taking the same risks as they did. There were few Victorians who were on nodding terms with both Karl Marx and Florence Nightingale.

Truelove was a radical himself. He was born early enough (1809) to be a follower and friend of early socialist Robert Owen; he attended his funeral in 1852. He was a chartist, a republican and freethinker, believed in women's rights and suffrage (his wife Harriet and two children were

106

suffragists too). He supported democracy in Europe and opposed the dictatorship of Napoleon III in France. Truelove, like Bradlaugh and the Wolstenholme-Elmys, supported Italian Unification. In 1849, he announced (in the Chartist newspaper the *Northern Star*) the birth of his son Edward Mazzini Truelove, after the Italian radical and nationalist, adding a little freethought aside by putting 'registered not christened'.[1] In November 1849 there was a non-religious blessing officiated by his colleague George Holyoake, whose own son had been named but not christened Maximilian Robespierre.

Truelove's contribution to radicalism was his work as a bookseller and publisher. He printed and distributed books on all radical subjects during his lifetime without fear or favour, and to his own considerable personal inconvenience. He started selling books at the John Street Literary and Scientific Institution in about 1842 and became the secretary in 1846. Florence Nightingale visited the Institution discreetly and struck up a friendship with his wife Harriet and an acquaintance with Edward.

The bookshop was a centre of social and political activity, raising money and organising events, but there was the ever-present threat of government suppression, partly because of the strong connection with the Chartists, as can be seen from this diary of the time:

> Another incident was about the time of my mother's death (1848). The Chartist riots were in full swing and an uncle of mine was one of the leaders. He kept a booksellers shop at 32 John Street, Tottenham Court Road, London where the meetings were held, many of which I was present at as I was staying with Aunt and often helped in the shop where most of the literature of the society was kept and sold, but as the Chartist riots are a matter of history I need go no further.[2]

It was a dangerous time to be a radical bookseller. Truelove also sold freethought, republican and atheist publications and supported birth control by selling contraceptives; he was in great danger of prosecution and this was not just in theory. There was a wave of blasphemy and sedition trials in the early 1840s. George Holyoake, the man who made up a secular birth ceremony for his son, had been imprisoned for blasphemy in 1841.

Another victim of the blasphemy laws was Charles Southwell, a brave but intemperate Bristol bookseller who published a newspaper, the *Oracle of Reason*, with the word ATHEISTICAL written in capital letters on the cover. He sold books that doubted the truth of religion and the historical accuracy of the Bible, but the authorities lost patience in November 1841 when he called the holy book 'This revoltingly odious Jew production'. The authorities used the established trick of arresting him late on Saturday afternoon in order to leave little time for bail to be organised; he stayed in prison till Monday. He served a year in prison for blasphemy – an imaginary crime in the minds of men like Holyoake, Truelove and Southwell. If God did not exist, it was a victimless crime, and if an omnipotent creator did exist, He did not need protection from a small Bristol newspaper.

Another freethought publisher, Matilda Roalfe, was as brash as Southwell, and faced similar consequences. She opened her shop THE ATHEISTICAL DEPOT in Edinburgh where she pulled no punches:

> I neither hope nor fear anything from authority, and am resolved to supply the public with works of a controversial and philosophical character, whether such works do or do not bring into contempt the Holy Scriptures and the Christian religion.[3]

Truelove and Southwell would have agreed; most other people did not, and her shop was stoned by a mob more than once. In January 1842, she was sentenced to two months in prison for blasphemy. It was easy to persecute atheists, as unbelief was very unpopular with all of the social classes, and the atheists knew it; 'Trial by Jury is trial by bigotry' said *An Account of the Trial of Charles Southwell*. Henry Hetherington, the indignant publisher, knew what he was talking about, having served four months for blasphemy in 1840.

What did a radical freethought bookseller offer to its customers? Truelove sold books by Southwell (*Superstition Unveiled*, 1854), Drysdale's *The Elements of Social Science*, the works of Robert Taylor, who had served two years for blasphemy, works by Carlile, Voltaire and Paine. There were also many books on economics, philosophy and science, especially the latter, and contraceptives for men and women. Truelove also published the *London Investigator*, later the *Investigator,* and continued with his twin-track of publishing and bookselling. His *London Investigator* of July 1854 advertised books from his own *Reformers Library* with titles such as *A few hundred Bible contradictions*. He knew that there was even more hostility outside London and offered a plain brown wrapper service; his advertising finished with this notice:

> E. T, having reasons to believe that many booksellers refuse to execute orders for the above, undertake to forward the work to all parts of the country upon the receipt of a Post Office Order.[4]

Truelove, like many freethinkers, was attracted to any scientific notion that was hostile to Bible teaching, and the weakest link seemed to be Genesis. In 1847, Truelove was selling *Vestiges of the Natural History of Creation* by Robert Chambers. The book suggested that the universe and everything in it, including man, evolved over time, with some failures, as seen by the fossil record. It was not the work of an atheist. Chambers marvelled at the great author of this system, which once created, did not require the creator to do anything. It was the work of a theist, but Chambers, a member of the publishing family, still decided not to reveal himself during his lifetime. It was still financial suicide for a publisher to publically disown the Judeo-Christian creation story but it was still relatively well received, being sold outside narrow freethinking circles. Charles Darwin later agreed that it had changed the mood of the people even though the science was bad.

Like many of the undesirable books of the nineteenth century, it was deemed more damaging if the poor read it. Truelove sold an abridged version of the book for two shillings and sixpence and advertised the fact. When the press would not take the advertisements, they were pasted onto placards and paraded through the street. *Vestiges* was not an underground production, bought and read by stealth, but known to have been read by both Prince Albert and Abraham Lincoln who liked the notion of a universal law for the universe. It was scarce not because it was obscure, but because many people wanted one. It attracted middle class intellectuals apart from the clergymen and the scientists. Charles Bradlaugh had an annotated secondhand copy in his library when he died.

Hetherington died of Cholera in 1849, affirming his atheism but also believing that his temperance would save him from cholera.

Hetherington was of a similar stamp to Truelove – a radical, freethought chartist who published the same material as Truelove and came from the same Owenite roots. One of his main aims was the abolition of the tax on newspapers and periodicals, introduced in 1819 after the Peterloo massacre and the consequent panic about mob violence and social unrest. The motivation was crude; it was designed to prevent radical material from getting into the hands of the working class by making it unaffordable – a 'tax on knowledge'.

In the 1850s newspapers were still taxed, albeit at a reduced rate, but the principle of pricing the poor out of knowledge still prevailed. At this point Truelove did his bit, risking, as ever, prosecution by the authorities. In 1853, he was prosecuted for selling a copy of the *Potteries Free Press and Weekly Narrative of Current Events*, a newspaper dedicated to news about Stoke-on-Trent and its environs. It seems an odd newspaper to sell in central London, and even more odd that he should be prosecuted by the Inland Revenue; but the paper was an unstamped publication, produced without paying the 'tax on knowledge' in a deliberate attempt by radical publisher Collet Dobson Collet to provoke a legal debate about the unfairness of the tax. This was a staged political act, designed to challenge the legality of taxes on newspapers in the courts; as far as the state was concerned, it was a matter of taxation only, which is why it was the Inland Revenue that led the prosecution. Truelove was fined a token amount, but the case publicised the injustice that periodicals about racing and hunting for the prosperous were untaxed, while the working class had to pay extra just to receive the news.

Truelove was out of tune with current beliefs and was prepared to be obstinate about it. In February 1854, a desperate medical student, who remained unnamed in the report, stole a copy of the *Lancet* from Truelove's shop in High Holborn. Truelove wanted his property returned and went to the Bow Street Office to retrieve it, and was asked in the normal course of the court process to swear an oath on the Bible, which he refused to do; 'I profess no religion. I claim exemption on conscientious grounds'. Truelove went on to assert that a recent Act of Parliament allowed this; he was told that the new law allowed Quakers and Moravians to claim exemption on religious grounds; 'your objection is based on irreligious grounds', he was told. Truelove then abandoned his prosecution and the alleged thief did give him his property back, but, as Truelove pointed out, he was denied the justice that would be extended to any citizen merely because of his conscience.[5] A similar event took place in 1857 when Truelove (and George Holyoake on a separate occasion) were rejected as jurors at the Old Bailey for admitting to having no religious belief. Clearly, any god would do, but 'no god' would not.

Truelove and his allies gained a victory when the newspaper stamp tax was abolished in 1855, but in 1858 he was prosecuted for publishing something more painful for the establishment. The immediate context was an attempt on the life of Emperor Napoleon III on 14 January 1858. Three bombs were thrown at the royal carriage as it made its way to the opera. Eight members of the escort and bystanders were killed and over one hundred people injured. The culprits were quickly arrested. The leader was an Italian nationalist, Felice Orsini, and the bomb that had failed to kill the Emperor had been made and tested in London.

Orsini was an Italian nationalist and thought the French Emperor was a barrier to Italian statehood and was convinced that he could bomb his way to Italian independence; it was an age-old political question: was assassination justified when the cause was right? Truelove supported Italian independence like many of our radicals.[6]

When a pamphlet was written entitled 'Tyrannicide – a justification', Truelove offered to publish it. He wanted a debate on principles; he did not recommend murder, he merely wished to print the opinions of others. Knowing that it was dangerous, he asked for the title to be changed to 'Tyrannicide – is it justifiable?' It was a slim, eight page pamphlet that sold for a penny, cheap enough for the masses to buy it and, the authorities feared, have their heads turned towards insurrection. It was written by another radical, W. E. Adams, but when the state took up a prosecution, it assumed the name to be false and went for the publisher instead. The authorities took up a prosecution in the usual way – making a test purchase and then arresting the publisher.

There were practical problems; the title of the pamphlet was phrased as a question, a question that was as old as politics itself. The French Emperor was not mentioned by name in the pamphlet. It was the government who decided what it meant and then arrested the guilty. It felt like an out of control executive to many, an executive that was making it a crime to discuss in theory the assassination of foreign rulers, and French at that.

There was a less famous prelude to this event. Three years earlier, prior to a state visit by the Emperor that included a ride past his shop, Truelove put a large placard outside his shop advertising *Les Châtiments (The Chastisements)*, a scathing attack on Napoleon, comparing him to Caligula and Judas, and to a worm, a wasp and a crocodile. Napoleon was upset by the book, and the authorities begged Truelove to remove it because they knew this. Truelove refused; on the morning of the ride past, a mysterious man came from out from the crowd with a large boat hook and pulled the placard from the open display in the shop.[7]

This time it was more serious:

> In the Court of Queen's Bench, on Tuesday, the indictments against Edward Truelove and Stanislaus Tchorzewski, charged with the publication of pamphlets vindicating the doctrine of assassination, and inciting evilly disposed persons to murder the French Emperor, came on for trial. The defendants, by the mouth of their counsel, stated that they had not the slightest intention of advocating in any manner the horrible doctrine of assassination.[8]

It helped that public opinion did not favour the bending over backwards to help the French, and that Prime Minister Palmerston was seen as too eager to use the laws of sedition to support an unpopular foreign leader. It all looked craven and a little ludicrous. Truelove, a middle-aged man, 'well dressed and respectable-looking', did not look like an ally of bomb-throwing anarchists.[9] Even his name was inappropriate for a putative assassin, thought the paper. A defence fund was created, but the prosecution came and went as a damp squib. The case was discontinued and a 'not guilty verdict' was directed by the judge. No action was taken, and he agreed not to publish the pamphlet anymore.

In 1867, Truelove gave way to the law literally when his bookshop was needed for the new law courts. His new High Holborn premises were that of the International Workingmen's Association from 1870; this is where Truelove would have met Karl Marx. The IWA were socialists and trade unionists, an international organisation dedicated to destroying capitalism, but slightly more dedicated to splitting into fractious rival groups. Truelove both supported them and published their work.

He was friends with Charles Bradlaugh and Annie Besant, who managed a moral victory at the famous 'Fruits of Philosophy Trial' of 1877. He suffered with them. In late May 1877, the same Suppression of Vice Society that were chasing Bradlaugh and Besant obtained a warrant for the police to raid his shop at High Holborn and seized around 600 copies of the *Fruits of Philosophy*, which Besant and Bradlaugh were shortly to go to court to defend.

The Vice Society, upset at their failure with the Besant/Bradlaugh trial, then attacked Truelove. In May 1878, he was indicted for selling Robert Dale Owen's *Moral Physiology*. Owen's book was, according to the *Portsmouth Evening News*, simply *The Fruits of Philosophy* under another name.[10] The most striking similarity was that both books had been on sale for decades. They also shared the conclusion that moral restraint was not the answer to family size and population increase, which was not what the Vice Society wanted to hear. Truelove saw some other similarities – the persecution by the Vice Society; the importance of allowing free discussion about birth control and female health; and the general use of obscenity law to suppress debate about philosophical or medical issues.

It was 1858, or 1877 all over again, except that he lost his case, after an inconclusive first trial. 'The course of Truelove never did run smooth,' joked the *East London Observer*; but it was not particularly funny.[11] He was imprisoned for four months. Although the £50 fine could have been paid many times over by his supporters, he did have to wear prison uniform, pick oakum and sleep on a hard plank bed. He was sixty-eight.

Truelove went back to work in his bookshop after the trial. He had the satisfaction of witnessing the demise of the Vice Society in 1880. The rest of his life was lived out uneventfully from his compact villa in Alexandra Road, Hornsey. In 1887, he was fined £5 for not having a dog licence; his mitigation that he had offered the money at the Post Office but it had been refused was not believed, but at least he did not have to swear to a God that he did not believe in. In 1889, one Alfred Dubree was given twelve months for stealing his watch. God was not involved in that either.[12]

He continued to work in his shop until 1893. Like Bradlaugh, books and radicalism had not made him any money. Like Bradlaugh, his extensive personal library had to be sold to pay debts after his death in 1899. Truelove is buried in Highgate cemetery with his wife Harriet and near his ally George Holyoake and his acquaintance Karl Marx. The sentiments on his gravestone are accurate:

> In Memory of Edward Truelove Publisher
> Regardless of the Obloquy and Suffering and Worldly Loss. He battled bravely through a long and troubled life to maintain the right of free speech and free thought.

Like Bradlaugh, he lived a long life and was just old enough for his assaults on the establishment to be forgiven, and be replaced with a patronising sense of fair play and praise of his personal qualities. His obituaries made this clear; Truelove 'may be said to have been a sturdy fighter in the ranks in the battles of lost causes and forlorn hopes, but his courage, endurance, absolute disinterestedness and self-sacrifice will always be remembered with appreciation by Englishmen of all shades of opinion'.[13]

The acknowledgement that Englishmen could possess, with impunity, 'all shades of opinion' was Truelove's legacy.

Chapter Nine

Atheism

Charles Bradlaugh

Charles Bradlaugh is Britain's most well-known atheist; he co-founded the National Secular Society, which still exists as Britain's premier secular pressure group. However, he was not the first atheist, and he was not the last; the earlier ones were slandered and persecuted, as can be seen in the previous chapter, and the ones that followed tolerated and later accepted. Bradlaugh was in the middle, and was the bridge between the two; he was reviled at the start of his life and grudgingly accepted at the end. He made atheism an acceptable intellectual conclusion for future citizens, at considerable personal effort and cost.

Atheism was the apex of freethought, or heresy to its enemies. There were many lower base camps – the theism of people like Frances Power Cobbe; the pantheistic/mystic approach of Anna Kingsford; the re-interpretation of death offered by the spiritualists, the secularism of men like George Holyoake, who wanted religion removed from public life, but it was Charles Bradlaugh who best represented the absolute rejection of religion on the basis that it was historically unlikely and scientifically unprovable.

Bradlaugh did not actually deny the existence of God. As he said: 'He did not deny that there was "a god" because to deny that which was unknown was as absurd as to affirm it. As an atheist, he denied the God of the Bible, of the Koran and of the Vedas, but he could not deny that of which he had no knowledge.'[1]

Atheism, like all bad ideas that the Victorians disapproved of, had its immediate origins in the French Revolution; the most famous British 'atheist' from the time was Tom Paine, whose book, the *Age of Reason* was hunted down and its retailers prosecuted in the 1790s. But Paine was not an atheist, he was a theist. Paine did, however, think

115

that organised, revealed religion that claimed absolute knowledge was absurd. A sentence from the *Age of Reason* proves it, 'I believe in one God and no more and hope for happiness beyond this life'.

Paine was also a republican and a democrat; so by the time of Bradlaugh, atheism was tarnished with these ideas. Bradlaugh made the problem worse by also advocating republicanism, democracy and more besides – Irish nationalism and land reform, birth control and Malthusianism – so confirming some people's worst suspicions that atheism was the mother of all destructive radical ideas. Throughout his life, he was 'Bradlaugh the____', and the blank was never anything good.

What would turn a Victorian into an atheist or a theist? For most of the freethinkers of the time, we do not know, but for Bradlaugh we have a story that may have happened a thousand times to much less famous people. Charles was from a religious, lower middle class London family, and he was born to work rather than to learn or have opinions. He was in school for only five years before he started working as a messenger boy for a coal merchant.

He worked hard. At twelve he was an unusually religious but clever child. He became a Sunday school teacher at fourteen at St Peter's, Hackney, and was a promising new addition to the church. His vicar, John Packer, thought so too and deputed him to be one of the people at the confirmation in front of the Bishop of London. What would be better than his best student responding to questions about the Thirty-Nine Articles, which defined the doctrines and practices of the Church of England? The sin of pride did not seem to be too far away from the Reverend Packer, and as events transpired it was clear that he was prone to other sins as well.

Charles, in his desire to get to the truth, researched the Thirty-Nine Articles when he was only required to learn and regurgitate them in front of the Bishop. This led to the same crisis that Annie Besant had when she tried to put the Easter story into order by using the four testaments, or Frances Power Cobbe when asking her father about the feeding of the five thousand. Most of our radicals who rejected established religion did so from an original position of naivety and trust; it was the truth, so it would bear examination; any questions could be answered by the experts.

Young Charles had questions. He then asked Packer for help in understanding them but was suspended from his job, and a letter was written to his parents saying that his inquiries were atheistical. This was powerful; Bradlaugh had reached no conclusions and the sin was *not* the questioning, but not accepting the 'truth' when told to him. So, like so many of our deists, he acquired his scepticism through a surfeit of knowledge that clashed and could not be reconciled with the claims of the church.

He was not an atheist yet, but he had doubts. Bradlaugh compensated by going out to public meetings at Bonner's Field on the banks of the Regent's canal, a favourite meeting point for Chartists. He was there to promote and defend Christianity but by default was exposed to the freethinkers who disagreed. These men and women were supporters of Richard Carlile (1790–1843) who was the prototype early nineteenth century radical, and a man who put his liberty at risk by selling Paine's *Age of Reason* on the streets. Eventually, Bradlaugh changed his mind; he accepted that the argument for atheism was unanswerable, and joined them. They ran a temperance hall and coffee shop at Warner Place, much to the fear and disgust of the neighbours. One night, his daughter recorded, the crying of a baby brought out the neighbours who feared a human sacrifice was taking place.

The Bradlaugh family were horrified at their promising obedient boy becoming an atheist, and the Reverend Packer had not been inactive either; he tried to save the rest of the family by inviting himself into their house, placing pious slogans on the walls, including 'The fool hath said in his heart, there is no God'. Bradlaugh had gone further – he told his new friends in speeches that he was now an atheist and a teetotaller. Packer also knew that he had attended Chartist meetings. Packer then threatened to use his influence with Bradlaugh's employers – he had three days to change his opinion or face poverty for himself and pariah status for his family. He chose the latter – leaving home, friendless, unemployed and aged only fifteen, a freethinker and an outsider. This was true courage. Like Frances Power Cobbe, he discovered what happened when he expressed his religious doubts to his family.

Our main source for Bradlaugh's life is the gushing and partial biography written by his daughter Hypatia Bradlaugh Bonner; if the book wasn't about a person who denied the existence of saints and martyrs, the word 'hagiography' would be appropriate. Hypatia was the ancient Greek philosopher, mathematician, astronomer, teacher and pagan who was murdered by a mob of Christians; her name was not a coincidence. She did not blame Packer for her father's atheism. Packer may have driven her father to unbelief but it would have happened eventually; her father's studious inquiry into religion's internal inconsistencies would have seen to that.

Bonner tells her father's story as if it was a constant battle and that was not necessarily the bias speaking. It was hard, with few friendly faces and the whole establishment against him. After leaving home, he lodged temporarily with another freethinker, a Mr B. B. Jones and tried to use his skills in the coal business to become a merchant, but lack of capital and the rumour that he was an infidel held him back. He was supported by the Carlile family at Warner Place, round the corner from the family that had rejected him.

He was only fifteen when he met Eliza Sharples. Eliza was the partner of Richard Carlile; not, shockingly his wife. They had been in what they termed a 'moral marriage', a three-sided affair with his legal wife Jane Carlile. Both she and Bradlaugh were influenced by Carlile's views. Carlile also had a daughter named Hypatia, who Bradlaugh would have known as a constant visitor to their home. In an age when radical thought was dominated by men, she was one of the first females to make public speeches about women's political rights. By the time they met, she was running a coffee and discussion café in Hackney. The only point of disagreement was on the subject of free love in marriage, perhaps the only subject where Bradlaugh did not take up a radical position.

Bradlaugh made his first public lecture, *The Past, Present and Future of Theology* at the Temperance Hall, Commercial Road, London, on 10 October 1850, aged seventeen. In June 1850, he wrote his first pamphlet, *A few words on the Christian Creed*, but he had no way of earning a living, so he joined the 7th Dragoon Guards, expecting to be sent to India, but ended up in Ireland.

His daughter portrays him as a popular character in the army, forever leaving his barracks to go to temperance meetings and reading books while standing up for the common soldiers. His nickname, we are told, was 'Leaves' due to his propensity to go AWOL, read books and drink lots of tea. His daughter claimed that everybody loved and admired him but he seems to have been a fish out of water. He did not like the army enough to build a career there; he was able to buy himself out with a legacy from the will of his great aunt Elizabeth Trimby. He found a job as a clerk in a law office from 1854 until 1863. This experience gave Bradlaugh the ability to defend himself in court over a lifetime of struggle and to devote an hour each morning to giving free legal advice to the poor. In his spare time, he started to write atheistical articles under the pen name 'Iconoclast'.

He married Susannah Hooper in June 1855 at St. Philip's, Stepney. She and her family were fellow radicals; they needed to be because of the life he was about to embark on. He was still a poor clerk at the time, and could only afford marriage by using the money that he had received as compensation for wrongful imprisonment by a solicitor who had unsuccessfully prosecuted him for stealing. Their marriage had broken up by 1870. Susannah had a serious problem with alcohol and they were estranged for much of their marriage, with her and some of her family living in Sussex, where she died of heart disease caused by her drinking.

In 1855, Bradlaugh was involved in the dispute over Sunday trading. It was proposed that there would be limits on the activities available on the one day of rest for the working people. Early in the year, evening pub opening hours were curtailed; now it was proposed to close small shops, reduce public transport and restrict recreation in order to keep Sunday 'special'. This would have destroyed the small Sunday shopkeepers and market stallholders who sold basic goods that were needed by the poor who were paid on a Saturday night. This legislation was proposed in a panic; the 1851 census of religious attendance had proved that large numbers of the working classes were absent from Church on a Sunday morning, and rather than make it more friendly and socially inclusive, the plan was to stop them doing anything else.

The first demonstration in Hyde Park was on 24 June 1855 and it was just about dispersed by the threats of the superintendent of police. The mob were still able to hoot their derision at the passing rich in their coaches, who were neither at home in religious contemplation nor giving their servants a day of rest. The next meeting was banned; Bradlaugh (and Karl Marx) were two of the 150,000 who turned up in defiance of the order. Marx thought the English revolution had begun; Bradlaugh saw it more as a matter of legality and justice, but then he saw everything like that.

Bradlaugh was one of the witnesses at the Royal Commission to investigate the unrest and his evidence was definitive – there had been no riot, the police had been violent, and there was no legal basis to forbid the assembly.

By 1856, he was lecturing around a small circuit of secular halls in London and Edward Truelove became his publisher. His tours around the country, which started around 1858, were physically demanding, badly remunerated and often downright dangerous. In April 1859, the principal citizens of Doncaster remonstrated with the mayor not to allow the infidel to speak and were outraged when he said that he, unfortunately, did not have the power. In other places, the meetings were either packed with his opponents inside the hall or as a hostile crowd outside. In the coastal town of Devonport in 1859, he addressed a meeting from a barge just a few feet off-shore so that he would be speaking outside the jurisdiction of the town's police.[2]

In June 1858, the religious establishment picked a fight with him. He was lecturing in Sheffield, a centre of support for freethought, when he was challenged to a series of debates by the Reverend Brewin Grant at the Sheffield Temperance Hall. Bradlaugh set the terms of the debate, and the titles of each night's debates explains a lot about the nature of his arguments. The lecture titles over the years were designed to provoke a strong reaction.

> The God of the Bible revengeful, inconstant, unmerciful, and unjust. His attributes proved to be contradicted by the book which is professed to reveal them
>
> Is the Bible history of the creation consistent with itself and with science?
>
> Is the Bible history of the deluge consistent and physically possible?
>
> The Bible; deficient in learning, logic, and fairness?
>
> Does Man have a soul?
>
> Were Adam and Eve Our First Parents?
>
> The Progress of Heresy

Bradlaugh was always a keen but amateur lawyer, and his seeking after the truth was a relentless interrogation of the Bible (or similar Holy Book) and its adherents, who he assumed were all lying to him. Sometimes meetings were held over three nights, with detailed arguments taking up four or five columns in the local newspaper; the whole of the back page of *The Ashton Weekly Reporter* and *Stalybridge and Dukinfield Chronicle* on Saturday 2 November 1861 was taken up in three nights of a discussion against the Rev. Woodville Woodman; the first night was devoted to *Is the Bible a divine revelation?* The Reverend Woodman was an old adversary; this was the second meeting this year. In February they had another four-night debate with Bradlaugh using his encyclopaedic knowledge of history and philosophy – The Koran, Book of Mormon, Greek, Roman and Persian History to prove that Christianity was neither special nor very different.

Bradlaugh was a famous opponent. Those clerics who came out relatively unscathed would boast about their debates with him in their lectures and book marketing; when the MP and news entrepreneur W. H. Smith invited him to discuss the truth of the Bible, Bradlaugh set up an informal committee to decide whether he was worth talking to.

The thrust of the opposition argument was that atheism was dangerous because it destroyed the basis of moral behaviour. Morality was impossible without a Christian moral framework; despite Bradlaugh and others pointing out that the Old Testament especially condoned some terrible acts, and that it was both possible and desirable to build a moral code without a supernatural element, it was an argument that resounded with many people. Lord Randolph Churchill believed that atheists 'were mostly the residuum, the rabble and the scum of the population; the bulk of them persons to whom all restraint – religious, moral or legal – is odious and intolerable'. When Bradlaugh ended up in the Commons in 1880, Churchill was one of his key persecutors.

He became a truly national figure in the 1870s. He was involved in the brief flourishing of republicanism in Britain (see Chapter Fourteen) and with the birth control campaign with his friend Annie Besant. He was reviled by the establishment by the 1870s, not just for his atheism, but as living proof that atheism led to a lot of other, equally undesirable sets of ideas. His newspaper, the *National Reformer*, confirmed these fears in its masthead slogan – *Atheistic in theology, Republican in politics, and Malthusian in social economy*.

Hecklers at rowdy meetings often accused him of supporting, sometimes even writing, the *Elements of Social Science*. He was aware of the book, and the real author, as Drysdale often wrote on population matters for the *National Reformer*. Bradlaugh's views on other subjects seemed to condemn him as well – he criticised inequality in marriage, encouraged divorce reform and allowed spiritualist magazines to advertise in his *National Reformer*. When he met Annie Besant in 1874, he gave her the option of breaking off their relationship because he was so unpopular.

Would it be possible for an atheist to be a member of parliament, or to be more precise, would it be possible for an avowed atheist to take his seat? There were already atheists in parliament, but they lacked both the bravery to admit it and the conscience to object to the oath. The wording was recent, used for the first time in 1868:

> I (name of Member) swear by Almighty God that I will be faithful and bear true allegiance to Her Majesty Queen Victoria, her heirs and successors, according to law. So help me God.

Bradlaugh had three problems; getting elected as an atheist; swearing allegiance to a royal family he wished to replace, and doing so in the presence of a God whose existence remained unproved. Like his insistence on holding public meetings without hindrance, this to him was an issue of free speech and citizenship. Atheists deserved the same rights as others – the same point that his friend Edward Truelove was making. This religious bar had gradually been removed; Irish Catholics were allowed to make laws in 1829. In 1849, Protestant nonconformists had their disabilities removed. In 1858, the first Jewish MP – Baron Lionel de Rothschild took his seat legally by saying 'so help me Jehovah', sworn on the Old Testament only. It seems that tolerance meant that any god was acceptable; but not the godless, who could not make a solemn promise because they were immoral.

Charles Bradlaugh is politically linked to the town of Northampton. He still has a public house named after him in the town, although his view of it would be mixed (until late in his life he remained teetotal). His first foray in the town was in January 1859, when he gave one of his lectures at the Woolpack Inn. It was a nonconformist town with some radical boot and shoemakers, but when he decided to get into parliament, he knew that he needed the Liberal Party to support him to get elected.

His first attempt was in 1868. The political establishment was appalled at the prospect of a republican, secularist, Malthusian, atheist Member of Parliament. The *Daily Telegraph* fulminated – how could the nation elect an atheist? The short answer was that they couldn't. 'I was beaten, but that was scarcely wonderful. I had all the journals except three against me,' said Bradlaugh. The leader of his own party was against him; William Gladstone made his views absolutely clear that he was not to be elected. Gladstone went to church twice a day; the facts were not unrelated. Many local liberals drew the line at his secularism; they liked most of his politics but why would you burden yourself with a candidate who was a proselytising atheist?

Bradlaugh had supporters – the working men of Northampton and a phalanx of reformers including John Stuart Mill, who sent in a £10 donation from his home in the South of France. The argument in his favour showed how deeply unpopular his atheism was; it was put by his supporter, the Unitarian minister J. K. Applebee. Atheism was so odious that no dishonest man who wished to win a seat in parliament would profess it; so therefore Bradlaugh was an honest man of principle. The second argument was more modern-sounding – his private religious beliefs were irrelevant if the MP served the voters of Northampton well.

He came bottom of the poll in the General Election and by-election of 1874, and squeaked in in 1880, benefiting from the huge swing to the Liberals, who remarkably won a majority of the national vote (54.7%). His election was national news, and there were going to be problems.

> There is a probability that an interesting and important question will be raised when Mr Charles Bradlaugh proceeds to take his seat in the new Parliament. Bradlaugh, as is generally known, is an avowed atheist, in the sense of denying that the existence of a Supreme Being can be proved, and accordingly he objects to take the ordinary parliamentary oath.[3]

The *Edinburgh Evening News* was able to produce a nuanced version of Bradlaugh's beliefs rather than merely call him a blasphemer, infidel or heretic as many 'letters to the editor' suggested. The insults were legion; he was the 'pet of the Northampton Shoemakers'.[4] One sympathetic paper noted that even 'Bradlaugh was subject to worse abuse than a costermonger would blush to bestow on his donkey'.[5] It still pointed out, a little gleefully perhaps, a weakness in his position.

Though a strong advocate of Republicanism, he has, it seems, an objection to promise fidelity to the throne, considering himself quite free all the while to agitate for the constitutional abolition of the monarchy; but he objects to professing a religious belief which does not hold.

The first part didn't quite fly; Bradlaugh's version of republicanism involved building a parliamentary majority for the abolition of the monarchy at the death of the reigning monarch, but it was pointed out that the oath extended to the 'her heirs and successors' and that these were the same people as Bradlaugh had condemned as 'costly puppets' only six years earlier.

The newspaper then correctly predicted the subsequent events:

By law, Christians in Parliament who conscientiously object to take oaths are allowed to make a solemn affirmation instead; and Mr Bradlaugh wants to get off with this. There is, however, a doubt whether his request will be readily granted. No such toleration is shown to atheists in courts of law, where, although Christians with conscientious scruples are allowed give evidence with a simple affirmation, unbelievers are not admissible as witnesses at all.

There was also some grudging respect for Bradlaugh:

He is not a man to endure tamely such a refusal of his natural rights and there is a likelihood that will not only get the way into Parliament made free for atheists, but will persuade the Liberal leaders to legalise the taking of evidence from atheists without oath. It would be especially unjust that Mr Bradlaugh should be debarred from Parliament, seeing that there is good reason to believe that several members share his opinions without imitating his candour.

When he appeared at the House of Commons on 3 May 1880, he asked to be exempt from the oath and to affirm instead. He had spent much of his adult life metaphorically tearing the Bible to pieces – he could not solemnly swear on it now. He quoted the Acts of Parliament he thought relevant. Since 1870, atheists had had the right to make an affirmation rather than an oath in the English and Welsh courts; when this was rejected he offered to take the oath anyway, on the basis that it was meaningless to him. It did not endear him to the House of Commons; they were expecting the worst, and this was it.

The next six years were turbulent. In 1885, at the height of the process, the conservative J.H. Bottomley told his working class audience at the Bedford Assembly rooms that it was part of the Conservative policy to keep such men out of the House of Commons. Herbert Gladstone, the Prime Minister's son, called it 'systematic persecution'.[6]

During that time, he was fined £1,500 for voting illegally, escorted from the Commons by police and was the last MP to be imprisoned. He had to fight his seat three times. In 1881 (unseated for voting before taking an oath), 1882 (expelled) and 1884 (resigned) where in a two-horse race he squeaked in with 51, 50.7 and 52.4% of the vote.[7] He took his seat without incident in 1886, the second of two winning Liberals.

Bradlaugh was to have only three years before his death as a 'normal' MP. He fitted into the institution much better than was expected for such a feared radical. He thrived in the House of Commons. His experience of turbulent political meetings held him in good stead; he was not going to be shouted down or embarrassed like our two other radical MPs – Hardie and Dilke. He also knew that his raucous methods of the town hall meeting were not appropriate in the Commons. He initiated new laws to allow atheists to affirm. The Oaths Act of 1888 allowed individuals professing no religious belief, or whose religious beliefs did not allow the taking of oaths, to 'solemnly affirm' rather than 'swear by almighty God', and in 1889, he introduced legislation to end the blasphemy laws which was lost on the second reading; but that was still remarkable progress as it had ministerial support. He advocated Home Rule for Ireland, took an interest in Indian affairs and supported Gladstone. In that time he did not agitate for republicanism or birth control and was clearly not a dangerous socialist, which encouraged his positive reception in the Commons.

Bradlaugh, unlike Besant, Truelove, Pankhurst and Hardie, never made the transition from radical Liberal to socialist; indeed he made enemies in radical circles by denouncing this new political creed. He had been denounced as a communist in the 1870s by those opposed to his republicanism, but he did not want the creation of an all-powerful state;

he had struggled against the establishment for nearly all of his life and did not want its power strengthened, although he did support reforms that improved housing and working conditions. He had been a success through his own hard work and talent, and the socialist call for collective action made him suspicious. He had been born in a tenement house in Hoxton and shared it with his parents and seven siblings and was now a Member of Parliament. Self-reliance had worked for him.

He died on 30 January 1891 at the age of fifty-seven. His life-long lung problems and hereditary kidney weakness were exacerbated by nearly forty years of ceaseless activity for unpopular radical causes. He knew this – he had burned the candle at both ends and in the middle. As he moved from unconsciousness to death, the House of Commons was clearing his name. They expunged the comments in their records that he was unfit to be an MP. His daughter discovered the news but seemed not to tell him to avoid further agitation.

He died an atheist; there was no panicky change of mind in the face of hell-fire that many of his enemies had predicted and hoped for. The rumour still spread, however; his daughter Hypatia Bradlaugh Bonner, who later became a peace activist, author, atheist and freethinker, felt the need to write a pamphlet entitled 'Did Charles Bradlaugh Die an Atheist?' The answer was: yes, he did.

He was no longer the controversial figure he had once been; he had made admirers during his time as an MP and his new status, while not always welcome, was tolerated. The *Northampton Mercury* noted that the grave was a great leveller but also a 'universal reconciler'; it was clearly no longer the first step to everlasting torment for the unbeliever, and the newspapers no longer bandied about words like 'infidel' and 'heretic' quite so freely.[8]

What was the verdict of the Northampton churches? Some thought that it was their own bigotry which had created Charles Bradlaugh. The object of their displeasure was Charles Packer. It was a pastoral failure – when Bradlaugh was young and enthusiastic but with unsettling questions, Packer let him down. 'Clergymen much dowered with bigotry [and] very much wanting in good sense,' said Dr Clifford of the Westbourne Park Chapel, who named no names, but the life story of Bradlaugh was well known in Northampton.

The Reverend Moulton of the Wesleyan Methodists also felt compelled to speak. He too blamed Packer for turning Bradlaugh away from Christ; all that intelligence, power and pluck could have been used for the church and not against it. Dr Parker of the City Congregation said that the man who did not meet the young enquirer in the right spirit was the real infidel; and at this point, some in the congregation shouted, 'Hear! Hear!'

There was no reference to eternal damnation in any of the reports from the six main Northampton churches. The Reverend Canon Hull of All Saints lamented that a man of such obvious talents had been lost to the church, but it was not his job to judge him. Canon Hull also took the opportunity to ask why so many sincere and public-spirited people became unbelievers – was it due to some people's shallow and inconsistent Christianity? The Reverend E. W. Bremner of the King Street Congregational Chapel also thought the event could not go without comment; yes, Bradlaugh was an unbeliever, but they must not judge – they should be too busy judging themselves. How far is the Church responsible for the present scepticism and doubt? The Reverend Harry Bradford of the Union Church broke ranks to some extent. While refusing to 'comment on recent events', he went on to comment on recent events by suggesting that there was nothing more serious than not being prepared to make your maker; that was as far as the criticism extended.

The plaudits were unceasing. Bradlaugh was a battler. The Reverend Street had known him for years; they were almost friends and he had no doubt that he was a moral man. The Reverend Rogers suggested that in many ways he was a Christian without knowing it – honest and public-spirited. He had turned out to be an excellent MP, a great friend to India and an ally of the poor without being an adherent of the new heresy, socialism. The Reverend Needham of the Grafton Street Chapel recorded the same good points and hoped that Bradlaugh's life could have been extended to give him a chance to repent. None of the clergy bought into the lie that he had repented on his death bed; they knew him too well. None of them had any difficulty with the notion that a man could be a freethinker and a man of good morality.

Three special trains were needed to move his supporters and admirers to the funeral in Woking. Although this was the site of a crematorium, this was not a cremation but an earth burial in a papier-mâché coffin with perforations to speed decomposition. It was a silent interment by order of the deceased, with no mourning clothes or lamentations, and the mauve, white and green rosettes of his Northampton election were thrown into the unconsecrated ground.

There were over 3,000 people present. Mr Gladstone sent the infidel a small wreath, as did the Women's Suffrage League. Annie Besant, the only person in black, was drifting away from his materialist view of life but remained his friend.[9] His fellow secularist George Holyoake, his publisher Edward Truelove, the Christian socialist Stewart Headlam, and the young David Lloyd George were present. The police who were sent to keep order also sent their own floral tribute, as did the Brighton Anarchists.

Mohandas Gandhi was one of many Indians there, paying their respects to a man who loved India, but he was not the most famous Indian present – that was Dadabhai Naoroji, who became the first Indian MP in Britain a year later, winning Finsbury Central by five votes in 1892. Some newspapers knew he was there and called him 'Lord Salisbury's black man'. This Conservative Prime Minister had predicted that the British would never want a black man as a representative in parliament. When he was proved wrong, Bradlaugh's work meant that Naoroji was not obliged to swear an oath on the Christian Bible.

Bradlaugh's daughter made this tribute:

> True, he was to win that fight, but his life was to be the price of the winning … but the laurel wreath was to fall upon a grave.

There was no braver man than Bradlaugh. He worked himself to an early death for a cause that he believed in; that cause was not, ultimately, atheism, but free speech and equal treatment under the law.

Chapter Ten

The Sexual Double Standard
Josephine Butler

One belief of the nineteenth century, and some would say, the century that followed, was that men's sexual incontinence was appalling and highly regrettable, but was still a fixed point around which other areas of social policy had to be modified, while women's poor sexual behaviour was a legitimate source of anger and condemnation. The law reflected this double standard. Under the Matrimonial Causes Act (1857), women could be divorced on the grounds of adultery alone, while it had to be proved that men had committed adultery alongside other offences. The message was that female adultery was a worse transgression.

The most infamous example of the nineteenth century double standard was the set of Contagious Diseases Acts (CDA) passed by a panicky and embarrassed Parliament in 1864, 1866 and 1869. It was not legislation for the whole country – at its widest extent, it covered the towns of Aldershot, Canterbury, Chatham, Colchester, Dover, Gravesend, Maidstone, Plymouth, Portsmouth, Sheerness, Southend, Windsor and Woolwich. These were all naval or army towns, regularly full of unattached men outside the control of normal family authorities, and it was here that prostitutes passed on sexually transmitted diseases to members of the armed forces, and of course, vice versa. As the behaviour of the men was something that could not be changed, it was decided that the best way to protect the armed forces from disease was to regulate, punish and fine the women only. Changing male behaviour was deemed to be impossible; so it was decided to regard women alone as vectors for diseases and control their behaviour.

Our radical in this area was Josephine Butler (born Josephine Grey in 1828). Her background was impeccably religious, prosperous and progressive. Her father, John Grey, was a cousin of the Whig Prime

Minister and was involved in the struggle for rights for Catholics, the poor and the anti-slavery movement. Like many of our female radicals, Josephine married an ally. She married theologian George Butler (Jan 8 1852) and they lived in Oxford, where he was an examiner and lecturer in art.

There was so much about Oxford and the university that she really enjoyed; the high-powered intellectual evenings with the leading thinkers in the country, including her Italian studies with her husband; the evening horse rides in spring and summer on the fine chestnut horse given to her by her father, and generally speaking being with her sympathetic husband, the 'faithful companion of my life'. Although they were not legal equals, they had the same value system and had the kind of companionate middle class marriage common amongst Victorian radicals but not common in the rest of the country for another century. The women's rights campaigner Millicent Fawcett understood the advantage of marriage to an ally, being in the same situation herself. 'She was never called upon to waste her strength of will and mind in combating domestic opposition'.[1] George may not have been the cause of her success, but he was the reason that she was able to endure the abuse and insults that were directed at her.

Outside her marriage bubble, Butler encountered problems:

> Every instinct of womanhood within was already in revolt against certain accepted theories in society, and I suffered as only God and the faithful companion of my life could ever know. Incidents occurred which brought their contribution to the lessons then sinking into our heart.[2]

There were lots of little pinpricks – she was allowed to be a member of the Bodleian Library; it was regarded by the men as an extraordinary concession to a woman, but Butler was perturbed by how big a deal it became. She once heard some male academics discussing Elizabeth Gaskell's novel *Ruth* and hearing them come to the conclusion that moral transgressions in women were more serious than those in men. *Ruth* was a work dealing with seduction and fallen women, and most of the men at Oxford would be pained if she had read it, never mind had an opinion about it. Middle class women were meant to be silent about male incontinence, unwed mothers, prostitution and any other 'embarrassing' social problems.

Butler was angered by the leeway given to the young gentlemen of the university and the misogyny of the unmarried dons that her husband worked with. She was shocked when a local girl was sent to prison for murdering her new-born baby, the product of a seduction and then abandonment by an Oxford don, who perjured himself in court. She blamed the murder of illegitimate babies as much on their fathers as their mothers, an opinion that was still not common two generations later.

Butler applied to Benjamin Jowett, the Master of Balliol College, not only for justice for the girl but to get the culprit to understand his wrongdoing. His reply was: 'It would only do harm to open in any way such a question as this. It is dangerous to arouse a sleeping lion'.[3] The Butlers supported the girl, visited her in Newgate Prison and eventually gave her a job as a housekeeper.

In 1857, the Butlers moved away from Oxford; despite being ordained in 1855, George Butler was more focused on education and he became vice-chancellor of Cheltenham College. The atmosphere, in all senses of the word, was better for Josephine, who had not been well at Oxford, but the college at Cheltenham was even more reactionary than the university; most staff supported the slave-owning Confederacy in the American Civil War (1861–1865). This would have pained her; anti-slavery was a key part of her upbringing. Little did she know that the worst pain was still to come.

On August 20 1864, the Butlers had just returned from three weeks away. Butler told the story to the *Women's Signal* in 1894.[4]

> Our dear little daughter, a child of seven, was dressed in her white frock and pretty sash to welcome us back. How lovely she looked, as she stood with her golden curls leaning over the balustrade, when we entered the hall door. Another second and she had lost her balance, and lay at our feet a crushed and lifeless mass upon the marble floor. I drank the cup of bitterness to the dregs that day.

For some people, such a terrible act of random and appalling mischance would create doubt in the existence of a beneficent God; but not in Butler, who was religiously the most orthodox of all our radicals. After the grief came the acceptance that a providential God had sent her a ray of light and a direction for the rest of her life. 'I became possessed with an irresistible desire to go forth and find some pain keener than my own – to meet people more unhappy than myself', she later wrote. She wished to help the poor, suffering, and underprivileged. She ignored her friends and family who told her not to do it.

The desire to help the oppressed was made easy when she found herself living near them. In the winter of 1865, George became Head of Liverpool College. She encountered once more the misogyny and double standards of Oxford, sharply enhanced by the grinding poverty and criminality of Liverpool, and it was here that she encountered prostitutes for the first time. She worked mostly in the Christian Mission at the Brownlow Hill Workhouse, the biggest one of its kind in England and now the site of the Roman Catholic Cathedral of Christ the King. It would have housed some of the most desperate women in the country; all the types of women that Butler was not supposed to worry about, never mind care for.

Men were separated from women and children in these workhouses. In September 1862, a few years before Butler's arrival, a fire destroyed one of the dormitories. There was not enough water pressure to put out the initial blaze, and the children who died were suffocated by smoke caused by cheap combustible bedding, or burnt by the falling roof. Some children were horribly mangled. Women waited outside to see if their children had escaped. Twenty-one children and two women were killed.[5] It could have been much worse. There were forty children inside; a week earlier there had been eighty.

Butler clearly wanted to help, but she was not the only middle class head teacher's wife who was concerned with poverty and injustice. She was different because she did not see her work as ameliorative, but principled. If philanthropy was her only aim and achievement, she would have been crowded out by tens of thousands of Victorian women who did the same. The urgency and ferocity of her campaigning, which later in life helped her take on and defeat the government, came not from polite disappointment at the lives of women in academic Oxford and slum Liverpool, but from the fundamental idea that the system itself was unfair. It privileged men who encouraged and condoned vice, and then looked the other way.

Her first major experience was with women picking oakum. This involved manually teasing out fibres from very large tarred ropes; the fibres were used in bulk to make ships watertight. It was appalling work – tiring, tedious, destroying the hands and the posture – and economically pointless, producing almost no income for the people doing it. That's why it was done in prisons and workhouses; it was too awful and unprofitable for free labour. Butler took direct action. She visited the women:

> It came as a surprise to the two hundred women and girls at work in the oakum sheds at the workhouse to find one day in their midst, a tall, beautifully dressed young woman, trying to untwist the tarry ropes with hands that were totally unfitted to the task. At first they laughed at her; but Josephine Butler went back regularly, and by talking to and befriending them learnt much of the sordid circumstances that had brought them there. Many of them were prostitutes who had become infected with disease and drifted in and out of the workhouse infirmary, where they were kept alive in conditions harsh enough to discourage them from returning too often.[6]

Josephine met a young woman dying of TB in the workhouse infirmary. Her name was Mary Lomax and her story was a common one, and the moral failure was clearly male. Mary was born in Derbyshire to a farming family who sent her to work as an under-maid in a well-to-do house.

> She was not fifteen when the gentleman sent her up to his room to fetch a cigar case, and followed her, and shut the door … There followed childbearing, shame, concealment, in which the parents, strong in North Country virtue, treated their child with a harshness of which they afterwards bitterly repented.

Liverpool was no better for Mary.

> She was 'literally kidnapped' by a Mrs Mandeville, the brothel keeper of one of the more 'select' brothels in Liverpool 'who goes about covered in diamonds and has 50 or 60 girls in her house'.[7]

When Butler heard the story, she invited Mary to live with them, with her husband waiting outside their house to show Mary her new room. Other poor women were invited to her home, to the dismay of the neighbours; sick and diseased prostitutes were not what the neighbours wanted. Her plan was to teach them skills that had economic use in society and to improve their education and morals. They made envelopes; and the skill was one that would help them in their lives, not just pass the time. In 1867, the Butlers secured a building near their own home, the 'House of Rest', to help those in danger of falling into prostitution.

Josephine wrote to the newspapers with problems about Liverpool that people should already have been aware of. Women's poverty was worse than men in Liverpool, as many of the jobs available were in the male-dominated shipping, trade and transport industries:

> The result is a mass of female destitution, with its triple choice of the workhouse, theft, and an alternative more shameful skill. There are hundreds of women in Liverpool whose life is spent in a hopeless oscillation between these. Homeless, or with homes in which industry is useless, chastity impossible, and, God unknown, their misery is once the shame and the injury of the community which looks on.[8]

She had met 200 women. They mostly wished to do legitimate work, and this was the best form of charity. Her Christianity told her that nobody was beyond redemption; she was angry and distressed that any confessing co-religionists could hold any other view. She called them 'muddled Christians'. In doing so, she came to the opposite conclusion to that of her old adversary, Benjamin Jowett, who told Florence Nightingale that such women were a 'class of sinners whom she had better have left to themselves'. They had made their own choice; they had made their own bed and now had to lay in it with strangers.[9]

Her analysis of society told her that these women were economic victims – women so poor that they had resorted to prostitution to feed their families. Some women entered prostitution so that they would end up in prison. Her house was a 'preventative institution', more than one step up from incarceration; she used this expression in her regular letters to the newspapers asking for money.[10]

It was while she lived in Liverpool that she heard of the 1866 Contagious Diseases Act. She knew that sexual double standards existed; now they were being put into law. The blame fell on male politicians and a cabal of male doctors. Butler later asserted that the Contagious Diseases Act (Women) was rushed through the Commons in four days and cleverly coupled with the Contagious Diseases Act (Cattle) so that the queen would not ask any embarrassing questions.

To Butler, this new law strengthened the sexual double standard. It was first and foremost a military measure, borne of a panic about the state of the armed forces, but based on the assumption that the behaviour of men could not be changed, so women should be punished. It did not apply to Liverpool, but the comparison was obvious. Major John Grieg who was the Chief Constable of Liverpool in 1877 pointed out that the floating population of, upon average, 20,000 seamen, increased by a west wind and decreased by an east wind. When these rootless seamen arrived in Liverpool, the trade they did with the desperately poor women of the city did not cause the same alarm. The upper class clients of prostitutes in the theatres and music halls of the Strand and Piccadilly were not part of the new law either, and the suspicion was that this was because of the upper class clientele that the girls served.

In December 1869, the Ladies, Association for the Repeal of the Contagious Diseases Act placed this angry announcement in the *London Daily News*. The Society had been formed two months early, led by Elizabeth Wolstenholme-Elmy, who requested that her then friend Josephine Butler took the lead:

> These Acts are in force in some of our garrison towns ... unlike all other laws for the repression of contagious diseases, to which both men and women are liable, these two apply to women only, men being wholly exempt from their penalties.
> Equality before the law, even for fallen women.
> Let your laws be put in force, but let them be for male and female.

The announcement was signed by 150 women, including Florence Nightingale, who particularly objected to the continental-style control of prostitution, Harriet Martineau and Lynda Becker. Butler became the

Honorary Secretary with an address in Liverpool, but was listed as 'Mrs G Butler'; she was, after all, a married woman.

The bravery of these women cannot be overestimated. By arguing against the Act, they made comments not just about prostitution, taboo in itself, but about male sexuality and the whole double standard. George Cavendish-Bentinck MP referred to her as 'a woman who calls herself a lady', while Sir James Elphinstone, member of parliament for the regulated town of Portsmouth and former army officer in India said: 'I look upon these women who have taken up this matter as worse than the prostitutes'. He continued in his interview for the *London Daily News*: 'women like Mrs Butler are so discontented in their own homes that they have to find an outlet somewhere, they have to be noticed at all costs, and take pleasure in a hobby too nasty to mention'.

Her husband was targeted and abused. In 1874, Canon Butler was howled down by clergy as he tried to speak on the subject of 'the duty of the Church of England in matters of morality' at a church congress in Nottingham. The chair that condoned such treatment was Dr Christopher Wordsworth, the Bishop of Lincoln, who was one of the supporters of the Reverend Besant when he took his daughter away from his estranged wife.

The first major target of Butler's campaign was Henry Knight Storks, the Liberal Party candidate in an 1870 by-election for the garrison town of Colchester, which was regulated by the new Act. Storks turned to politics late in his career – he had been a soldier beforehand, mostly stationed within the Empire, had supervised British military bases in Turkey during the Crimean War and had supported the efforts to improve nursing standards for injured soldiers. On the basis that the comfort of his male sailors and soldiers had always been his number one priority, Storks maintained that prostitution was a necessity for the armed forces. His last post was as Governor of Malta where he claimed (wrongly) to have eradicated venereal disease by regulating prostitution. To his enemies, he had made a necessity out of sin; it was almost as if he was not merely protecting the health of the British soldier, but encouraging whoring as one of his few inexpensive pleasures; an obvious aid to recruitment when other working conditions were poor. Storks also wanted the venereal disease tests to be used regularly on army wives. Butler and her allies were determined that he should be defeated.

He was the establishment candidate. Storks himself was standing as MP because Gladstone wanted his help in reforming the army; Storks made no concessions to the strong feelings against the Contagious Diseases Act. The arguments in favour were a powerful mixture of morality and appeals to national security; this was an age of insecurity about the strength of the armed forces and the creation of a powerful new Germany. Storks wanted the Act to be extended to the whole country. The call for its extension was at least as popular as calls to abolish it. Once again, his defeat was a political necessity for Butler.

Storks was in the unusual position of being supported by the military establishment *and* the town pimps and brothel keepers. The criminal elements of Colchester helped the campaign by intimidating hotel owners and anybody else helping Butler. Her hotel was surrounded by a mob and she had to hide in the attic. She was followed by paid thugs and hecklers. She was pursued out of the Assembly Hall and had to be dropped out of a back window, where she wandered lost in the streets while a mob looked for her. The newspapers were quiet; they did not want to talk about prostitution and equally did want to report on women taking on such subjects, but in Colchester, the voteless working class women were supported by 600 former Liberal voters who abstained and 100 who changed to the Tories, and Storks was defeated. At home, the Butlers received a telegram saying simply 'Shot Dead' and they knew what it meant.

After Storks' defeat, there was a Royal Commission; it took evidence over forty-five days from seventy-nine men and Josephine Butler. The arguments were the same – pragmatic versus moral. As well as the parliamentary lobbying, Butler also publicised terrible stories of the abuse of women that the establishment believed she should not even know about, never mind bring to public attention.

One story that stands for thousands is that of Caroline Wyburgh, a nineteen-year-old who lived with her mother in a two room slum in Chatham, Kent. She washed doorsteps and basements for a living and was walking out with a local sailor. 'Walking out' suggested that she was dating or courting this young man, but the result of her perfectly normal behaviour was that she was hauled out of bed in the middle of the night after a 'tip off', and was accused on that evidence alone of being a prostitute.

Imprisoned, she submitted to a 'virginity test' after holding out for five days being strapped to her bed. She was legally defenceless. Only a police officer's suspicion was needed to arrest her. She had the much more difficult task of proving a negative. The punishment for not cooperating was three months in prison, including the option of forced labour.[11]

She could only be found innocent by submitting to a virginity test; tied in a strait jacket, Carolyn was declared 'not guilty' by the doctor who had, in effect, deflowered her. The minimum age that examination could take place was twelve. Yet, her soldier was never pursued or questioned. Some reports say it was a sailor, some a soldier, but the truth is that the identity of the man never mattered. This was slavery – the worse kind, you were guilty until proven innocent and rights over your own body were taken away for the convenience of the state and its armed forces.

Another key technique was the mass meeting. Like most of our Victorian radicals, Butler was a fluent and charismatic speaker. She had particular resonance in the provincial inland towns of the North of England, not because they were hotbeds of immorality but because many of the working class saw the Contagious Diseases Act as a direct attack on poor, working women.

When Butler spoke in working men's clubs such as the one at Crewe, it was men who complained that the police were harassing poor women working in ordinary jobs in urban areas. Many of these women worked at night; a cheery greeting to a male friend in the street could lead to arrest and a forced genital examination which the CDA allowed. Josephine said, 'No lady in her carriage would ever be stopped for examination.' This was a powerful draw; at one meeting in Newark, she was introduced as 'this lady has something to tell us about our daughters'. She was comfortable in the presence of the working class; some meetings consisted almost entirely of working class women; her work with the women of Liverpool was coming to fruition.

Butler was not just fighting for prostitutes, but for all women, rich and poor. It was a matter of citizenship and basic legal rights. The CDA was framed as a health-based piece of 'sanitary' legislation and was considered too unimportant to warrant a jury trial or any if the other basic rights when somebody was accused of a crime. After 1866, plain clothed officers of the Metropolitan police were used to enforce the law – men who had volunteered to leave their homes to do this moral policing, and to assault and accuse women with only a tenuous reason to believe that they were prostitutes:

Any woman can be dragged into court, and required to prove that she is not a common prostitute. The magistrate can condemn her, if a policemen swears only that he "has good cause to believe" her to be one. The accused has to rebut, not positive evidence, but the state of mind of her accuser.

Even worse were the consequences of being found guilty:

To have her person outraged by the periodical inspection of a surgeon, through a period of twelve months; or, resisting that, to be imprisoned, with or without hard labour – first for a month, next for three months – such imprisonment to be continuously renewed through her whole life unless she submit periodically to the brutal requirements of this law.[12]

Many women, intimidated by the police had made a voluntary, but false submission of being a 'common prostitute' to avoid the imprisonment but still had to suffer an annual intimate examination. In either case, the examination was not really medical or therapeutic but supervisory. The women would be brought before a magistrate, who would order them to register and be medically examined if he agreed with the policeman's opinion. If the examination proved VD, she could be compulsorily detained for three months in hospital, or longer if the male doctor thought it necessary. It was the rule of men, as one witness pointed out:

It is men, only men, from the first to the last that we have to do with! To please a man I did wrong at first, then I was flung about from man to man. Men police lay hands on us. By men we are examined, handled, doctored. In the hospital it is a man again who makes prayer and reads the Bible for us. We are had up before magistrates who are men, and we never get out of the hands of men till we die![13]

Proponents of the law suggested that it would make women think twice before embarking on this line of work. Some MPs suggested that there was no point trying to save girls who were already doomed by their sordid environment. All this infuriated Butler. Another criticism was that prostitution, as a convenient vice for men, had become regulated and therefore normalised. Those women who *were* prostitutes, and followed the medical requirements, were left alone. They congregated in houses, with pimps and regular customers, more or less under the protection of the law.

Opposition within the establishment was patchy. The mainstream Church of England was not of much use. Christian support came from Non-conformists – Quakers and Unitarians especially. There was no political party that could be relied on, as the Acts were introduced and extended under both Liberal and Conservative administrations.

Butler had some allies in parliament; the greatest of these was James Stansfield MP. He devoted his political career to fighting the Act. He was an up-and-coming Radical/Liberal politician but he refused to consider promotion into the cabinet until the Act was repealed, which turned out to be more than fifteen years. He pointed out that the rate of VD in the army did fall as a result of the Act and that the only way of proving it would be to examine both men and woman for diseases; and this was never, of course, going to happen. He was attacked by other men for taking part in 'filthy work', but he did help to change the outlook towards the Act. When the Act was repealed in 1886 (the compulsory medical examination had already been abolished in 1863), it was Stansfield who telegraphed the good news to the Butlers, who were in Naples. Stansfield returned to the cabinet briefly in April 1886 but the government fell three months later.

Another line of attack was that the whole business was suspiciously continental. Regulating prostitution was being done on the same principles in francophone Europe. Belgium taxed their state-run brothels. Immorality had been cleaned up and nationalised for the benefit of men and taxpayers. Being no better than the French was a strong moral argument, and Butler extended her campaign to Europe in 1874, where she used her fluent French to harass and embarrass the police chiefs and politicians of Europe on the subject of vice in general. 'Belgium, as far as vice is concerned, is rotten to the core,' she told the press in 1891 and showed her traditional side by attributing this to the socialist tendencies of the Belgian working class, which meant they were godless and not interested in eliminating vice.[14]

She was also concerned about sex trafficking, mostly the abduction of girls and women to brothels on the continent and, even more shockingly, the lack of any prosecutions. The question was asked – why did so many men in positions for influence not get prosecuted?

She continued her campaign against vice. She supported the work of W.T. Stead and was involved in the staged procurement of an underage girl (see Chapter Eleven). She was involved in the raising of the age of consent for girls – one of the worst abuses of the 'steel rape', the internal examination, was that it could be performed from the age of twelve. Butler moved her attention to India, where women were being sold into prostitution by the British army with a system that looked worse than that at home because it seemed clear that the authorities were not just tolerating it, but providing a service.

She remained a supporter of women's suffrage. She wrote a pamphlet on the subject as early as 1855 and was an active member of Millicent Fawcett's National Union of Women's Suffrage Societies. Fawcett called Butler 'the most distinguished Englishwoman of the nineteenth century'.

Butler, like Fawcett, saw the connection between the abuse of women and their lack of political status:

> During these twenty years there was one thing which made our battle harder than it would have been … we have been knocking at the door of the constitution all these years, and there are men who, even now, tell me that they would give us anything in the way of justice, except the Parliamentary vote. Think what we could do in the cause of morality; think of the pain and trouble and martyrdom that might he saved in the future if we had that little piece of Justice.[15]

She believed in marriage; hers had worked well, but she was aware that this was not the case for all. She wanted women to have education and prospects so that they could make a choice from love rather than necessity.

Her fellow radical Florence Fenwick Miller gave her this accolade:

> Generally, with the hour comes the man. In this case, men could and would not have done whatever was necessary had not the ideal leader been found amongst women.[16]

Butler's achievement, in her own words was to fight the 'false and misleading idea that the essence of right and wrong is in some way dependent on sex'.[17]

Chapter Eleven

The New Journalism
W.T. Stead

What kind of person would you get if you combined Oliver Cromwell, Martin Luther, P.T. Barnum and the fictional Don Quixote?[1] The Victorian radical you would end up with is William Thomas Stead (1849–1912). Now more or less forgotten, except for two vignettes; when he bought an underage thirteen-year-old girl to prove that it could be done, and was rewarded with three months in prison, and when he died on the Titanic's maiden and only voyage in 1912.

Like many of our Victorian radicals, he was a journalist, but he was a new breed that changed the nature of the profession to something that we can recognise today, which could either be a compliment or a damning criticism depending on your view. He was the country's first crusading journalist, with the power of a relatively free and powerful mass media behind him and was motivated by a desire to uncover evil and bring wrongdoers to account.

'Crusade' is absolutely the correct word; despite the reputation of journalists today, Stead was intensely religious all his life, even later in life when he became theologically unorthodox. Like Josephine Butler, Stead was from a Northumberland religious background, in his case from the family of a relatively poor Congregationalist minister and a campaigning, reformist mother. It was a family which valued work and service rather than personal enjoyment. Later, his critics pointed out that he was thirty-five before he entered a theatre, perhaps a result of having in his mind better things to spend time on, as the result of the work ethic drummed into him by his parents.

He left school at fourteen to work as a clerk, having had two years' formal education. His employer, Charles Smith, was a wine and spirits merchant; this was never a problem in the Stead family, who, despite being earnest and industrious, were not temperance. Smith was also the vice-consul for the Russian Empire, which was to matter later as part of Stead's interest in international affairs and world peace.

Stead's heroes were Oliver Cromwell and James Russell Lowell. From Cromwell, he admired his religious faith, his uncompromising morality and his defence of religious liberties for non-conformists such as himself. Lovell was a New England poet and writer and was a Christian abolitionist who stressed the humanitarianism of Christ in the same tradition of Stuart Headlam.

Before he became a journalist, Stead helped his father in Howden in evangelical charity work and wrote strong Christian reformist articles (mostly for nothing) about social issues. He had been writing for eighteen months when he was made editor of the Darlington *Northern Echo* at the age of twenty-two, the youngest editor in the country and one who had never actually worked in a newspaper office before.

He was not a modest man. The *Northern Echo* was going to be his pulpit. His hero Lowell had become a newspaper editor himself and used the platform provided to oppose slavery; he was going to be God's agent against sin like his other hero Cromwell. When he was appointed to the editor's post he told a friend that it was a 'glorious opportunity for attacking the devil'. He wanted to be a Christ that kicked over the tables of the money-lenders; in later years while in prison, he declared that being a Christian was not enough and instead people should 'be a Christ'. This sounds arrogant, and it was certainly an opinion that many had, but to Stead, it simply meant taking action. He was confident; despite having no credentials; he negotiated a huge annual salary of £180, total control of the newspaper, no Sunday work (for religious reasons), and an exemption from the usual work attire; he didn't have to wear a top hat.[2]

His *Northern Echo* was on the up; bankrolled by wealthy non-conformist backers and, after 1873, delivered to London on the railway system by W.H. Smith by 10 a.m. on the day of publication. The paper under Stead crusaded in many areas simultaneously – the eight-hour day for coal miners; compulsory secondary education, votes for women and the abolition of the Contagious Diseases Act. He opposed slavery, was lukewarm about the monarchy (Stead called the Prince of Wales 'the fat little man in red'), and opposed the Turks in their treatment of the Bulgarians.

He married Emma Wilson in 1873; she was a childhood friend and fellow Congregationalist. They missed out the word 'obey' from their wedding vows. His view, much more controversial then than now, was that marriage was a marriage of equals with the same interests. Later in life, he ran one of the first dating agencies called the Wedding Ring Circle (1897–1900). He ran it with scrupulous regard to etiquette and privacy, but this did not stop complaints. He was a weird man, they said, by bringing together odd, detached individuals who should have known better. He was the ringmaster of these odd people, the 'P.T. Barnum of Matrimony,' said his enemies, but to him, this was a compliment.[3]

He was a friend and confidant of Josephine Butler and he could be spotted wherever there was political agitation. He was in Trafalgar Square in 1886 during the demonstrations of the unemployed whipped up by Hyndman and the SDF; he knew the Pankhursts and defended Richard when he was accused of atheism; he was a close friend of Annie Besant by 1890. He also supported people who were atheists, like Bradlaugh, and took a keen interest in the new members of the Labour Party in 1906, despite not being a socialist himself.

He became a national figure in 1883 when he was appointed deputy editor of the *Pall Mall Gazette*. The *Gazette* was a serious and influential paper, an important evening read for the liberal classes. It was also staid and traditional until Stead became the editor in 1885. Then it changed; he introduced illustrations (rare in a serious daily paper) and banner headlines. His headline 'TOO LATE!' (a response to Gladstone's failure to relieve General Gordon in Khartoum) was the first-ever to use 24 point type. There were shorter paragraphs, interviews with famous persons, a review of what other newspapers were saying, and generally more strident, angry and occasionally titillating articles. In 1883, he had published *The Bitter Cry of Outcast London* which highlighted life in the slums in deliberately lurid anecdotes, while at the same time being an appeal for social justice.

One of the most pressing issues was juvenile prostitution, called 'white slavery' when the victims were shipped unwillingly to the continent. Prostitution had not been mentioned much in polite society but had been changing since the campaigns of Josephine Butler aided by Stead himself. In 1885, his *Pall Mall Gazette* published a series of articles called the 'The Maiden Tribute of Modern Babylon'. Audaciously, he bought a thirteen-year-old girl, the daughter of a poor chimney sweep, who he named Lily, but was in reality Eliza Armstrong, had her certified as a virgin and went through the formalities of selling her to a brothel.

Stead's investigations were far from objective and measured; they were anecdotes, gleaned from weeks of 'slumming it' in the vice dens of London. He rented a room off the Strand for use at any time of the day or night. He confided to his mistress, 'I go to brothels every day and drink and swear and talk like a fiend.' Stead took to calling himself Charles, painting his face with rouge, smoking and drinking champagne. Cynics may have thought he was thoroughly enjoying his moral crusade.

1885 was an election year, and Stead wanted to influence the incoming government to raise the age of consent to sixteen. The Offences Against the Person Act 1861 set the age at twelve, a figure that had been used in English law since the thirteenth century. It was increased to thirteen in 1875, but Stead believed that any age less than sixteen would lead to the sexual exploitation of children.

Stead did not detect any great desire for a change in the law – 'The Home, the School, the Church, the Press are silent,' he said in his newspaper. He was more or less correct, with a few remarkable exceptions such as the work against the Contagious Diseases Act. Stead was particularly scathing about the inactivity of the established church; they were not 'being a Christ'. There had been a child prostitution panic at the beginning of the 1880s, but the establishment did not seem moved to change. He wondered why this was, and like many others, his mind turned to it being a conspiracy.

Stead was going to use his newspaper to change the law. It was a carefully crafted journalistic campaign. Firstly, he needed to attract people's attention, and there is no better way to do this than warning people that they are going to be appalled by something. Stead published a warning in the *Pall Mall Gazette* on 4 July 1885 that his readers were in for a shock, a 'journey into hell'. His timing was excellent, and not accidental; the Criminal Law Amendment Bill was stalling in parliament, with the implication by its enemies that nobody was particularly interested in a further increase in the age of consent. Stead's plan was that he would make people interested; the stories that he had found were 'abominable, unutterable, and worse than fables yet have feigned or fear conceived'. On 6 July, he further justified himself by pointing out the complete silence of the establishment on the subject. 'There is nothing more pleasing for the common and powerless to bust a conspiracy of silence,' said the *Pall Mall Gazette*. This was what Stead called 'government by journalism', something that still exists today, for better or worse. The seduction of the poor by privileged men was not new. The novelty was the source of the condemnation – the *Pall Mall Gazette* was a metropolitan newspaper for the gentlemen of London not the *News of the World, Reynolds' Newspaper*, and *Lloyd's Weekly Newspaper*.

It was without much doubt the most successful piece of tabloid journalism in the Victorian period. With titles like 'The Confession of a Brothel Keeper', 'Virgins Willing and Unwilling', and 'Strapping Girls Down', the newspaper was in great demand both by the social justice enthusiast and the plain prurient.

Over four weeks, Stead spent 'hours alternately in brothels and hospitals, in the streets and in refuges, in the company of procuresses and of bishops'.[4] This may have been a melodramatic statement but his readers would have been used to the slum literature of the 1880s which involved this. His mention of bishops was the opening cannonade in his main line of attack, against the rich and privileged who were the consumers of the vice, and marked them down as the enemies of humanity.

It was research by anecdote; a virgin could be bought for £20, he was told by an experienced police officer; followed by two paragraphs of graphic detail about the girl's screams when being raped going unnoticed – 'the limit of screaming of any kind is only five minutes'. A reader of Victorian pornography would have recognised the genre, but then it moves on – the constable has no right to intercede; the victim could not prosecute as she knows nothing and her word would be taken as worthless.

The women are portrayed as vulnerable and weak, and the victims of rich men. The people of the slums were the victims and the residents of the West End were the perpetrators. 'The East is the great market for the children who are imported into West-end houses, or taken abroad wholesale when trade is brisk'. He had worked previously with Josephine Butler and agreed with her that these were not fallen women, but victims who had been corrupted by rich men. This trade in English girls was a form of slavery – one section was called the 'THE LONDON SLAVE MARKET'. Doctors, for a fee, would issue certificates guaranteeing that twelve year olds were *virgo intacta* to debauched old gentlemen.

Josephine Butler remembered his emotional response:

> He threw himself across his desk with a cry like that of a
> bereaved or outraged mother, rather than that of an indignant
> man, and sobbed out the words, Oh, Mrs. Butler, let me
> weep, let me weep, or my heart will break. He then told
> me in broken sentences of the little tender girls he had seen
> that day sold in the fashionable West-end brothels, whom
> he (father-like) had taken on his knee, and to whom he had
> spoken of his own little girls.[5]

To the newly emerging Labour and socialist movement, his reportage
rather proved their suspicion that the rich were degenerate. W.H. Smith
refused to stock the *Maiden Tribute* which increased its appeal and
strengthened the conspiracy theories. Stead employed newsboys to sell
it on the street; there was a shortage of part three and there was some
public disturbance as people jostled for copies. The socialist George
Bernard Shaw offered (rhetorically) to sell a thousand copies on street
corners.

Government by journalism worked; both the classes and the masses
were influenced. On 22 August, 250,000 people converged on Trafalgar
Square/Hyde Park to demand an increase in the age of consent. The
1885 Act made the age of consent sixteen (this was for girls only; there
was no rule about the age of consent for boys although there was a
minimum marriage age).

This was not the end of the issue for Stead; in October 1885, he stood
accused of procuring Eliza Armstrong and was found guilty. The Eliza
Armstrong case was the same mixture of melodrama, titillation and
social outrage. Through a procurer, he offered £3 for Lily and never for a
moment hid his intention to set her up in a brothel – and another £2 when
her virginity was verified. Stead was also charged for the chloroform
that was used. He was found guilty, despite widespread sympathy for
him. He was sent first to the appalling Cold Bath Fields, sleeping on the
same type of rock-hard plank bed endured by Edward Truelove, but after
three days he used his influence to get a transfer to Holloway Prison (it
did not become a women's prison until 1903) where he lived in moderate
comfort with lots of visitors. He was sentenced to three months and
served two.

For Stead, this was a price worth paying, and excellent publicity. The 1885 Act was often called Stead's Act; he emerged as a martyr for social justice and purity when some would say that he was a tabloid journalist who had successfully panicked the public into believing that sexual exploitation of children was a bigger social problem than it was, creating an age of consent that was higher than other European countries.

He was proud of himself. He continued to wear prison garb on the anniversary of his imprisonment until his death in 1912. It was a costume more than an actual uniform – in 1910 it was a knickerbocker suit decorated with dainty arrows and a neat pair of golfing stockings.[6] He changed into his costume at work in the morning and wore it all day and evening at a social gathering at home in Wimbledon. He never hid the fact that he enjoyed his time in prison, and enjoyed reminding people about it.

After the events of 1885, W.T. Stead became a prominent member of a new organisation called the National Vigilance Association. Their aim was to use the law to suppress criminal vice and immorality. This proved a problem for former allies like Josephine Butler and a distance appeared between them. In her eyes, he wanted to go too far and intrude into people's private lives using the blunt instrument of law. Josephine Butler gave more emphasis to individual conscience and morality.

In 1892, he announced that he was getting messages from the afterlife. Specifically, they were messages from the recently deceased US journalist Julia Ames, who contacted him via automatic writing. He had always been inclined in this way. He had always had premonitions; he attended his first séance in 1881. In 1909 it was Julia herself who asked Stead for a special room to allow the pent-up demand for the dead and living to communicate. So, in 1909 Stead set up Julia's Bureau, an agency where the public could contact their loved ones through a group of resident mediums that assembled regularly each day. It was used by 600 people over three years, with about 75% success rate claimed.[7] People would wait in an outer office, fill out a form saying that the departed would 'desire such an opening of communication as earnestly as does the applicant'. The only cost was a guinea contribution to his spiritualist library.

In 1909 Stead was granted a private interview with former Prime Minister William Gladstone, who died in 1898. Nothing, not even human mortality, could stop Stead's journalism. He had launched *Borderland* in

1893 – a spiritualist quarterly magazine that ran until 1898. Many of his friends were sceptical, and on the whole, the 'spook business' did him little good. Some believed he was a fraudulent believer, others thought he was a dupe, noting the great influence of his spiritualist daughter, Estelle.

Stead had radical views on foreign policy. After 1888, he set himself an even more ambitious target – world peace through arbitration and international courts – the reason he was on the *Titanic* in 1912 was to attend a peace conference. He opposed the Boer War of 1899–1902, or to be more precise, opposed those who supported it, who he saw as dangerous Little Englanders who risked a world war. 'These swollen-headed jingoes would probably ere now have landed us in war with Russia or Germany, or the United States.'[8]

He was no pacifist. He wrote the 'Truth about the Navy' which advocated outbuilding the German Navy to reduce their own ambitions – he used a pithy journalist's phrase to make this point – 'Two keels for one when taking on the Kaiser'. His early connection with Russia as a child and his fame led to diplomatic relations at the highest level with a country Stead believed would help Britain keep the peace.

His internationalism included an interest in Esperanto. He had formed the Esperanto Club in 1903 in the Strand. After his death the *Hastings and St Leonards Observer* presented a tribute to Stead in the language of world peace; this was eleven months before the start of the First World War.[9]

Stead owned a holiday cottage on Hayling Island, Hampshire. Every summer he gave it over to the poor and unfortunate, giving them a holiday near the sea, filling the house, the houseboat and tents in the garden of Hollybush Cottage. He liked sailing in Chichester harbour and even joined the local lifeboat crew. Journalism was still everything, though. The grateful poor at his holiday home were more or less obliged to produce their own paper, *The Hollybush Gazette*, which would be read out with great solemnity at the end of the week's holiday. Everybody had a job; children were posted at the door to make a note of when letters were collected.[10]

It was from Hayling Island that Stead hurried to Southampton to board the *Titanic*, partly in order to attend a World Peace Conference at Carnegie Hall, and despite the advice of a clairvoyant to avoid it. When the iceberg hit, he quietly read a book in the first-class smoking room, and reputedly surrendered his life jacket to one of his fellow passengers. He behaved with the calm certainty of a man who had been to the other side of death many, many times and knew that there was something better there. His body was never recovered.

His friends in Britain put up their own memorial on a granite plinth beside the Thames and within sight of parliament.

> This memorial to a journalist of wide renown was erected near the spot where he worked for more than 30 years, by journalists of many lands in recognition of his brilliant gifts, fervent spirit and untiring devotion to the service of his fellow men.

Underneath it are written the two words which his admirers believe summed up this man of courage and charisma – 'Fortitude and Sympathy'.

In 1914, William Crookes the scientist and spiritualist, predicted that Stead would come back from the dead to speak to them; it was all about communication and free speech. Perhaps the last word came in June 1914, two years after his death, when Stead appeared at a séance held by a General Sir Alfred Turner. Stead reported that he had drowned quite quickly and had passed to the other world, being conscious all the time. When pressed for a message, Stead told the audience that his message was to 'pursue truth ... all truth' – which, whether truthful or fraudulent, were plausible last words.[11]

Chapter Twelve

Radical Christianity
Stuart Headlam

When the radical atheist Edward Truelove was released from prison on 12 September 1878, he was favoured with a welcoming committee headed, inevitably, by Charles Bradlaugh and Annie Besant. Truelove was given an illuminated address and a purse to the oddly exact amount of £177, and some laudatory speeches. Besant handed over the money, Bradlaugh made the main speech which was seconded by a local radical, Stuart Headlam, who:

> sympathised with Mr. Truelove for what he had suffered in the cause of progress and liberty, and stated that if a man was not morally guilty they were bound to give him their support. The more he differed from a man the more he would wish that man's opinions to be freely published.[1]

Headlam knew how Truelove felt. He had been in this situation as well; four months earlier, it has been *his* testimonial evening, after being sacked by his employer and persecuted by the newspapers in a very similar fashion. In June 1878, a large appreciative audience at the Commonwealth, a club for working people in East London, had presented him with an illuminated vellum scroll praising his good work in the community. The scroll and a purse of £100 were presented by Florence Fenwick Miller, who praised him for working unselfishly for the poor and knowing their needs.

The event that led to his sacking had taken place nine months earlier at the same location. On Sunday 7 October 1877, while the artisans of Bethnal Green supped their beers, Headlam told them something they already believed; that the music hall and theatre were excellent recreations for the working classes. He pointed out that the rich had their operas and garden parties, and that a night of music and acting was preferable to the gin palace and the public house. Actors and dancers could not be excluded from the Kingdom of God merely because of their profession; they were bright and pretty people, who injected joy into the lives of the labouring classes and should not be condemned because some fell short morally, because everybody was a sinner. He was backed up by the show business elite of London, who appreciated his support against the prejudices of the establishment and the specific intrusion of the Suppression of Vice Society. Sir Henry Irving was particularly appreciative of Headlam's efforts.

Why would this free speech loving, freethought supporting, friend of actresses be sacked for holding these views? It was because his employer was John Jackson, Bishop of London, and Headlam was curate of St Matthew's Bethnal Green, and the Bishop was waiting for an opportunity to dismiss him. Headlam had already made a name for himself as a socialist, secularist and high church ritualist. He defended both the Catholic Church against common prejudices and was a witness at Bradlaugh and Besant's *Fruits of Philosophy* trial in 1877. Bishop Jackson had tried to prevent his ordination from happening at all; this was his chance to remove a turbulent priest.

There were a couple of meetings between the radical priest and the conservative bishop where punches were not pulled. When he was asked if St Paul would have gone to the music hall, he replied that he did not know, but was sure that Jesus and his mother would have loved it. Christ was in the music hall, ballet and pub, according to Headlam, and they fell out over the specific subject of ballet girls. Jackson thought they were a source of sin and lust; Headlam thought that they had Jesus in them as much as Holy Communion.

Headlam actually knew what he was talking about; in his earlier position as a curate in Drury Lane, he had met them. Nobody knew more about the truth of their lives, and nobody wished to help them more, without judgement. He had also built up an interest in dance. He was the only Church of England cleric to ever make a theological case for ballet.[2] When faced with Episcopal authority, Headlam made no attempt to be conciliatory, did not care if he was not liked and doubled down in his positions. The bishop had told him, in one of his tellings-off, that you could be a church-goer or a theatre-goer, but you could not be both. Headlam disagreed, and was sacked.

Bishop Jackson was most well-known for his unforgiving sermon 'The Sinfulness of Small Things' and for hypocrisy; in his early days, John Jackson had himself combined his hobby of comic singing and acting at Pembroke College, Cambridge while at the same time being one of the specially selected preachers. Those newspapers opposed to the Bishop suggested a fundraising performance of Moliere's *Tartuffe*.[3]

There was a wave of both indignation and supportive letters. The Rev. George Sarson, curate of St Martin's-in-the-Fields, pointed out that nobody did more to bring to the church those who had been entirely indifferent to it. Not only did Headlam perform the ordinary tasks well, he spent his own time and money doing more. Headlam was a slum priest, and his sincere efforts made more people come to church. He had re-established the Sunday school at St Matthew's, introduced more convenient services to encourage the poor and even raised money for the very club that he gave his talk in. He had helped fund the Commonwealth Club and introduced faith as a talking point amongst the singing, dancing and drinking.

Sarson's supportive letter did not mention that Headlam organised a Sunday school that was mixed boys and girls; he did not want to offend unnecessarily, and he also failed to mention that he knew Headlam well. In 1873, both men became members of the radical Junior Clergy Society, designed to 'promote sympathy and mutual help' among younger clergy and give the opportunity 'of freely discussing matters of practical interest in parish work'. Even before the incident with Bishop Jackson, Headlam was already on the way to being one of the radical churchmen.

Who was this secular priest who defended theatre girls and atheists? Stuart Duckworth Headlam was born in Wavertree, then an upmarket part of Liverpool, in 1847. His family were rich; his father Thomas made a fortune in insurance underwriting, and like most of our radicals, Headlam's ability to outrage the establishment was generously facilitated by the absence of the need to make an employer happy.

In 1861, the family were living in Camden Park, then (and now) a highly prestigious part of Tunbridge Wells. The house, which is still there, had been built a few years earlier and was named *Wavertree* after their first home. The family were living off their investments and the labour of a general servant, a cook and a housemaid. Between the ages of thirteen and eighteen (1860–65) he attended Eton, which was commonplace for his class, and became a socialist, which was certainly not. He also became much more High Church than his father. The family must have wondered what they had paid for.

Headlam thrived at Eton and this was due to the influence of his teacher William Johnson. Johnson was famous for three things – writing the words to the *Eton Boating Song*, being a Christian socialist, and being forced to leave Eton in 1872 under a cloud for an inappropriate relationship with one of the pupils. The influence of the song on Headlam is unknown, but the importance of the other two was immense. His religious and political views were shaped by Johnson, who was a follower of the Christian socialist F.D. Maurice (Maurice was to teach Headlam at Trinity College, Cambridge), who believed that God would replace a 'competitive, unjust society with a co-operative and egalitarian social order'.

Headlam left Cambridge with the very lowest pass degree – a low third – but knowing exactly what he wanted to do with his life. He wanted to do good; his private income, the kind of thing he condemned in others, was going to allow him to do it, and think radically. Headlam's tolerance to all was established by his acceptance (but not approval) of William Johnson's sexuality. Thirty-five years later, when Headlam found it possible to support Oscar Wilde, his willingness to help may have been due to the fact that 'others close to him had been caught in a similar sexual tangle'.[4]

In 1868, he left Cambridge and had plans to be ordained into the Church of England. His father arranged for his son to be trained by Herbert James, a Low Church evangelical whose theology exactly fitted the Church of England as it was. All this was to happen in sedate and uncontroversial Bury St Edmunds. James liked Headlam as a person but found him impossible as a student. Headlam had already decided on the type of Christianity he wanted to profess; he moved to London and worked under Revered Charles Vaughan, probably the second gay man he encountered.

Men like Headlam were not what the Church thought it wanted. He was never going to climb up the greasy pole of the Church of England hierarchy, although if truth be known he did not slide down the pole, he actively threw himself off it. He never rose higher than a curate and was dismissed from all five of his lowly positions during his lifetime, and to his dying day never had a congregation of his own.

He did, however, form one of the first socialist groups in Britain. In June 1877, before his terminal arguments with the Bishop, he formed

The Guild of St Matthew, which has been described as being the first explicitly socialist group in Britain. It was similar in motivation to the later Fabian Society; it was a small group, never more than 400, that organised tours and lectures and was in the business of changing minds – making Christians into socialists rather than the other way around.

In 1878, Headlam married Beatrice Pennington but the marriage soon became in name only when it transpired that Beatrice was a lesbian. They were well matched in every other way; their theology and love of the stage and theatre were the same; Beatrice particularly loved ballet. They lived together formally until 1885 and the reason for the estrangement did not come out until decades later when George Bernard Shaw confided in a letter that Headlam 'had a wife who was a homo'.[5] Headlam once again was able to show toleration of others and acknowledge their right to live how they wanted. Headlam bore the shame of separation so that Beatrice could be herself.

In 1879, Headlam formed the Church and Stage Guild to bring the clergy and the acting profession closer together. His wife read a paper there on the ballet in 1879; there was even some overlap with the Guild of St Matthew. Headlam continued to consort with atheists and secularists, who were some of the least popular people in Britain in the 1870s. He was friends with the arch-atheist Bradlaugh, sometimes arguing with him in lectures and sometimes supporting his attempts to start science classes that would have included an attack on the same scriptures that Headlam based his worldview around.

He also knew the difference between atheists and secularists; he opposed the former with civil arguments and had some admiration for the latter. He was opposed to pure secularism, but believed that in a world where the vast majority of the poor were truly miserable, nothing could be truly secular; the suffering of the poor really mattered and while this was clearly a material matter, they also had the essence of Christ about them.

Both atheists and secularists had the same human rights; when Edward Truelove was released Headlam meant it sincerely when he said that 'the more he differed from a man the more he would wish that man's opinions to be freely published'. It was a free speech issue. In 1880, when Bradlaugh was struggling for his seat in the House of Commons, Headlam wrote and offered him the blessings of Christ. He saw no paradox or contradiction in supporting the godless: 'Bradlaugh may not know God, but God knows Bradlaugh'.[6]

Headlam was to play his part in the radical 1880s, described in more detail in Chapter Thirteen. In 1883, he called for the abolition of the House of Lords, and his licence to preach was withdrawn; in the same year he told the Guild of St Matthew that its members were:

> bound to support all movements which tend to the secular well being of Humanity [and bound] to be Radical Social reformers; to protest vehemently against injustice being done to blasphemers and atheists.

Socialists Sidney Webb and George Bernard Shaw attended the Guild of St Matthew occasionally, and the organisation went from strength to strength. He was a lukewarm monarchist. On the celebrations for the fifty years of Queen Victoria in 1887, he proclaimed that 'the Queen's Jubilee is good, but the People's Jubilee is better'.

Headlam played a prominent part in the aftermath of Bloody Sunday in Trafalgar Square (described in a later chapter). A week after the carnage, the clerk Alfred Linnell joined a gathering in Trafalgar Square to protest against the authorities' violence; in a cruel and ironic twist, he was knocked down by a police horse and died on 2 December and Headlam presided over his funeral with 200,000 assembled people.

He does not seem to have actually witnessed the events of 'Bloody Sunday' of a week earlier. In 1888, the *Record* newspaper suggested that he was at the Trafalgar Square demonstration. This was disproved and damages paid, but not before Headlam made his support clear by declaring that if Jesus has appeared at the demonstration, he would have been arrested or worse. On the basis that the earth 'belonged to the Lord not the landlords', he also described the Dukes of Bedford and Westminster and other landlords as no better than robbers.

Headlam had no problem whatsoever in turning Jesus into a socialist, and turning socialism into a moral course for all Christians. Jesus, Headlam pointed out, very rarely talked about life after death, which Headlam believed had become an obsession with the Victorian church, but did talk a lot about a righteous kingdom that needed to be established on earth; Christians who thought only about salvation in the afterlife missed the point of Jesus' teaching. He pointed out that Christ's miracles involved welfare and well-being; so, when children died of horrible, preventable illness it was not good enough to just say that they were happy in heaven and it was all for the best – action needed to be taken here, on earth.

Jesus' parables were about harmony and cooperation. Capitalism was the death of co-operation and competition created lives of miserable, joyless struggle for millions, with his East End poor being the most glaring example. When his critics quoted Jesus 'the poor ye always have with you', Headlam suggested that this was more of a reprimand than a support of the status quo. Poverty was a human creation, and so suffering that was caused by poverty could not be condoned by Christians.

Headlam was a socialist, but socialism was not his religion, it was, in his mind, the logical consequence of his faith. Socialism was a practical problem solver, not an ideology. It came straight from the teaching of Jesus. Headlam was never a Marxist; with Marx's view of religion as the opiate of the people, that was impossible. However, he showed the same tolerance to Marxists as he did to anything else. He was also a high churchman, enjoying the elaborate rituals and further alienating him from the Church of England, but that was not the main purpose of his faith either.

> The Christian Church is intended to be a society not merely
> for teaching a number of elaborate doctrines, not even for
> maintaining a beautiful ritual and worship but mainly and
> chiefly for doing on a large scale throughout the world those
> secular, socialistic works which Christ did on a small scale
> in Palestine.[7]

He remained unpopular with the established church. In 1890, he was invited to St Agatha's in Portsmouth for a Guild of St Matthew lecture. It was the mission Church of Winchester College and it served the poor of the Landport area of the city, where it still stands. The Warden of Winchester College expressed the prevailing view of the whole church – 'With your ultra high church proclivities on the one hand and your socialist teaching on the other, no sober minded and loyal citizen could support you'.[8] The packed audience did not agree, and the lecture was not about religion but on the reform of the ownership of land without which, the poor would always be poor. God created the earth, but nowhere did it say that he allowed a small ruling elite to take it for themselves.

He joined the socialist Fabians in 1886 and kept his membership until his death. He was soon a key speaker, and chaired meetings. He wrote pamphlets for them, stressing the compatibility of socialism and Christianity and calling for Christians to be socialists, and not, crucially, the other way around, which would have made more enemies as most Fabians were indifferent or hostile to organised religion. He still had the knack of courting unpopularity. In April 1889, he suggested that the Fabians organise more drawing-room meetings and attract the upper middle class by lectures at fashionable centres.[9] In later life, he drifted away from the Fabians as their members became more secular, but he was always broad-minded. George Bernard Shaw noticed that he avoided religion and stuck to politics.

British socialism is famously more indebted to Christianity than Marx; certainly Headlam did not need Marx when he had the revolutionary Jesus, but he was influenced by the American economist Henry George. In his 1879 book *Progress and Poverty*, George posed the question that was beginning to irk American and British radicals; technology and industry had created a wealthier society, but the poor had become poorer and the gap between the rich and poor was growing. Where was the money going? George believed that the answer was land values and rent. Technological change and the labour of millions benefited those who owned the productive assets and they were accumulating wealth as the poor became poorer. His answer was a land tax to replace the revenue from the taxes on the poor or even the end of private ownership of this resource. 'Land gets its value from its location, nothing to do with the merits of the land or whoever owns it'. The tax raised by a levy on this unjustified wealth would be used by a reforming government to benefit everybody in society.

Georgism was more influential than Marx, who had died in utter obscurity in 1883. *Capital* was unavailable and then later not read much; *Progress and Poverty* was much more influential, and Headlam met the author several times in the 1880s.

Headlam was active in London politics and in 1888 he and Annie Besant were elected to the London School Board. His socialist programme was free secular education; free school meals; an eight-hour day at decent wages; nationalisation of land, Home Rule and disestablishment of the Protestant church in Ireland. Together they attempted to persuade the School Board to abolish compulsory religious instruction and to provide free meals for the poor. He was a London County Councillor from 1907 to 1917, and when the cinema arrived in the 1910s, he supported their request to open on Sunday as it provided colour and entertainment to the life of the poor and was a healthy alternative to the public house. He remained more popular among secularists than Christians. In 1907 the Marxist Social Democrat Federation newspaper *Justice* called him 'the well known friend, the genial and broad minded socialist cleric'.

Like many of our Victorian radicals, he was an inveterate traveller and lecturer. In February 1895, he accepted an invitation to lecture at the Leicester Secular Society on the subject of teaching religious education in state schools. After some initial hostility, his audience warmed to him when he declared that it was not the business of the state to teach religious principles. When approached with what we might call today a 'gotcha' question about reading the Bible, he replied that it should be read as Shakespeare or Shelley ought to be read. It was not much of a surprise that he was forbidden from preaching and did not regain his licence between 1888 and 1898.

In 1895, he once again accepted the title of 'socialist' for the Guild of St Matthew, seemingly a little tired that people thought it was both a novel term and an insult.[11] His socialism was clearly Christian – he wanted the greatest economic and social change with the least possible interference with private life and liberty; this would include placing the means of production into the hands of the working class with the minimum of puritan intervention into the lives of others.

During the trial of Oscar Wilde, Headlam posted bail for him, much to the alarm of the Church authorities. He wrote in his own newspaper, *The Church Reformer*, to assuage people's concerns; he posted bail for his reappearance at court, not as a character witness, but then he lost trust again by saying that he hoped Wilde a fresh start and a fruitful life after he had completed his sentence. He was taking the action to support the theatrical industry as well. 'My confidence in his honour and manliness has been fully justified by the fact ... he stayed in England and faced his trial'. It was certainly an act of faith; when he pledged half of Wilde's bail of £5,000, he had not met him.

Later, on 18/19 May 1897, Wilde visited Headlam's Upper Bedford Place house, after his release from Pentonville Prison. His décor was tasteful and had been cutting-edge two decades earlier.

The drawing-room was full of Burne-Jones and Rossetti pictures, Morris wallpaper and curtains, in fact an example of the decoration of the early eighties, very beautiful in its way, and very like the aesthetic rooms Oscar had once loved.[12]

Wilde was transferred to Pentonville to prevent any demonstration by Lord Queensberry or his friends, and very early the following morning he was released. Two people met him: his loyal friend Robbie Ross, and Stewart Headlam. Headlam was still there to give him support, which is more than many of his more established friends managed to do. Headlam was later one of the first twenty-four people to receive a presentation copy of Wilde's *Ballad of Reading Gaol*. Headlam's support for such a controversial figure as Wilde cost the Guild of St Matthew many members – he was also threatened by a reactionary mob, and his housemaid fled his house in horror.

The most important woman in his life was Martha 'Pattie' Wooldridge. She was a showgirl and ballet dancer; her first leading role was in *Alice in Wonderland* at the age of ten. The pair had met in the 1880s and Headlam thought so much of her that he introduced her to the Bishop of London in 1885. It was a test; the newcomer Francis Temple had a reputation as a severe but sympathetic cleric; Headlam decided to test this new tolerance by introducing him to twenty-two-year-old Martha.

Temple, unlike Jackson, tried his best, but could manage no more than the ultra-ambiguous, 'I am sure you are a good woman. I hope you don't imagine I think any harm of you,' to which Martha replied indigently and undeferentially, 'I should think not!'

Headlam had invited the Archbishop to actually see a ballet; Temple believed that it should be purged of sin first; Headlam believed that it was as free from sin as any other activity. Today the ballet is suitable for archbishops; it was much more disreputable in Victorian times, being no better regarded than music hall.

Headlam and Martha lived together as devoted friends from 1899 in another house called Wavertree, in St Margaret's near Twickenham, designed by his friend William Morris. Martha is described in some records as his niece (1901 Census) and housekeeper, but in reality probably neither. The household appears on the 1911 Census; Martha, forty-eight, is the first on the list, listed as head and Headlam is listed as a boarder, aged sixty-four, a cleric and county councillor who had been married for thirty-three years to Beatrice Pennington. Martha may or may not have been a servant, but there were two other hired helps in the eight-roomed home,

Life was good. They toured the world and had famous celebrity friends. His views became more acceptable to the establishment. In his last year, he received a favourable letter from the Archbishop of Canterbury thanking him for his work. When he died in 1924, Martha's devotion continued until her own death thirty-four years later. 'Wavertree' was sold and she moved to a smaller house next door which she named Stewart House.[13]

He has a commemorative plaque in his local church at St Margaret's and a school named after him in Bethnal Green. He is still remembered by both Christian socialists and atheists. Comments like this sum up the Headlam contradiction:

> [he] is the nearest thing I have come across to a patron saint of atheists. In his lifetime he was certainly regarded with respect and love by the sort of atheists who would have regarded any other Anglican in a dog collar with scant respect.[14]

Chapter Thirteen

Socialism

Keir Hardie & Henry Hyndman

On the last day of December 1866, a ten-year-old boy turned up at the house of his employer, wet and hungry; wet because of the weather and his poor clothing, hungry because there was no food in their one-roomed house. This was the second time he had been late for work and both were for the same reason – to keep his family from disintegrating. His father was on strike. All their possessions had been sold. His family were living on strike pay of one and sixpence a week, so the boy's pittance of a wage was a matter of life and death.

The boy earned three and sixpence for a twelve hour day delivering baked goods; these customers wanted their breakfast on time, so the errand boy had to be both pitilessly early and very punctual. After waiting so that the pious prayers of the family were not interrupted, the boy was sacked, and his outstanding wages denied as a punishment. He tried to blurt out his reason – he was helping his dying brother in his last hours. This was not just rejected; it was not listened to, and the boy was dismissed with a sweep of the hand. He was given a bread roll by a kindly maid; he rushed home; it was still raining and his food got wet. His new brother was born the same evening.

In the same year, a young journalist for the Conservative *Pall Mall Gazette* was working in Europe reporting on the war between Austria and Italy. He was twenty-five and had recently finished his education. His father was rich, the family had made money from Caribbean plantations and he followed the well-worn path of the privileged; first Trinity College, Cambridge, and then whatever he liked. Here are his own, rather complacent words:

> I had the ordinary education of a well-to-do boy and young
> man. I read mathematics hard until I went to Cambridge,

where I ought, of course, to have read them harder, and then
I gave them up altogether and devoted myself to amusement
and general literature.

Mathematics was followed by two years studying law; playing first-class cricket for Sussex and the MCC; and after deciding to become a journalist, being able to achieve this with ease.

What did these two disparate lives have in common? They were both radicals, who played their own important part in the growth of socialism; James Keir Hardie (1856–1915) and Henry Hyndman (1842–1921), representing the two main strands of the Labour Party; simply put, Trade Unionism and Marxism.

Hardie is better known than Hyndman and is infinitely better regarded – the Labour Party leader at the time of writing is called Keir, not Henry, and the Labour Party does not award the Henry Hyndman award annually to a long-standing activist. Hardie is, without doubt, the father of the Labour Party, but both men made a vital contribution, and their parallel lives reveal a lot about the way the party developed. Hyndman, who was eventually to find the Labour Party a disappointment, could be called the pioneer of British socialism; but this is not the same as being the pioneer of the British Labour Party.

In 1867, Hardie was working as a trapper in a privately owned coal mine, Newharthill Colliery, North Lanarkshire. He was not quite eleven years old. He had to work from 6 a.m. to 5.30 p.m. plus four hours on Sunday and received 3s. 6d. a week and was not paid for the three-mile journey to the pit. Trapping was an appalling job; boys worked in the dark all day, seeing more rats and ponies than people, and lacking the solidarity of the older men working the coalface together. His job was to regulate the air supply in the pit through a door, which also had to be opened when train loads of coal passed through. He did this for two years, when he was promoted to looking after the pit ponies.

Hyndman had sailed through home schooling and Cambridge and did not take his education very seriously; Hardie had to fight for his. The 1872 Education Act guaranteed schooling for five to thirteen year olds, but Hardie had started paid work at the age of eight and had missed this opportunity. His job at the bakers was his fifth job; his mother removed him from one – sharpening and carrying potentially lethal tools – when two children were killed at work and from another when it was clear that he would have to work for free in his apprenticeship year. It did not matter how much ingenuity they showed, how much resilience, the system as it existed would always keep them poor.

Hardie, who later claimed that he was never a child, had to learn quickly. His parents taught him the basics, especially his mother Mary, a dedicated autodidact who gave him a love of reading. More formal instruction was next; in the hours of darkness after work, he attended Frasier's Night school in Holyton, where he would need both the constitution of an ox and his own candles in order to learn reading and writing in the dark and cold.

He also learned about the dangers of alcohol. His stepfather had taken to drink around the time of the unsuccessful 1866 strike and it was this experience that made Hardie a temperance campaigner. He signed the pledge aged seventeen in 1873. Although later in life, and in his pictures, he seems moody and serious, he spent his spare time following football, going to concerts and playing his banjo and accordion.[1] He was strong, bearded and red-headed and had several girlfriends in his youth, and, for that matter, after he married Lillias Balfour Wilson in 1879.

Hardie did not need to reject Christianity to come to his radical conclusions – unlike many Victorian radicals. His mother Mary and his stepfather David seemed to have abandoned organised religion under the influence of Bradlaugh and Besant but avoided indoctrinating their son. So, Hardie was brought up as an atheist and converted to Christianity by a local mission in the year 1878.

He learnt to love Christianity but loathe many of the people who claimed to follow it. He belonged to Sunday schools and churches which helped him and his family, but he rejected the hypocrites who owned coal mines and made him work on Sunday or shop owners who prayed over bacon, eggs and coffee but let a young man go home without his wages to a cold foodless house. He condemned the established church for condoning poverty. He hated the sectarianism in Scotland between Catholic and Protestant; both for its own sake and its use as a strike-breaking weapon – normally bringing Irishmen in as blackleg labour, which both exploited and exacerbated existing religious tensions.

By 1876, aged twenty, he was a skilled miner, a hewer who cut coal by hand with an axe. In 1879, he took up his first Trade Union appointment. This was soon noticed and he was blacklisted, as were his two younger brothers, Alexander and Willie. The colliery owners held all the cards;

the over-supply of labour meant that workers lived in fear of their jobs. Strikes regularly failed due to poor finance, haphazard organisation and lack of coordination between pits – indeed his first job in 1879 was as a corresponding secretary for the Lanarkshire miners. In 1880, he was involved in the Eddlewood Strike; it lasted six weeks and the men were eventually starved back into work. Such failures were depressingly common.

In 1880, Hardie was organising soup kitchens for strikers while Henry Hyndman was standing for parliament. Hyndman was still working as a journalist, had travelled through the United States praising British rule in Ireland and the Empire. In 1880, he tried to stand to become the Liberal candidate for Marylebone, but the Liberal Party machine condemned him as a Tory. Gladstone himself spoke against him, and he pulled out of the selection.

In 1880, his politics were unclear; by 1881, he was a socialist. He had read Henry George's *Progress and Poverty*, like Stuart Headlam. He read the *Communist Manifesto* (1848) and the works of Marx in French and was converted. From then on, he had the rigid dogmatism of a convert and the passion of somebody who became a socialist as the result of an intellectual process. At this point, a cliché appears; Hardie, the radical through experience, and Hyndman, the radical through reading; but it doesn't quite fit, as Hardie did a lot of reading and Hyndman proved himself ready to take part in conflict in the 'real world' as well.

Marx was living in London in the 1880s and Hyndman paid him a visit, or more accurately a series of visits, sometimes by invitation and later by turning up unannounced.[2] After one uninvited visit, when the family had to retire to bed to get him and his wife to go home, Marx called his new mentee 'a complacent chatterbox'. Hyndman claimed to be eager to learn, but still managed to do all the talking. Hyndman then wrote a book on socialism – *England for All* – with a chapter on the evils of capitalism that Marx would have recognised; it had been copied, sometimes verbatim, from Marx's own work without even a name check. Hyndman's rather lame reason was that the great British public would be resistant to the damning economic critique of a foreigner, and a German at that. The eager protégé eventually became *persona non grata*.

He finally formed his own small radical Party – the Democratic Federation (after 1883 the Social Democratic Federation) in June 1881. At the inaugural meeting, Hyndman bemoaned the infighting between radical groups and called for unity; a tradition that has continued ever since. Each founding member was given a copy of *England for All*, ensuring that more people would have heard about socialism from him rather than Marx, whose *Capital* was not available in English until 1887.

Hyndman's action plan was radical; the abolition of capitalism and landlordism, and the nationalisation of all the means of production. The SDF demanded triennial parliaments, adult suffrage (the original proposal was for adult male suffrage, and it was only extended to women after a lively debate). The landlords were to be attacked in two ways – the nationalisation of land, and the abolition of the House of Lords. Ireland, regarded by socialists as the worst victims of landlord power, was to have Home Rule.

He presented it as a class struggle – 'From the luxurious classes, as a whole, I expect little support'.[3] Throughout his career, he always dressed impressively as a member of the elite, while at the same time plotting their downfall. He was the first, but not the last, affluent, high born socialist; the paradox was noted at the time. The *Daily Mail* (founded 1896) made a point of adding 'wealthy socialist' to his name.

In 1882, Hardie was a long way from this socialism or wealth but he had the same experience as Hyndman in that he became a journalist on moving to Cumnock in 1880 at the request of the Ayrshire miners. It was now impossible for him to add to his sixteen years as a miner and he could not be a Trade Union organiser because the mine owners threatened to sack anybody who was associated with him. He became a journalist, not like Hyndman because he had the money to subsidise his own party and publications, but through a contact at the local Congregationalist Church. He earned £1 per week from 1882 to 1887 writing about mining conditions for the Liberal newspaper the *Ardrossan and Saltcoats Herald* and its sister paper the *Cumnock News*, under the pseudonym '*Trapper*'.

While *Trapper* was writing in the local paper, involved in the intricacies of Scottish Trades Unionism, Hyndman more or less owned Britain's first socialist political party. The SDF was a tiny organisation of around 500. The meeting and the party were dominated by Hyndman's personality and his money. The press, noticing that this was the same man who proclaimed himself a Liberal only four years earlier, thought he was organising a vanity project. This view from a hostile newspaper was typical:

A commanding mind may gather a party round it; but a mere
wire-puller like Mr. Hyndman can no more create a party
than he can create a planet. The man is ambitious. He is
young, and a glib talker … He, however, told his unlucky
companions that he would make his name known, and he
had done so.

A rich and ambitious Oxford man with a monstrous ego proclaims his
support for labour in order to get on; that sounds very modern. Like
most radical reformers, Hyndman thought that revolution was in the air;
he said as much in his *Dawn of A Revolutionary Epoch* (1881). It was
written for one high-brow London magazine, and duly reviewed in the
others, then spread to the popular press.

Hyndman argued that it would soon no longer be possible to exclude
the workers from their legitimate place in the running of the country.
Hyndman, unlike most early English socialists, knew Europe well and
was able to form the false conclusion that Communism was coming – 'the
Jews furnish their leaders,' said one reviewer of his article, amplifying
one of the newer anti-Semitic conspiracy theories of the nineteenth
century. Economic and political crises were coming; radical bodies
needed to unite; the working class needed direction and organisation to
stop the non-producing classes exploiting them. Hyndman had a man in
mind for the leadership of this movement, and he did not need to look
far or think hard to name him.

Hyndman alienated people. He was a pioneering socialist thinker,
a brilliant speaker and communicator but he was also domineering,
fractious, selfish and unempathetic. Other socialists like Eleanor Marx,
future Labour leader George Lansbury, and William Morris soon split
from him. This was one of the negative characteristics of Britain's first
home-grown radical socialist; he could not be told anything, even by
Karl Marx. Friedrich Engels continued to hate him even when Hyndman
reconciled with Marx before his death. In 1894, the dogmatically
inflexible Engels accused Hyndman of inflexible dogmatism.[4] When
Hyndman remarried in 1914, he thought that the first edition of his 1881
book was a good wedding present to give to his new wife, Rosalind
Travers. His ego was enormous.[5]

In 1885, Hyndman, without consulting his comrades, accepted
£340 from the Conservative Party to run candidates in Hampstead

and Kensington, to split the Liberal vote and therefore enable the Conservative candidate to win. This strategy did not work and the two SDF candidates polled fifty-nine votes between them; in the same year, John Burns stood in Nottingham and gained 5.4% of the vote – a mere 657 votes in total.

At the same time, Hardie was a church leader and a trade unionist and was still a Liberal; but a radical one, increasingly dissatisfied with the willingness of the Liberal Party to do their best for working people. The break from the Liberals for trade unionists like Hardie was protracted and painful. Other Victorian radicals had to make the decision about sticking with the Liberals or sticking it to them. Hardie and Pankhurst opted for Independent Labour and Bradlaugh and Dilke stayed with the Liberals.

In 1888 there was a by-election in Mid Lanark, the constituency that Hardie knew best. He attempted to get the Liberal Party nomination; which he must have done through gritted teeth. Since the 1867 Reform Act gave property holders in urban areas the vote, many miners were elected to Parliament under the Lib-Lab banner, the Lab standing for labour rather than Labour. Hardie at this point was deeply unimpressed by the lack of support he had received from them; particularly the ex-miner and Lib-Lab MP Henry Broadhurst, who voted against an eight-hour working day for miners, and others who generally failed to respond to strike breaking and starvation tactics by mine owners. The nomination went to a lawyer J.W. Philips who was parachuted in from London, who was neither working class, Scottish nor a miner, so was in Hardie's mind unsuitable to represent the constituency.[6]

Hardie decided to stand as the Labour and Home Rule candidate. Two coal miners, David Murray and William Walker, signed his nomination papers, much to the disgust of the London newspapers. The Liberals claimed he was splitting the anti-Tory vote, but their moral superiority was diminished somewhat by their (secret) offer to Hardie of a paid party job and a safer seat next time around if he would withdraw from this one.

It was uphill all the way. He was supported by the Women's Suffrage Movement, but they by definition had no vote. His Liberal opponent supported both the eight-hour day and Home Rule for Ireland, removing Hardie's potential advantage. He differed from Phillips by offering himself as the representative of the Scottish working man. He pointed out that the colliery owners already had eighteen MPs, and there were even more representing the land owners, the lawyers, the armed forces and the brewers. One of his supporters at his packed meetings (meetings were open to all and were free, so it was wrong to use that to judge support) estimated that the working class had eight people in the House of Commons who actively pursued their interests. The Liberals spread the untrue rumour that he was being paid by the Conservatives, which had been true about Hyndman. Hardie achieved 617 votes (8%) to the winning Liberal 3847; but this was the point where the break with Liberalism started.

His defeat mattered to the Liberals. Mr Gladstone beamed with pleasure at the result, it was said.[7] The Liberals were saved from a split and the nation saved from a working man in parliament, as one newspaper reports:

> If Mr Keir Hardie had polled anything like the formidable number of votes the "labour" party would have been heard of again in artisan constituencies all over the country, and the result might have been very serious schism in the Liberal party. As it is, the "labour" party is apparently not dangerous and the bravado and bluster of its representatives will in future cause less apprehension.

They were right that a Liberal split had been averted, and that the rise of a labour party had been stopped; but something had been started – a Trade Union based labour party, with Hardie as its eventual leader.

His journey towards socialism had started. In 1887, Hardie went down to London in order to join Hyndman's SDF but never did. He discovered two things – one that party conferences involved a lot of heavy drinking (another tradition which has not changed much), and secondly that Hyndman was not very interested in trade unions and a little too fond of the kind of revolutionary rhetoric that did not win elections. He did, at this point, meet Friedrich Engels and Eleanor Marx, who both admired him and shared his rejection of Hyndman. During the 1887 election, the SDF newspaper *Justice* published a letter from a Comrade J. Waugh of the Glasgow Central Branch accusing Hardie of being little more than a Liberal and 'anything but revolutionary' – which was demonstrably true, and the fact that the SDF thought this was a problem worth airing shows the distance between them.

Hyndman was not following a parliamentary road in the 1880s; instead, he was exploiting the first major downturn in the economy for twenty-five years. The word unemployment (as opposed to an individual being 'unemployed') was first used in this decade. He proved himself to be more than just a bookish Marxist; he was ready to use the power of the mob to force the pace of political change. Trade unionism was never his preferred route to socialism. He pointed out that the established Trade Unions were conservative in that they only defended the present conditions of their own members. They defended the wages of their members but had little consideration for the poorer part of the working class, and they would become part of the problem if they continued down this route, being merely a soft cushion against capitalism for privileged workers. Here, he had a point. Trade Union legislation passed by the Liberal government in the 1870s had given skilled workers what they needed. Hyndman and other SDF thinkers had views of strike action that would cheer modern-day conservatives; they were a waste of time and resources. Trade Unionism was not socialism but the capitalism of the proletariat.

It was in the 1880s that socialists like Hyndman were able to exploit the rise in poverty and inequality for their own propaganda. Many thought that they were overstating the case; Charles Booth thought so, but at least started to collect data in London from 1886 onwards and discovered that the socialists had not been exaggerating. The capital was fertile ground for the SDF and one of the achievements of Hyndman was to make London the centre of British radicalism, which had not been the case since the 1790s. Although the leadership was largely middle class, they were also ready to lead the working class – not the working class of the skilled Trade Unions but the mass of striking and starving workers in London.

Hyndman proved that he was more than just a theorist in the winter of 1885/86 when he and John Burns led a demonstration of the unemployed around Trafalgar Square, demanding relief for the unemployed and the re-introduction of protectionism; free trade was just another function of the free market that served only the capitalists. The docks were stagnant and the sugar refineries had failed. The Red Flag was flown; Burns opened the meeting with a reference to the 'Revolutionary' Social Democratic League, adding a new and dangerous adjective to the name of the organisation; about 1,500 people were there and Burns did threaten violence if there was no justice for the working man. One of the journalists at their later Old Bailey trial (they were acquitted; Hyndman defended himself and loved every minute) admitted that he did not know how long Hyndman spoke for because he did not dare get his gold watch out. The journalist W.T. Stead was also there; he judged that the crowd were rough, but not as coarse as Bradlaugh's atheists. Hyndman spoke at the end, saying the time for moderation was gone. He said the people out of work had been asked to be moderate, but how could they be moderate when they were unemployed and starving? If the thousands there had the courage of a few they would very soon alter the existing system of things.

The meeting was tense but basically peaceful, but afterwards 5,000 marched down Pall Mall, looting shops and smashing windows. 'To the clubs' was the cry, which was not surprising considering the way that Burns (and to a lesser extent Hyndman) had spoken to the crowd. Burns had allegedly said that hanging was too good for some people, as it would spoil the rope, and in a more fatal version of the eighteenth century cry of 'bread or blood' called for 'bread or lead'. The Carlton Club was attacked and shops raided, then they insulted gentlewomen openly in the street. It ended up with a baton charge in Oxford Street that finally dispersed the demonstrators.

In the following days, there was a rush on behalf of the rich to help the poor. The Lord Mayor's Mansion House Relief Fund had languished, containing no more than £3,000 on the day of the riot; two days later it was £75,000. Hyndman was cynical about their motives. Their 'swift-born pity' was 'quite undistinguishable from craven fear'.

This event became 'Black Monday', at least for those afraid of the mob. Hyndman felt differently. Hyndman enjoyed the potential power of the working class, with him at the helm. Despite his addiction to the rhetoric of revolution, he was not trying to overthrow the state – the plan was to show the potential for disruption when people felt mistreated and getting his small socialist party well known. It worked on both counts, although his temporary importance did not translate into mass membership. The SDF was tiny even in 1889. It had forty branches, dominated by London, with less than a thousand members.

The authorities were in the mood for revenge after their apparent defeat; they did not have long to wait. The scene this time was Trafalgar Square itself; since the spring, the square had been occupied by the poor and the unemployed of the East End; the summer had been hot and dry, which suited the celebrations for the Queen's Jubilee in June but now people were starving; being fed by charity and incited by radical speakers. On 19 October, and regularly afterwards there were unsuccessful heavy-handed attempts to remove them that caused resentment. It was soaking up police resources – 2000 officers every weekend – and nothing was being achieved apart from highlighting the precariousness of the system. One of the many four to six hundred homeless was Mary Ann Nichols. She had been dismissed from a job as a servant in May 1887, and like many at Trafalgar Square, preferred tramping and living outdoors to the workhouse. She later settled in Whitechapel, where she was murdered by 'Jack the Ripper'.

A major rally was planned at the Square on 13 November 1887; it merited the title later given to it by Annie Besant of 'Bloody Sunday'. William Morris wrote that he 'was astounded at the rapidity of the thing and the ease with which military organisation got its victory'.[8] The marches to the square, and the rally itself had been banned. George Bernard Shaw, a naïve twenty-one-year-old, set out from Clerkenwell Green with a large group, most of whom were charged by police batons at Holborn. They made a rational decision and ran away; Shaw called it 'the most abjectly disgraceful defeat ever suffered by a band of heroes outnumbering their foes a thousand to one'[9] but he learned the same lesson as Morris; that the revolution was not going to be physical. It was a victory for the state monopoly of legal violence – a well-armed police force with the resources to do anything against the poorest classes that capitalism had produced.

Lots of other marchers were intercepted by violence; at Trafalgar Square, they were set upon by the police, the cavalry and the Grenadier Guards, helped by middle class special constables who hated and feared these kinds of people. It was Peterloo plus a police force. Two hundred were seriously injured and at least two killed; most, but not all of the protesters were unarmed.

Despite their leader's views on Trade Unions, members of the SDF and others made significant strides in the 1880s in organising what is condescendingly sometimes called 'unskilled Labour'. The period 1886 to 1889 was particularly turbulent, with some success for the radical movement and for unskilled workers in new types of Trade Unions. SDF members played a big part – Annie Besant and SDF member Herbert

Burroughs helped to organise the poor exploited match girls at Bryant and May. The unskilled women workers in a London match factory were receiving 4s a week for a fourteen-hour day. They were frequently injured by the poisonous chemicals used in making matches. SDF members John Burns and Tom Mann led the great dock strike which gave the workers a tanner (6d) an hour. SDF member Ben Tillett helped to win the gas workers an eight-hour day in the strike of 1889, creating a union of 20,000 members and over sixty branches across the country.[10] These successes helped expand the trade union movement beyond its traditional preserve of skilled craft workers, something that Hardie approved of.

Tom Mann (1856–1941) was another great figure in the Labour movement with links to both the Hyndman and Hardie strand of organised Labour. Like Hardie, he worked as a trapper in a coal mine. By 1880, he was in London, reading the same books that converted Hyndman to socialism, and joined the SDF in 1884; but, like Hardie, he was always a Christian and Trade Unionist first. By 1886, he had read Marx, and become a communist but in 1888 was the man who ran Hardie's campaign in Mid Lanark. Like Hardie, he was a crucial part of the creation of the Independent Labour Party. Like many other socialists, he eventually split from Hyndman.

The gap between the two men was still great. In 1888, Hyndman's party declared that it would accept no parliamentary candidates who did not endorse class war; a year later Hardie founded the Scottish Party which was the broadest of political churches, and it was no surprise when it was the pragmatist rather than the class war warrior who was elected to parliament for the constituency of West Ham South (1892). However, in order to succeed he needed both the Marxists and the Liberals; the Liberals to withdraw their candidate, which they did, and for the SDF to support him. The minutes of the Canning Town Branch of the SDF (membership 110) have survived, and one entry reads 'Keir Hardie has declared in favour of nationalising of land and all means of production through Parliament, this Branch recommends him as a candidate for the House of Commons for S. W. Ham'.[11] Hardie knew that the support of the SDF did matter, especially in London where they were strong, but it shows the weakness of the nascent Labour party that it needed the cooperation of both Liberals and Marxists.

Hardie became the first independent Labour MP in 1892. It was to be mostly a place he hated and despised – 'a place that I remember with a haunting horror' and the experience was neither very fruitful nor very successful. His arrival in the clothes of the working class is famous and infamous; 'Dressed like a navvy,' exaggerated the *Leeds Mercury*; navvies did not wear tweed suits with a red tie and flat cap. The newspaper was correct in one sense – Hardie *was* creating a mini-drama, marking himself out as the only working man in parliament, and one that had not been put there by agreement with the Liberals. He wore his cap as he entered the Commons, and only removed it when called to order by the Speaker. Hardie later claimed ignorance of procedure, although this did not prevent him wearing a neckerchief in the Commons and regularly appearing half-shaved. If Hyndman had ever been elected to the Commons, he would have worn a morning suit while still claiming it was a victory for the working classes – perhaps two sides of the same ideological coin.

After his victory, the *South Wales Daily News* asked whether he would act independently.[12]

> 'Most decidedly,' replied Mr Hardie, 'I shall always sit on the Opposition side of the House … I regard my election for South West Ham as a protest against the dilatory methods of social legislation observed by the Conservatives and the Liberals. My sitting on the Opposition benches will show there can be no trifling with Keir Hardie'.

He was being a little unrealistic about what a single voice could achieve. That the Liberals were no better than the Conservatives was an extreme position, and there *were* people who trifled with him and got away with it. In 1895, when the Liberal government was about to fall, Hardie lamented that he could not trust people who said they might support him; 'Some men should never to be allowed to sleep on anything'.

Hardie's maiden speech was about unemployment, and the misery it caused to real people; he told MPs that people starved because of shortage of work, while others committed suicide before starvation killed them. Others had been made so ashamed of their situation that they hid away and died in other ways. As far as he was concerned, casting poverty as a moral failure was just a way of ignoring the call for collectivist state action. The speech was heard in silence as the tradition with maiden speeches demanded; his later speeches were met with derision and scorn, and the rules of parliament were used against him.

The most famous incident was Hardie's reaction to the birth of a son to the future George V, then the Duke of York, on 23 June 1894. In early July, the Commons was invited to congratulate the royal couple on the birth of their child and Hardie refused to do so. Instead he produced what his enemies say was a caddish and churlish diatribe which started with his announcement that he owned no loyalty to any hereditary monarch. Any form of royalty was an impediment to the progress of the people. As far as his enemies were concerned, this was a gross breach of faith for a man who had sworn an oath of allegiance to the queen. The Tories then asked him why he had taken the oath, exposing the weakness of his position.

He was powerless and alone, both on this occasion and generally in the House of Commons. After a speech which seemed to blame the week-old child for the moral turpitude of his grandfather the Prince of Wales, his call for a division against the motion to congratulate had only one vote in favour. It was an acclamation, and his voice would have been alone in a sea of indignant opposition. Hardie was equally passionate; 'A scotch accent stronger than usual also bore evidence to the severity of his agitation,' said one hostile newspaper.[14] The *Leeds Times* accused Hardie of launching an avalanche of sewerage on the Royal family; perhaps this shows their lack of interest in public health reforms, as the correct word is *sewage*.[15] The poor blameless infant in question grew up to be Edward VIII, playboy and dilettante who abdicated in 1936 to be with the divorced woman he loved.

The national Tory press fell on Hardie. Colonel Sanderson MP, who had called for the unnecessary vote that he not be heard, called him a cad. 'Thus ended ingloriously the republican assault on the throne. The only member who could be found to prefer a republic to monarchy is the one member who will certainly lose his seat at the general election'. He was compared unfavourably with other Liberal-Labour MPs. He was condemned for not having much influence *and* for not really attending the Commons very much:

> He takes little part in the real work of the House, is rarely seen there, misses important divisions, and does little or no Committee work. But he usually turns up when there is opportunity for rather cheap display.[16]

He was compared unfavourably to the recently deceased Charles Bradlaugh, who had been able to help the working man as a Liberal. He was also compared unfavourably to John Burns, who was able to influence the government under the Liberal banner – the same man who had threatened revolution with Hyndman in Trafalgar Square six years earlier. It was true that he did not spend much time in the Commons; he travelled the country making speeches, so the accusation that his attendance was sparse and his interest in committee work was limited was actually true, but it was a strategy that made sense – he could have more influence as Labour's only MP in a packed meeting hall than in the Commons.

Hardie was responsible for the formation of the Independent Labour Party in 1893. It was based on the widespread assumption that the Liberals were never going to be sufficiently supportive of the working class. They were a socialist party; the policy 'to secure the collective ownership of the means of production, distribution and exchange', remained Labour Party policy until 1995.

The Labour movement failed its first electoral test in 1895. There was a Conservative landslide and the two main parties gained 3.4 million votes and the combined vote of the Hardie's ILP and Hyndman's SDF was 37,555 of which the SDF achieved 3,122. Hardie lost his seat in South West Ham on a straight fight with the Conservatives. In this case, many Liberals, lacking a candidate, stayed at home or voted Conservative, and Hardie rather petulantly blamed them for a lack of support despite doing nothing to reassure them. He also blamed the newspapers and the fracture of the Irish national vote which mostly went to him in 1892. He always carried around three farthings in his pocket to flourish when accused of taking Tory gold – an accusation made more ridiculous by the fact it was the Tories who defeated him.

Hyndman suggested that they had won the argument despite losing the election and that the large swing from Liberal to Conservative was a result of the fear of real fundamental change that the inevitability of socialism would bring. The right-wing press saw it differently; they chortled as both Hardie's *Labour Leader* and Hyndman's *Justice* begged for money and advertisers and then asked (rhetorically) why the working class were not prepared to pay to read their newspapers.

Money was always a problem. The outdoor rally, beloved of the left at elections, was originally a reluctant result of a lack of money. Candidates for parliament were expected to pay their own expenses and contribute towards the administrative costs of the election as an upfront cash deposit even before nomination. When Hardie was elected in 1892, he took a contribution of £100 from the American Andrew Carnegie; on the day of his election, the Hoxton Branch of the SDF condemned the gift and demanded that it was returned. Carnegie was a social progressive who actively campaigned against monarchy and gave money to radical causes, but the objection from some was that he was a multimillionaire businessman as well.

The unity between the two men was more apparent than real. Hardie and Hyndman would clash again in 1900 when the Labour Representation Committee was formed. The members of the committee – two from the SDF and the ILP, one member of the Fabian Society, and seven trade unionists – showed the balance of power in the organisation and there was no strong support for Hyndman's version of class warfare. The result of the 1900 election was underwhelming; two seats, one for Hardie in Merthyr Tydfil, and one for Merthyr-born Richard Bell, who was more inclined to Liberalism. So the first ever two-member Labour party was split.

Another big difference between Hardie and Hyndman is reminiscent of some of the problems of the Labour party in recent times. One problematic aspect of Hyndman was that he was an anti-Semite, and still managed to create offence in an age where casual anti-Semitism was endemic. Anti-Semitism was present in both the left and right of politics. The stereotype came easily to both. Jews occupied both the top and the bottom of the economic pyramid. Jews both controlled and undermined capitalism, depending on the choice of conspiracy theory. They were international finance capitalists and sweated immigrant labour, both inimitable to the interests of the nation. When Jews were victims of riots in Vienna in 1885, Hyndman explained away the violence, blaming them for the resentment they caused by controlling finance capital.

Hyndman was unable to visualize the Jewish immigrant as a victim of capitalism; the Jew was a foreigner and product of the free movement of labour that depressed wages and weakened the negotiating position of indigenous workers. Other socialists, like Beatrice Webb and William Morris, diagnosed the situation differently. Jewish immigrants were exploited by Jewish entrepreneurs in sweat shops producing cheap clothes and furniture; as desperate refugees from Eastern European pogroms and violence, they were the ultimate in working class misery.

It wasn't just anti-Semitism – in 1882 when it was still the Democratic Federation, a resolution from Hyndman committed the organisation to opposing Chinese immigration because the Chinese 'always remained a distinct race wherever they went. They could swamp us industrially and crowd us out of almost every occupation'. The unions were often no better. In 1894, the Trade Unions Congress complained that the low paid Jews were ready to work for fifteen hours a day on a diet of 'cold coffee, bread and cheese'.[17]

Hyndman's nationalist version of socialism was one of the reasons for the departure of Eleanor Marx, William Morris and others for whom socialism was an international creed. Morris's rival organisation the Socialist League was scathing when the SDF demanded the end of free movement of labour. When Hyndman blamed the Jews, Morris was sarcastic in his *Commonweal,* a paper he subsidized in the same way Hyndman subsidized *Justice*; 'In regards to Ireland, the poor foreign Jews have, as yet, not penetrated...hence, the standard of the Irish peasants and workers is an almost ideal one'.

Hyndman's opposition to the free movement of people was consistent; he did not want the British to leave the country either, and his explanation was tinged with eugenic and race theory; 'Why was the race deteriorating?' he asked.

> Most important of all, in my opinion, is the continuous stream of emigration of the more vigorous, capable and discontented of the working class to the United States and the Colonies for two whole generations.[18]

Hyndman was a nationalist; to his enemies, he was a Marxist-Jingoist; when he told Karl Marx that he had omitted a credit to *Capital* in his *England For All* because the English did not like Germans, he was not making an excuse. It was not merely his noxious personality that created splits in the movement; he opposed the Boer War in 1899–1902, disliking both sides but not being prepared to use up his time and resources to oppose it, much to the disgust of his SDF members. Hardie opposed the Boer War and died in 1915 completely opposed to fighting the Great War against fellow workers.

Hardie and Hyndman had different views on women's suffrage. Hyndman's view on the women question was ambiguous; through the prism of class rather than social issues, he wanted the vote for women to be achieved at the same time as all the working class. Emmeline and Richard Pankhurst first met Keir Hardie at the International Workers Congress in 1888. Hardie became a friend and often shared platforms with them. Hardie supported women's suffrage throughout the suffragettes' struggle. Hardie resigned as leader in 1908 and focused his efforts on campaigning for votes for women, developing a close relationship with Sylvia Pankhurst, daughter of Emmeline. Hardie was prepared to spoil his relationship with the Labour Party to focus on supporting the demands and tactics of the suffragettes; official party policy was to focus on the vote for all. When he died in 1915, Sylvia Pankhurst called him 'the greatest human being of our time'. They were lovers, but it was suffrage and pacifism that united them more strongly.

In 1903, Hardie produced this description in the Labour leader of the type of 'supporter' who would actually postpone the arrival of his kind of socialism:

> It is a quaint spectacle to see a top-hatted, frock coated member of the prosperous middle class sweating on a platform to prove his "class consciousness" with the poor worker. Do these men de-class themselves when they become socialists?
>
> The class war dogma is admittedly based on the theory of Socialism set forth in the Communist Manifesto of Marx and Engels ... It does not touch one human sentiment or feeling. However correct it may be as a form of words, it is lacking in feeling, and cannot now be defended as being scientifically correct. It entirely leaves the human element out of account. Evolution is not a class struggle; and even where it assumes that form it is but the outward expression of an inner fact.

When the first Labour Party appeared in the Commons in 1906, it was much more Hardie than Hyndman, indeed it was not really Hyndman at all. Hardie's Labour stood in fifty seats and won twenty-nine with an average of 5,000 votes. Hyndman's SDP stood in eight constituencies with an average of 2,000. It was a progressive, Trade Union dominated party, clearly more Methodist than Marxist. The 1906 success was due to the Lib-Lab pact; Hardie had learnt to tolerate the Liberals; they stood aside in thirty seats in exchange for the Labour Representative committee only contesting fifty. Hyndman the purist, did not support it and the SDF left the LRC in 1907.

There was a real interest in these new MPs. The radical journalist William Stead sent them a questionnaire and wrote an article based on the twenty-five replies he received, rather clumsily entitled 'The Labour party and the books that created it'. It also showed a deep misunderstanding of the men he had written to; they had formed their opinions from their disadvantaged background and their work in the Trade Union movement, not from books.

As the leading and most dynamic members of their class, they had of course read books which influenced them. Where had their socialism come from? The answer was not Karl Marx. Only two cited *Capital* as an influence, and only one had read his work systematically. The socialism of the first Parliamentary Labour Party came from the Bible, Methodism, and their own experience, mostly as Trade Unionists. Only one of the Labour MPs of 1906 had ever been an activist member of the SDF.

When Hyndman died in 1921, the leader of the Labour party, John Clynes was called on to mark his passing with some positive thoughts. He did not find it easy. Hyndman was isolated, and had been for a generation; he was rich and a great speaker but the SDF went far ahead of working class opinion. 'He was always uncompromising and impatient of those who knew that a Labour Party could be built up only when the Trade Unions were converted to independent political action,' said Clynes, through the most gritted of teeth.

It was, of course, Keir Hardie who had achieved that success – independent action mostly through unions, but his career ended in apparent failure. Hardie had died in 1915, in agony over the war but refusing to renounce his pacifism. He was about to walk away from the House of Common; like in 1892–1895, he was alone, but this time because his colleagues had deserted him to support a European war with workers at both ends of the bayonet. The newspapers did not relent – *Punch* called him *Keir Von Hardie*; he needed to be guarded just passing through the street.[19] It all hastened his death, aged fifty-nine, on 26 September. When Hyndman died he was better remembered as a jingoist supporter of the First World War rather than as an agitator on behalf of the unemployed a generation earlier. They died as they had lived; differently and unapologetically.

The spirit of Hardie and the ghost of Hyndman still live in the Labour Party today. Labour remains a hybrid organisation, a tense alliance of Social Democrats, Socialists, Marxists and Trade Unionists, and the lives of the two men show that that tension was apparent at its birth. The man who taught himself to write with a piece of shale in a coal mine mostly triumphed over the rich Marxist gentleman, but the struggle continued for the soul of the Party, even though the two sides have different guises today.

Chapter Fourteen

Republicanism
Sir Charles Dilke

The British monarchy has never needed popularity and has only courted it in the last fifty years. This has been a historical anomaly, the wisdom of which has yet to be established. Prior to that, they aimed to be respected, revered and feared but remained secure in their position even when they were denied all three. The Hanoverians met with a large degree of apathy; to some, they were a usurping dynasty. George IV was actively hated by the time of his death in 1830 and the subsequent reign of William IV was neither exciting nor endearing. When the young Alexandrina Victoria became queen in 1837, the bar was very low. They neither needed nor wished to be liked, which was convenient, because they weren't.

It is also a myth that Queen Victoria was always a popular monarch. She was at the beginning and end of her reign, but this was not the case in the middle. In fact, the opposite is probably true. She and her family became unpopular in the 1870s and there was a brief but intense streak of British republicanism that blazed and then faded away. Its roots were shallow and its followers were divided on their strategy, tactics and aims.

Republicanism had a bad name, even before the establishment alarm at the Chartists. Britain was a republic for eleven years after the execution of Charles I in 1649; this was regarded as a regrettable experiment, not to be repeated. When it was repeated in France in 1789, republicanism was regarded as traitorous and the works of English republicans like Thomas Paine were burned in the street and banned from publication. Paine criticised the monarchy, not only as an anti-democratic part of the constitution but as part of the system of 'Old Corruption' where the main criticism was that they were not pulling their weight, not earning their money or a mixture of both; and later Victorian republicanism showed the same theme. Chartist newspapers in the 1840s refused to be jubilant at the birth of Victoria's many children and dubbed them the 'Royal Cormorants'.

When republicanism revived in the late 1860s, it came back as a 'value for money' issue. By 1870, the queen had been out of the public eye for a decade, mourning her husband and determined not to repeat the mistake of her beloved Albert, who she believed had worked himself to death. This fear of work would have come as an unpleasant surprise to the millions working in mines and factories or slaving away as domestic servants for six and a half days a week, but there was a common view that the queen was not performing her public duty. Charles Bradlaugh, the secularist and republican, commented that the country had had no effective monarchy for a decade after 1860 and the state survived, so what was the point of it?

Victoria's eldest son and heir was also unpopular. Edward, Prince of Wales was a living, breathing, taxpayer-funded example of the double standard of expected male behaviour, with another layer of hypocrisy created by his leeway as a royal. His gambling, womanising, and specifically, his dalliances with actresses were already well-known, and he was considerably less popular than his mother. He was hissed at at Epsom race course, at the theatre or even when appearing in public in his coach.[1]

Part of the problem was that Edward was unable to build up a more serious public persona because the queen forbade him from doing anything more than social and trivial public appearances. The oldest people alive in 1870 could still remember the thunderous denunciation of George IV as lazy, arrogant and spendthrift. To their critics, the Hanoverian vices were returning; the new Prince of Wales was like the old Prince of Wales, and the system was as corrupt and expensive as it had been then.

British republicanism was revived in 1871 by the unlikely figure of Sir Charles Dilke (1843–1911). Dilke was a radical liberal MP and an important progressive force in Victorian Britain. He was an early supporter of women's suffrage, working in the same organisation as Cobbe and Wolstenholme-Elmy. At a time when many franchise organisations asked only for the vote for single and widowed women, Dilke wanted the vote for women on the same basis as men, and, unlike others, did not hide the fact that female suffrage in local elections was merely a stepping stone to votes at General Elections.

He also held other radical opinions; he supported the secret ballot, equal-sized constituencies and the ratepayer paying the expenses of elections rather than candidates. He wanted free and compulsory state education, employment on merit to the civil service, the better taxation of land, and the end of promotions in the army being bought rather than earned. He supported the rights of Trade Unions to picket lawfully and the demand for an eight-hour working week when even most Liberals thought the former would bring national anarchy and the latter national bankruptcy. No cause was too unpopular; in 1870 he became a member of the Aboriginal Protection Society and presided over their annual meeting. The society was designed to promote the welfare and human rights (but not the culture) of all indigenous peoples in the Empire; it was charity of the 'supporting backward peoples' variety, part of the unthinking racism of Victorian society which Dilke accepted without condemnation.

He worked very hard, read considerably and was a talented communicator – he was a fluent French speaker. He was a rich man, with an income of £7,000 per year. He inherited his father's fortune, his two newspapers (The *Athenaeum* and *Notes and Queries*) in 1864, and four years later his father's seat in the House of Commons representing Chelsea. That may sound an unlikely home for a radical MP, but the Chelsea of the 1860s was not the same as today. It was a partly artisan community, with rows of working class streets in Kensal Town, intellectuals and lawyers around South Kensington and Holland Park, and an artistic and literary set in Notting Hill. It was the 'most intelligent place in Britain,' said Dilke. This was brilliant campaigning and had the necessary element of truth to flatter people effectively.

Dilke had spent much of 1871 in Paris, following the events of the Prussian defeat of France and the setting up of a republic over the water from Britain. The authorities feared the chaos that ensued while still worrying about the political consequences. It was at this point that Dilke became Britain's most famous republican, almost by accident and certainly not by design. On 6 November 1871, he set light to smouldering grievances with a speech at Newcastle entitled *Representation and Royalty*. As the title hints, it was more about the massive difference in the size of the constituencies. He pointed out to the artisan audience something that they already knew – Newcastle (electorate 18,565) had the same number of MPs as the sleepy border town of Berwick-upon-Tweed (electorate 1,415). They knew because many of them were enfranchised for the first time after the Reform Act of 1867, and their vote, while now real, was less powerful than that of more middle class electors.

This, according to Dilke, was inefficiency, dishonesty and possibly corruption. At this point, he moved onto the Civil List, the cost of the monarchy and suggested, hypothetically and speculatively, that a republic would be a more honest form of government. The queen had been absent for a decade, and now more taxpayers' money was being demanded for her children Louise (a dowry of £30,000) and Arthur (an allowance of £15,000 when he came of age). Could the queen not use the Civil List to pay these gifts to the already privileged, rather than ask the taxpayer?

He claimed that the one million pound Civil List was used to offset the expenses of the monarch and for the upkeep of the royal household, and so provided no national benefit. His speech listed all dependents and household members supported from the public purse, which included Victoria, nine children and their dowries, and the future support of the Prince of Wales and his subsequent children. She did not even pay income tax, introduced in 1842 and deliberately aimed at the very rich.

One possible solution was a republic – one that would bring would transparency to public spending, and any money lavished on a head of state would be with the consent of the people.

> If you can show me a fair chance that a republic here will be free from the political corruption that hangs around the monarchy then he would say, and he believed the middle class in general would say – let it come!

This was not a revolutionary point of view. It wasn't even a concrete suggestion. 'Let it come' is neither a ringing endorsement of republicanism nor a plan of action on how to achieve it. Dilke believed that the middle classes would eventually accept a republic if it produced pure and efficient, rational and cheap government, in the fullness of time after a long period of citizenship education – but to the popular press, it sounded like pure treason.

The response was vicious and immediate. What annoyed the establishment was the impertinence of bringing up the subject at all – it was all grubby and undignified. Dilke was the ungracious bean counter, trying to monetarise the value of an esteemed institution, poking his nose into the laundry bills and the regularity of new uniforms being issued. Indignant correspondents complained to the newspapers that at the time the queen *had* offered Sir Robert Peel to pay tax and the offer was not taken up. Dilke was a cad, and worse.

Considering that he was a hereditary baronet who would want to pass this title to his son (if he ever had one, sniffed one newspaper) and the very honour was the responsibility of the queen, this all stank of hypocrisy. In an echo of the twentieth-century cry of 'why don't you go and live in Russia?' it was suggested that he should sell all his property and go to the United States, or even worse, to the chaos of republican France. More than one newspaper called him *Citizen Dilke*.

What rankled most with the establishment was *who* Dilke had shared his thoughts with. Discussing whether the respectable classes would theoretically warm to a republic was the wrong approach to his Newcastle audience of radicals, secularists and Irish nationalists. It gave the lower classes *ideas*; many in the audience were members of the Newcastle Republican Brotherhood, formed in 1855 as a loyal body designed to educate the population in the ways of republican thought. The *Times* made the same point when it huffed that the claims for nepotism and corruption were incorrect, and even if true, were not to be discussed in a meeting of the lower classes.[2] Many Liberals in his own constituency also thought that this was more than one step too far. One voter in Chelsea, who had canvassed for Dilke in 1868, withdrew his support because of his speech to the 'uneducated men' of Newcastle.

Dilke was wilting under establishment pressure. Charles Bradlaugh joined the fray and made himself as unpopular as a republican as he had as an atheist. Bradlaugh toured the country in the mid-1870s using the railway network to arrive in the early evening, make a speech at a local assembly room (unless the booking had already been cancelled or sabotaged by the local authorities) and mostly talked about the cost of the monarchy. In 1871, Bradlaugh became President of the London Republican Club, and a year later he published 'The Impeachment of the House of Brunswick'. Bradlaugh's name was linked with Dilke, to the detriment of both; the establishment could see why republicanism might be profitable for an upstart journalist from East London, but a baronet?

At his Leeds meeting, Dilke started to backtrack. The word treason was ringing in his ears; his claim not to be frightened by it made its own point. Like all former politicians accused of treason, he shifted the blame, condemning the monarch's advisers for mishandling the queen's finances. The best defence for a monarchy in this country was that it was harmless and that it existed inside a democratic system, and perhaps saved the nation from a certain amount of political intrigue. He did not budge from the point that they had enough money. He felt that being able to talk about the monarch's finances was a principle of free speech.

The Leeds meeting attracted 5,000 people, all of whom had to apply for a ticket for security reasons. There was no trouble because the event was under the control of a local radical Leeds MP, Robert Carter. When the locals were less welcoming, the situation could deteriorate quickly. In Bolton on 30 November, 'Tory Roughs' threw iron bars through the window at the 2,000 ticketed supporters inside. One man was killed in the fracas and Dilke's life was threatened, although he was either naive or arrogant enough to take no notice, strolling out through the demonstrators nonchalantly smoking his cigar. The eight ringleaders were later prosecuted and a patriotic local jury found them not guilty.

On 6 December he was back in the more friendly territory of Birmingham, where his friend Joseph Chamberlain brought out the local police force to protect Dilke; each interrupter was removed by two police officers during a dull speech about public finance. When he returned to Chelsea, he narrowly won a vote of confidence at the Vestry Hall, but not before a mob had destroyed all the furniture and disabled the gas lighting. It was all a perplexing fuss for a position that was purely theoretical, and set in the distant future; as Dilke said 'history and experience show that you cannot have a Republic without you possessing at the same time the Republican virtues.'

That Britain did not have a republican people was proved in the winter of 1871/1872 when the Prince of Wales nearly died of typhoid. There was an outpouring of concern when he caught it and national jubilation when he recovered, and the vast but shallow republican tide slowly receded. Some of the working classes, still collecting signatures opposing the Civil List, may have wondered why one man getting typhoid from his Scarborough holiday should be more important than the thousands who died of it in filthy British cities, and one infected sewer pipe in a well-appointed haunt of the rich should be improved before the cess pits of the poor, but that was not the view of those who mattered.

Queen Victoria was so relieved that the disease that killed her beloved Albert did not quite kill her son that she sprang back onto the public stage, which is all that most of her critics actually wanted. In February 1872, she opened parliament, for a change, and directed her thanks to the whole nation for praying for Edward during his illness. For those who were doubtful about the power of prayer, there were public health and housing improvements announced soon afterwards, partly when it was realised that princes could die too.

When the Civil List was debated in March 1872, Dilke received almost no support. The House of Commons was disruptive and hostile; a motion was put forward that, as he had broken his oath of allegiance, he should not be heard to speak, which was met with cheers. When he did speak it was dull, merely asking for better information about the Civil List. Many MPs, tired of groans and ironic cheers, just left the chamber. Then Dilke's more robustly republican colleague Auberon Herbert made a speech that was howled down; he was widely regarded as a silly young man whose pretensions were enormous – 'Had a mad dog made his appearance on the floor of the house a scene of wilder excitement could not on the instant have been raised,' said one hostile newspaper. Sir George Bentinck's contribution to the debate was (allegedly) to make a sound like a cock crowing; perhaps indicating the view of the MPs that the enquiry about the queen's finances was cowardly and tasteless.

Dilke's motion was defeated by 276 to 2 – so that was four votes if the two tellers were included. The value for money argument was going nowhere; some radical republican MPs rejected the emphasis on the cost of the Civil List. Henry Fawcett MP (husband of the Suffragist Millicent Fawcett) was unimpressed 'over the miserable haggle over a few pounds'.[3]

Dilke had stirred something; both old Chartist resentments about the monarchy, and more recent complaints. The earlier economic depression from 1867 had revived discontent. By mid-1873 there were about ninety republican clubs in Britain, together with another fifty societies that were republican in sentiment. These organisations were small, mostly between twenty and fifty members, and very few with a working class majority – Sheffield and Newcastle being the main exceptions.

At first, these organisations thought that Dilke was their ally. In January 1872, a republican rally organised by Dilke's close acquaintance George Odger passed a vote of thanks for his work. The Newcastle Republicans passed a similar motion, as did the Leicester Democratic Association (who re-branded themselves as the Leicester Republicans).

Would he please talk to them? It seemed not. Dilke gave the Glasgow
Republican Club the same message:

> Sir Charles added that, although he was a republican, he
> preferred for the sake of the cause and Liberal principles
> generally, not to visit the city under the immediate auspices
> of the Glasgow Republicans.

Dilke was no republican propagandist; he arrived in Glasgow in
October of the same year as he promised, he gave a talk entitled *Class
Legislation*, where his first example was the cronyism involved in the
1872 Birmingham Sewerage Bill. The 3,000 capacity hall was half
full. The weather was bad, said the press, but others suggested that the
attendance was actually increased by the prospect of seeing his new
wife, Katherine Mary Sheil.

Katherine died in childbirth two years later; Dilke was distraught.
Too upset to deal with the funeral, he left the arrangements to his brother
Aston Dilke. This was made even more complicated by the fact that
Katherine wished to be cremated; Aston Dilke took advice from the
newly formed Cremation Society, who informed them that it was not
definitely legal. Katherine was embalmed and her body sent by train to
Dresden. Dilke suffered some opprobrium for allowing this to happen; it
was banned soon afterwards in Germany.[4]

His speech at Glasgow was not all boring. He did move on to more
radical matters in the speech, like redistribution of seats and the problem
with the House of Lords, and finished with a restatement of his theoretical
republicanism but also that 'most radical opinion agrees that all the
reforms he wanted were perfectly compatible with monarchy'. It is clear
why he did not want to say this in front of the Glasgow Republicans.

The proper republicans were small and split. There was, by 1873,
a National Republican Brotherhood, a confederation of seventeen
organisations whose members were all styled 'citizen' and had a green
(for fertility), white (for purity) and blue (the colour of the sky that
all men inhabit) tricolour as their emblem. Most clubs did not have
a membership of more than fifty; some no more than twenty.[5] They
wanted a federal, secular republic with one house elected by PR (and
therefore the abolition of the House of Lords), secular education and
the nationalisation of land. They supported Irish Independence; opposed

capitalism, and lords and usury. These policies were all one step further than a radical like Dilke was prepared to go. They specifically disavowed atheism as part of their creed, noting correctly that the two were often linked.

Bradlaugh despised their socialism and their attack on atheism and formed a rival body. The National Republican League planned a parliamentary road to republicanism by electing enough MPs to repeal the 1701 Act that created the Hanoverian succession and block the succession of Edward VII. Like the republican Brotherhood, he detested the monarchy, not on a 'value for money' basis, but because it was a front organisation protecting a bloated and land-hogging aristocratic landlord class and a national privileged church.

Dilke continued to watch the royal pennies rather than plot a change in government and society. In 1876, he joined Bradlaugh and Besant in a further campaign against the Civil List, especially the £142,000 that was being spent to send the Prince of Wales to India. Their 'monster' petition was paraded to the House of Commons and looked impressive, but the tour went ahead.[6]

Dilke is our only Victorian radical who became both a Privy Councillor and a Cabinet member. Dilke's name was on a list of five that Victoria did not want in Gladstone's 1880 cabinet (it included another republican, Henry Fawcett) but Gladstone ignored it. She watched his progress with suspicion but was mollified by the cabinet post he was given. The President of the Local Government Board was not a leading role, but was one he was well suited for; it was a 'details' job.

By 1885, his republicanism had been forgiven and forgotten by all except Queen Victoria. His reputation was at an all-time high and he was being spoken of as the next Liberal leader (and therefore possible Prime Minister). Then his high flying career was brought down to earth by an infamous adultery case made more disastrous by his cack-handed response. Virginia Crawford, a relative by marriage, was being divorced by her husband, Captain Henry Forster. In her confessions to him, she named Dilke as her main lover; they had had secret trysts in Sloane Square and Kensington for two years between 1882 and 1884. She also threw in other accusations; Dilke had had an affair with her own mother Ellen, and a three-in-a-bed romp with her and a servant girl called Fanny, much to the delight of the salacious press. In the great British tradition of blaming the foreigner, Dilke was accused of introducing the women 'to every kind of French vice'. Crawford said 'He used to say that I knew more than most women of 30.'

The first trial showed the complexity of English divorce law; Crawford and Dilke did not speak; Crawford was found guilty of adultery; there was no case to answer for Dilke and the judge awarded him costs. The law decreed that Crawford had committed adultery, but for Dilke, the vice had not been versa. There is plenty of reason to suggest that Crawford was lying; she needed a divorce; she chose to make the accusation against Dilke because Dilke had been both her mother's and her best friend's lover.

The optics were awful; this was 1885. There were shades of *Maiden Tribute*; the establishment figure, destroying marriages and taking advantage of his power over the lower classes. It was no wonder that W.T. Stead started up a campaign against Dilke, insisting that he defended himself. Stead and others were campaigning against the sexual double standard and here it was right at the top of society. Stead continued his campaign against Dilke for years after the trial, continually raking up the muck. Dilke was unlucky to cross a man who regarded himself as 'the chosen instrument of public morality'.[7]

Dilke decided to clear his name; egged on by his own ego and the denunciations of Stead, he went through the elaborate process of challenging the decree nisi but in order to do that, he was in the unenviable position of trying to prove that something had not happened. Fanny Grey, the third person in the romp, claimed that it was a lie, but that was not believed. He performed poorly against three women who said the same thing on oath; his own odd habit of keeping a diary and cutting bits out was given the worst possible interpretation. It took the jury fifteen minutes to confirm the decree, and therefore his guilt. Queen Victoria was amused. The lawyer who had destroyed him, Henry Matthews, became an MP and at Victoria's insistence made Home Secretary in 1886.

What destroyed Dilke was not his radicalism, but his reputation as a womaniser. He had been defeated by his own reputation; even if innocent, which he may well have been – most historians think he was – it *was* the kind of thing that he did. Like his theoretical ruminations about republicanism, his affairs would have been tolerated if these indiscretions stayed inside the Westminster bubble. Perhaps he should have quietly ridden out the storm, but that would probably not have worked. He lost his seat in Chelsea in 1886 *before* the second legal proceedings had finished. However, it was close – he won 49% of the vote in a two-horse race in the context of a Conservative landslide in the rest of the country. Had the election been a year later, he would have lost by more; you can't be an MP if the London music halls were writing bawdy songs about you – or at least you couldn't in the 1880s.

Despite his support for women's suffrage, he lost the support of feminists who now saw in Dilke the same sexual double standard that held them back. When he was being considered as a London County Council alderman in 1889, the whole of the women's movement petitioned against him.[8] He was actively opposed by leading feminists including Annie Besant and Elizabeth Wolstenholme-Elmy, whose own views on marriage were far from orthodox, and by the time he had returned in 1892, Gladstone did not want public adulterers in his cabinet. He had tried to persuade him from standing in parliament; he could just about stomach atheists as he had proved in the Bradlaugh case but adulterers were beyond the pale.

In the 1890s, he successfully resurrected his career as an MP. After his political re-launch in the Forest of Dean, he told the *Gloucester Citizen* that the whole republican frenzy had been taken out of context.[9] He had planned six speeches in 1871 on various subjects, all pertinent to his belief in radical reform, of which the civil list was just one. This rang true; even at the famous Newcastle speech, the monarchy was the second subject of the night. He claimed that there was one phrase that he regretted, but did not say what it was; a good guess would be the verbatim report from a scurrilous pamphlet entitled *What Does She Do With It?*

Dilke was moving leftward after his return to the Commons in 1892; there were rumours that he would join the Independent Labour Party. He remained isolated; he had hopes of joining the famous Liberal Government of 1906, which would have allowed him to have more of a historical legacy and be associated with some of the Liberal reforms that he had devoted his life to.

He died in 1911, having exhausted himself in the two General Elections of 1910, but he had some real achievements to his name. He was a fervent supporter of the Liberal reforms in general but made specific contributions to the 1884 Reform Bill which gave the vote to more working class men in the counties. He was responsible for the

Redistribution of Seats Act in 1885, which ensured that constituencies were similarly sized, and did something to ensure that each vote was of equal value. He also wished to abolish two forms of plural voting which undermined the idea of one person one vote – the extra vote that graduates had voting for the university seats and the right of people to vote in more than one place if they had the property qualification. George Bernard Shaw knew an MP who had thirteen votes and a vicar who voted forty times legally.[10] This reform had to wait, and it was as late as 1948 in the case of the university plural voting.

The minimum wage is often viewed as a modern idea, but the first one was introduced by the 1909 Trade Boards Act, which regulated conditions in industries with an oversupply of labour and a consequent weak negotiating position for the workers. Initially, it was only in sweated trades such as chain-making, ready-made tailoring, paper-box making, and lace finishing. Dilke was the inspiration rather than the instigator; he had been calling for this protection for a decade. He also helped the shop workers. When they formed their union, they named their headquarters Dilke House. The warm tributes of socialists like Hardie and Tillet show that he was regarded as a friend of the working classes.

Thus a man who never worked in his life showed his interest in the very poorest, and it is clear that he had more to offer if scandal had not hit; but it says a lot about Victorian Society that it was adultery that finished him off, not republicanism, which was a threat to nobody in the establishment.

Chapter Fifteen

Eugenics

Francis Galton

In the reputational afterlife, most of our Victorian radicals became either revered or forgotten. Only one is still actively disliked. The radical in question was the English explorer, traveller and scientist Francis Galton (1822–1911). He was undoubtedly one of the greatest scientific polymaths in British history. He still has his own Institute which focuses, quite rightly, on his immense scientific achievements in the areas of meteorology, psychology, genetics, forensics and statistical methods. He produced the first newspaper weather map in 1875, revolutionised police work with his breakthroughs in fingerprints, and more. There is no room here for all his achievements, because his fame has been eclipsed by his infamy; as I write, University College London, where he did much of his work, is renaming the laboratory which carries his name, a name which has been linked with racism and genocide. His own Institute accepts that his so-called scientific views on race improvement are morally reprehensible and completely discredited.

Galton is the father of eugenics, a term he invented in 1883, meaning no more than 'to live well'. Its meaning is bland and uncontroversial, but as with any utopian theory, the controversy starts when the general aim becomes a set of specific proposals. Eugenics is essentially the science of selective breeding. It is a contentious subject, at least when applied to humans; selective breeding of plants and animals has become commonplace and has produced improvements in animals and plants that have benefited humanity. This important point was made by the evolutionary biologist Professor Richard Dawkins in 2020:

> It's one thing to deplore eugenics on ideological, political, moral grounds. It's quite another to conclude that it wouldn't

work in practice. Of course it would. It works for cows, horses, pigs, dogs & roses. Why on earth wouldn't it work for humans? Facts ignore ideology.[1]

This tweet does not make Dawkins a eugenicist; the consequences are 'morally deplorable', he later added, and the unacceptable moral consequences are well known. The idea that you can improve the physical and intellectual quality of human beings by planned breeding – that is, being selective about who breeds and by definition, who doesn't – is a very radical thought. Some would say it is also a very reactionary thought, as it is so different to our preferred way of improving human beings; through education, health and environmental reform. Eugenics is linked with authoritarian and dystopian shortcuts; compulsory sterilisation of the mentally unfit and racism used as a pretext to genocide. Galton is accused by some of being a proto-National Socialist, the inspiration behind Nazi racial policies.

Here is our 'fascist', as imagined by the US journalist Jim Holt:

> In the eighteen-eighties, residents of cities across Britain might have noticed an aged, bald, bewhiskered gentleman sedulously eying every girl he passed on the street while manipulating something in his pocket. What they were seeing was not lechery in action but science.[2]

Galton was collecting data. The key to understanding Galton's both immense achievements and errors is his faith in analysing numbers; 'Whenever you can, count,' Galton said. He was skilled in lots of areas but first of all, he was a mathematician, a collector of data and a statistician. Galton was a scientist who believed that correctly interpreted data would produce irrefutable conclusions. On this occasion, he was travelling around the country looking at women, sometimes individually and sometimes in crowds at race meetings through his opera classes, and ranking them for beauty using a counting device hidden in his pocket which he (without innuendo) called his 'pricker', a needle and paper affixed to the finger and palm of his glove. The categories were 'attractive', 'indifferent' and 'repellent'. When he finished, he turned his data into a conclusion about the women of Britain which he called his 'beauty meter'.

There is so much wrong with his methods – the premise is distasteful, the criteria are very culturally loaded, and the method is random and misogynist. At the time this scheme was seen as silly and eccentric as well. Galton did not see it in this way. He felt he was judging and measuring dispassionately; he was, in his mind, a statistician who was convinced that differences between individuals and races existed and could be tabulated. He felt that he had found out where the ugliest women in Britain could be found.[3.]

He was a rationalist too; he rejected the traditional form of religion but did so using data rather than more theology; he was similar to Sir Henry Thompson in that regard. Their backgrounds were similar too – born of privilege, highly intellectual and acutely aware of it, and moving rapidly and sometimes quite frenetically from one subject to another.

In 1872, Galton and Thompson became part of the 'Prayer Gauge Controversy'. Galton was both mildly amused and appalled at unsubstantiated statements about the efficacy of prayer. He also noted that this belief was shared by Christian churches that were divided on other issues; Catholics, Anglicans and Non-conformists all prayed to avoid or mitigate problems and declared fast days and days of humiliation. They all believed that God intervened in an otherwise rule-based universe. In 1872, Dr. Hook, the Dean of Chichester, stated that 'the general providence of God acts through what are called the laws of nature. By this particular providence, God interferes with those laws, and he has promised to interfere on behalf of those who pray in the name of Jesus'. Dean Hook was specifically implying that the Almighty was intervening to help the Prince of Wales who, after national prayer, had recovered from typhoid.[4]

Both Thompson and Galton proposed to challenge this dogma. Thompson's longitudinal story of hospital wards (Chapter Five) was not necessary in Galton's view. Large amounts of data already existed. It was not only to hand but was not compromised by being created for the sake of the experiment. Galton collected and collated; he noted that life expectancy for members of royal families was the lowest of the ten occupational groups that he studied, and they were prayed for in every church in Christendom. He noted that the clergy, the experts on intercessionary prayer, lived no longer than anybody else. To back up his own evidence he noted that the insurance and actuarial companies, who made their profits when working out when people would die, never asked if they prayed. Ships that carried missionaries were statistically no safer than others. The data was conclusive.

He was no authoritarian dogmatist. The critics of scientists, people like Anna Kingsford and Francis Power Cobbe, suggested that scientists were replacing one priesthood with another, but for Galton, his work was an investigation, not an assertion. He was fully able to change his conclusions. His achievements in the areas of fingerprinting were inspired by his hypothesis that they could reveal details about genealogy, race, and social class. The evidence he gathered proved that hypothesis wrong; so he changed his mind.

Galton's thinking was transformed by the publication in 1859 of his half-cousin Charles Darwin's *Origin of Species*. There was no more radical thinker than Charles Darwin in this era, but he plays no part in this book because by the end of the century his views were accepted. In 1894, it was noted that evolution was being discussed by the British Medical Association annual meeting 'disputed by no reasonable man'.[5] However, some of the ideas generated from Darwin's theories were radical and much more controversial. The long title of Darwin's work was *On the Origin of Species by Means of Natural Selection, or the Preservation of Favoured Races in the Struggle for Life* – and it was the second part which caused all the controversy. Darwin mostly described plant and animal breeding to provide better specimens and was referring mostly to physical characteristics like eyes and wings. Galton's work was to extend the argument into other areas.

The expression (not penned by Darwin) that is most associated with his book, and later of the eugenics movement, 'the survival of the fittest', merely meant that organisms that were best adjusted to their present environment were more likely to survive into the next generation, where 'fit' was meant in the nineteenth century meaning of appropriate rather than athletic. It did not take much imagination to make this sound like a heartless, life-or-death struggle between competing nations and races.

Galton *was* a racist; he believed that races existed, and could improve or deteriorate over time, so logically some must be inferior to others at any given point in history. He believed that the white race was superior to others; in Victorian Britain, his views, while extreme, shocked nobody. He also asserted that the Chinese were superior, or more accurately, capable of faster improvement than the Black African and suggested that millions should be moved there. The Chinese would then breed better people who would push out the indigenous people. More controversial, and in the same year, 1873, Galton wrote an article 'Hereditary improvement' in which he created a eugenic utopia where the rich and intelligent would be actively encouraged to produce children and the genetic underclass would be prevented from doing so, by force if necessary.

Galton believed that good characteristics such as intelligence, proneness to good health and general moral character could be inherited and that the opposite was true – unfortunate outcomes could be prevented by selective breeding. This is controversial only in part; in the twenty-first century, unborn babies are scanned for Down's syndrome and other similar conditions and we do not call it eugenics; this is what Dawkins meant when he pointed out eugenic interventions can work.

What worried Galton was that the survival of the fittest was not taking place anymore. Darwin's model of evolution was too slow for Galton; modern society was in the process of destroying its productivity, by allowing the unfit to be born, survive and reproduce.

> One of the effects of civilization is to diminish the rigor of the application of the law of natural selection. It preserves weak lives that would have perished in a more barbarous land. (1865)

Modern science had reduced death rates and increased survival rates amongst all classes. Better babies needed to be born. But it was worse than that; unless marriage partners were selected to be physically and intellectually similar, there would always be a regression to the mean, a move towards mediocrity. Galton wanted to protect genius just as much as wanting to maintain the overall level. For example, he argued that the ancient Greeks lost their racial superiority when they began breeding outside their own people.

If natural selection was no longer operating, eugenics was needed to stop the drift to mediocrity. Animal selection worked; every championship-winning racehorse proved it, but it sounded horrible when applied to humans. Galton was well aware of the aversion to this and regularly denied that he wanted compulsory human breeding. However he freely admitted that, on meeting somebody for the first time, he put them into categories – 'desirables', 'passable' and ' undesirables'.

His basic eugenic plan was to leave the passable majority alone and deal with the 5% or so who were outliers at either end. The elite at the top would have incentives to reproduce. Galton fantasised about a society where the right people marrying would be rewarded by Queen Victoria giving the bride away. 'Negative Eugenics' was less attractive, involving state-sanctioned birth control and sterilisation.

There was considerable opposition to his radical ideas. Evolution and Eugenics did not go together automatically; Alfred Russel Wallace, who is now regarded as the co-founder of the theory of natural selection, had no faith in the notion that it was possible to identify the best people and that the social problems of an unfair capitalist society made the division into fit and unfit too arbitrary. It was Galton himself who invented the term 'nature v nurture'; his enemies stressed the absolute importance of environment. Men like Wallace and others would point out that better diet and health would solve the problem of the so-called underclass better than state-sanctioned control of birth.

It was also argued that moral characteristics like energy, entrepreneurship, bravery and laziness were social constructs determined by the prevailing ruling class. Galton did not go as far as to suggest that characteristics acquired in life could be inherited, but his belief that nature triumphed over everything was offensive to those who wanted to change the world now.

Galton supported some social changes. Like the Fabians, he wanted a route into higher education for the working classes, but in his view, it was only *some* of the working classes, the useful ones who had found themselves in the underclass but could be rescued. So eugenicists in the twentieth century devised and created intelligence tests for children, leading, in England, to selection at age eleven based on a tripartite division in the provision of schools.

There was admiration for eugenics, especially by the turn of the century. There was support from Darwin and other eminent scientists and celebrities. Virginia Woolf, T.S. Eliot, D.H. Lawrence, Julian Huxley and Marie Stopes all held eugenic views. Winston Churchill was vice-president of the first International Eugenics Conference, held in London in 1912. Two years earlier, Churchill had told Prime Minister Herbert Asquith that 'the multiplication of the feeble-minded is a very terrible danger to the race'.

Other radicals and progressives had no time for eugenics. Their interests were not the same, despite both needing massive state intervention to achieve their aims of improving the environment. Galton's main worry was that industrial capitalism had created an underclass that was dangerous, disruptive and nationally inefficient, and would grow out of control. The desire to breed them out was never going to make eugenicists popular with many ordinary workers.

Some leading socialists did support eugenics, especially in relation to the aristocracy. Both socialism and eugenics were opposed to the status quo implications of the hereditary class. The landlord class married their relatives to keep the money in the family rather than basing marriage on health and mental ability or even love. An attractive and vivacious daughter was regarded as a good trading asset and almost auctioned off to the richest bidder, who by virtue of being rich may also be older and more vitiated breeding stock. Aristocrats were interested in the inheritability of money for their selfish interest; the eugenicists believed in the passing on of civil strengths and virtues for the improvement of race and nation.

Some key socialists – Sydney Webb, George Bernard Shaw and (for a short while) H.G. Wells, flirted with eugenics. When Galton published data about the disastrous fall in quality when rich men married heiresses, the socialists could nod their head in agreement that the system was corrupt. The Webbs called this inefficient breeding 'money selection' and noted that it applied to the working classes as well. The lower end married among themselves, multiplying the same problems and the prudent and the providential having a lower birth rate.[6] H.G. Wells believed that improvement would only be possible with the 'the sterilisation of failures, and not the selection of successes'. George Bernard Shaw, a political opponent of Churchill, agreed with him about eugenics.

Socialists and Eugenicists could also agree that – whatever the reason – the working class were suffering under capitalism. The belief that the race was deteriorating – dysgenics – was clear for all to see in the slums of London, Manchester and Glasgow, and social studies from the 1880s onwards proved the point.

The urge to investigate the state of the nation came from the profound shock after the Boer War (1899–1902), a colonial war that Britain should have won easily. The failure to defeat the lightly armed, poorly organised farmers in South Africa was partly due to an army of working class volunteers who were physically not up to the job. The defence and expansion of Empire, the very thing that made Britain great and prosperous, was in doubt. The consequences of the Boer War made eugenicist talk more respectable, as it could be couched in the language of national efficiency, a notion that the Victorian establishment could sign up to.

It was no accident that it was military inefficiency that started the panic about the state of the working class; it was the working class that fought the wars. The state had collected data during the 1850s and could make a direct and frightening comparison. During the Crimean War, 10% of those recruited were under the standard army height of 5 foot 6 inches and in 1900 the figure was 65.5%.[7]

The 1904 report was shocking. The conclusions were that ignorance, poverty and neglect were creating children who did not get enough to eat and could not be efficient in anything they did, be it schooling or fighting. At the Johanna Street School, a ten minute walk for MPs across Westminster Bridge, children were living on bread, tea, margarine and fried fish. The Medical Office of the London School Board estimated that 90% were too ill, disabled or sick to operate efficiently. The conclusion was to exercise, examine and feed children and take steps to make their parenting better by focusing on the training and welfare of working class women. Only the state could do this, and for the sake of national efficiency, it had to be done, with worries about weakening the sense of self-respect and self-reliance put to one side.

There were no eugenic conclusions implied by the report, but they could be inferred, and they were. Karl Pearson, the most prominent supporter of Galton, concluded that negative eugenics could be used to support the race. State spending on the deserving poor might still be necessary but there was always going to be an underclass for which it would be a waste of money; whether this residuum was created by capitalism or genetics, it could still be eliminated by eugenic policy; fellow socialists Bernard Shaw and H.G. Wells came to the same conclusion. There were some people – an underclass – who would not respond to an improvement in the social environment and social justice; if the state gave them a bath, they would put coal in it.

Events were moving Galton's way in the last decade of his life. While the new Liberal Government was improving conditions for the poor, it was still possible to argue that this was not fast enough. 'Evolution was too slow, and merely improving the race through environment, health and education took far too long. What nature does blindly, slowly, and ruthlessly, man may do providently, quickly, and kindly,' he declared in 1904.

In 1908 Galton published *Memories of my Life*, in which he recognised that 'an appreciative audience is at last to be had'.[8] He was knighted two years before his death in 1911, with an immense scientific reputation, of which his eugenicist work was only a part. The Mental Deficiency Act of 1913 was a piece of social legislation with a eugenic element. It did prevent those whom the state considered 'mentally feeble' or morally defective from reproducing by separating them from the population; it was the type of stern measure that Galton would have approved of, but there was also new legislation by the Liberals such as free school meals and old age pensions designed to improve the race by non-eugenic means.

Galton was married for forty-three years to his wife Louisa. They remained childless, which was eugenically very inefficient for a man who was such a genius. Galton died in his sleep at home in Haslemere in February 1911, after what the newspapers called an 'injudicious airing', which went on to cause bronchial and heart complications. The obituaries agreed that he was the last of the great Victorian scientists; eugenics was seen as one of his many great achievements at the time. The fact that it was picked up and perverted by fascists after his death is not his responsibility – it was a mainstream middle class belief when he died. If you blame Galton for the Nazis, you also need to blame Theodore Roosevelt, William Beveridge and Bertrand Russell. More to the point, as Javier Yanes noted, 'Hitler did not practise eugenics, he practised genocide'.[9]

Conclusion

Words Not Deeds

If you are interested in twentieth century British history, you will understand the slogan *Deeds not Words*. Our Victorian radicals put their faith in the *word*. All of them, apart from the painfully shy George Drysdale and the slightly buttoned-up Edward Truelove, could make speeches to hundreds of people without fear; all of them were authors of some sort. They wrote, they lobbied, they lectured, they petitioned and they published hand bills, tracts, manifestos, magazines and books. Five of our eleven men stood for parliament; Hardie, Dilke and Bradlaugh succeeded and Hyndman and Pankhurst failed. Those who did not speak in the Commons had other ways of disseminating the word – publishing, pulpits, law courts or scientific eminence. For the female radicals, life was harder, but every single one of our women learnt to speak and write, often in opposition to men, and opposed by men. Every single one of them – man or woman – refused compromise with public opinion. Some of them – Holmes, Thompson, Galton and Cobbe – were conservatives but were still progressives in their area of expertise and concern. The key idea was *persuasion*.

They did not set fire to anything or go on hunger strike. No barricades were mounted by our radical Victorians; with the possible exception of Henry Hyndman, whose desire for revolution was never as strong as he claimed and certainly not as strong as his enemies asserted. Those Victorian radicals who survived into the 'direct action' twentieth century did not prosper; Keir Hardie, the pacifist, died in despair in 1915 as the Labour Party supported the Great War; Elizabeth Wolstenholme-Elmy was unable to support the militancy of the WSPU. W.T. Stead was still engaging the modern world in 1912; he was planning a trip to the USA in an attempt to use words to bring about world peace until his choice of modern transatlantic transport let him down.

Our Victorians radicals wanted change via peaceful means. As they were not going to change the world by violence, so they were never going to get into the GCSE and A-Levels or the popular history programmes. The WSPU were men and women of action; the camera was now widely available, and so the evidence for the popular television documentary was everywhere. Yet you cannot find the motivation to slash a picture, storm parliament or starve yourself without the intellectual arguments to support it. The twentieth century campaigns against cruelty, abuse and domestic violence are Victorian. The first petition for women's suffrage was in 1866. The British version of Social Democracy is a nineteenth century compromise. The Trade Unions that challenged the state in the twentieth century were born by resolutions and committee meetings in the nineteenth. Twentieth century deeds were created by nineteenth century words.

References

Chapter One

1. *Whitstable Times and Herne Bay Herald*, 3 March 1888
2. Pert, *Red Cactus*
3. Kingsford, *Health, Beauty and Toilet*
4. Van Arsdel, *Anna B. Kingsford, M.D.: Catholic Convert, Yea or Nay?*
5. ivu.org/history/kingsford/commemoration.html
6. History of Vegetarianism – Anna Kingsford M.D (via ivu.org)
7. Kingsford, Maitland, *Clothed with the Sun*
8. Gandhi, *The Story of My Experiments with Truth*
9. Maitland, *Anna Kingsford, Her Life, Letters, Diary and Work*
10. Ibid
11. Ibid
12. Pert, *Red Cactus*
13. *Woman's Signal*, 14 October 1897

Chapter Two

1. Philips, *Ascent of Woman*
2. Mitchell, *Frances Power Cobbe: Victorian Feminist, Journalist, Reformer*
3. Ibid
4. Ibid
5. That is the equivalent of seven full pages of this book
6. Cobbe, *Life of Frances Power Cobbe*
7. Ibid
8. Ibid
9. *Mary Carpenter of Bristol*, via bristolha.files.wordpress.com

10. Schupf, *Single Women and Social Reform in Mid-Nineteenth Century England*
11. This double standard was to persist until 1923
12. Cobbe, *Celibacy versus Marriage.*
13. richardjohnbr.blogspot.com
14. *Bedfordshire Mercury,* 25 December 1875
15. Cobbe, *Science in Excelsis*
16. *The Animal's Defender and Zoophilist*, Volume 7, 1888
17. *Globe*, 28 October 1892
18. *Gloucester Citizen*, 9 April 1904
19. ukunitarians.org.uk

Chapter Three

1. zythophile.co.uk/2010/01/15/a-short-history-of-bottled-beer
2. Sherlock, *Fifty Years Ago: Or, Erin's Temperance Jubilee*
3. hidden-gems.eu/monaghan%20-%20carlile.pdf
4. Sherlock, *Ann Jane Carlile: A Temperance Pioneer*
5. Blocker, *Alcohol and Temperance in Modern History*
6. Sherlock, *Ann Jane Carlile: A Temperance Pioneer*
7. *Belfast Newsletter*, October 1851
8. Lysaght, *Father Theobald Mathew Apostle of Temperance*
9. *Leeds Times*, 6 June 1846
10. Mcallister, *Picturing the Demon Drink*
11. Bernard, *Prove I'm Not Forgot: Living and Dying in a Victorian City*
12. *Ipswich Temperance Tracts*, 1856
13. Sherlock, *Ann Jane Carlile: A Temperance Pioneer*
14. Mcallister, *Picturing the Demon Drink*
15. *Belfast Telegraph*, 25 October 1947
16. https://ulsterhistorycircle.org.uk/anne-jane-carlile-plaque-unveiling

Chapter Four

1. Jupp, *Death in England*
2. Crookes, *Researches in the Phenomena of Spiritualism*
3. *Spiritualist*, 5 June 1874
4. Crookes, *Researches in the Phenomena of Spiritualism*
5. Bournemouth Spiritualists www.bsnuc.co.uk/page15.html

Chapter Five

1. *Illustrated London News*, July 1974
2. *Manchester Courier and Lancashire General Advertiser*, 29 February 1888
3. Turner, *Rainfall, Plagues, and the Prince of Wales: A Chapter in the Conflict of Religion and Science Journal of British Studies*, Vol. 13, No. 2 (May, 1974)
4. An old prayer for modern medicine (nih.gov)
5. www.gutenberg.org/files/54176/54176-h/54176-h.htm
6. @hellohistoria twitter account
7. *London Evening Standard* via *Edinburgh Evening News*, 6 April 1874
8. *Cork Constitution*, 2 June 1876
9. *Bedfordshire Mercury*, 21 March 1874
10. *Eastern Daily Press*, 3 June 1879
11. *Edinburgh Evening News*, 11 May 1875
12. *Pall Mall Gazette*, 25 April 1902
13. aparcelofribbons.co.uk/2012/08/london-graveyards-the-wonderful-mrs-basil-holmes
14. Malchow, *Public Gardens and Social Action in Late Victorian London*
15. *Ealing Gazette and West Middlesex Observer*, 29 December 1900
16. *Ealing Gazette and West Middlesex Observer*, 24 December 1898

Chapter Six

1. radicalmanchester.wordpress.com/2012/04/08/elizabeth-wolstenholme-elmy-manchesters-free-love-advocate-and-secular-feminist
2. Wright, *Elizabeth Wolstenholme Elmy and the Victorian Feminist Movement*
3. radicalmanchester.wordpress.com/2012/04/08/elizabeth-wolstenholme-elmy-manchesters-free-love-advocate-and-secular-feminist
4. *Common Cause*, 22 March 1918
5. prospectmagazine.co.uk/magazine/lily-maxwell-first-woman-voter-britain-suffrage

6. Prospect Magazine, *The woman who voted in 1868*
7. Holmes, *Natural Born Rebel*
8. *South London Press*, 12 September 1885
9. Pugh, *The Pankhursts: The History of One Radical Family*
10. *South London Press*, 14 November 1885
11. *Manchester Evening News*, 25 January 1887
12. *Clarion*, Saturday 9 July 1898

Chapter Seven

1. Darby, *George Drysdale: Forgotten prophet of the sexual revolution*
2. Ibid
3. Ibid
4. Darby, *Sceptics and libertarians in the day of laissez-faire*
5. Pert, *Red Cactus*
6. *Halifax Guardian*, 14 July 1877
7. www.npg.org.uk/collections/search/person/mp98509/george-drysdale
8. www.nationalgalleries.org/art-and-artists/66284/george-drysdale
9. Bland, *Banishing the Beast: Feminism, Sex and Morality*
10. Besant, *An Autobiography*
11. Griffin, *Bread Winners*
12. Besant, *An Autobiography*
13. Ibid
14. *Reynolds's Newspaper*, 17 November 1889
15. Besant, *An Autobiography*
16. spartacus-educational.com/Wbirth.htm
17. *Labour Leader*, June 17 1904
18. Thompson, *The Rise of Respectable Society*
19. *Reynolds's Newspaper*, 17 November 1889
20. *Manchester Guardian*, Archives 6 July 1928

Chapter Eight

1. *Northern Star and Leeds General Advertiser*, 30 June 1849
2. Chartist Ancestors Blog
3. Stein, *An Anthology of Atheism and Rationalism*
4. *London Investigator*, July 1854

5. *Cork Examiner*, 13 February 1854
6. Notably Bradlaugh, Butler, Wolstenholme-Elmy, and Besant
7. *The Bookseller*, 7 November 1893
8. trove.nla.gov.au/newspaper/article/2464134
9. *Jersey Independent and Daily Telegraph*, March 1858
10. *Portsmouth Evening News*, Monday 28 April 1879
11. *East London Observer*, 18 August 1877
12. *Islington Gazette*, 26 September 1889
13. *Portsmouth Evening News*, 20 April 1899

Chapter Nine

1. Bonner, *Bradlaugh: A Record of his Life and Work*
2. humanism.org.uk
3. *Edinburgh Evening News*, 10 April 1880
4. *Newbury Weekly News and General Advertiser*, 15 April 1880
5. *The Referee*, 11 April 1880
6. Lutgentdorff, *Slaughtering sacred cows: rebutting the narrative of decline in the British secular movement from 1890s to 1930.*
7. Wikipedia: Northampton Election Results
8. *Northampton Mercury*, 6 February 1891
9. www.john-clarke.co.uk/bradlaugh.html

Chapter Ten

1. Fawcett, *Josephine Butler: Her Work and Principles*
2. Butler, *Recollections of George Butler*
3. *London Calling*: Josephine Butler (general-southerner.blogspot.com)
4. *Woman's Signal*, 13 September 1894
5. *Western Daily Press*, 9 September 1862
6. Peacy, *Josephine Butler: The Great Feminist* (international-review. icrc.org)
7. Neal, *Sex, Gender, and Religion: Josephine Butler Revisited*
8. *Liverpool Daily Post,* 19 September 1867
9. Benjamin Jowett, letter to Florence Nightingale, quoted in Bell, *Josephine Butler. Flame of Fire*
10. *Liverpool Daily Post*, 15 November 1869
11. Hamilton, *Opposition to the Contagious Diseases Acts, 1864-1886*

12. *The Shield*, 14 March 1870
13. *The Shield*, 9 May I 870.
14. *Leicester Daily Post*, 2 October 1891
15. *Woman's Dreadnought*, 24 October 1914
16. *Woman's Signal*, 17 December 1896
17. Butler, 'The Double Standard of Morality' in *The Philanthropist* (1886)

Chapter Eleven

1. *The Scotsman*, Thursday 19 November 1925
2. *Northern Echo*, July 5 1999
3. Phegley, *Courtship and Marriage in Victorian England*
4. Stead, *Maiden Tribute of Modern Babylon*
5. Josephine Butler on W.T. Stead
6. *Framlingham Weekly News*, 12 November 1910
7. *The Sketch*, 22 September 1909
8. *South London Chronicle*, 11 January 1902
9. *Hastings and St Leonards Observer*, 13 September 1913
10. *Hampshire Telegraph*, 21 April 1933
11. *Leeds Mercury*, 8 May 1914

Chapter Twelve

1. *Portsmouth Evening News*, 16 September 1878
2. Headlam, *The Ballet,Theory of Theatrical Dancing*
3. *Derry Journal*, 30 January 1878
4. Today in London's rebel history: May 19, 2016
5. Tyson, *Bernard Shaw's Book Reviews*
6. Sinnot, *The Rev. Stewart Headlam and Friends* (existentialistmelbourne. org/pdf/2006_August.pdf)
7. Headlam, *Christian Socialism*
8. Osborne,*The Life of Father Dolling* (via anglicanhistory.org)
9. *The Letters of Sidney and Beatrice Webb*
10. henrygeorge.org
11. *Burton Chronicle*, 12–26 September 1895
12. Leveson, *I Want a Change of Scene*
13. Stewart and Martha (stmargarets.london/archives/2009/05/stewart_ and_martha.html)
14. http://www.existentialistmelbourne.org/pdf/2006_August.pdf

Chapter Thirteen

1. Holman, *Keir Hardie: Labour's Greatest Hero?*
2. Wheen, *Karl Marx*
3. Hyndman, *The Record of an Adventurous Life*
4. libcom.org/files/SU03.15.2.Skelly.pdf
5. marxists.org/archive/hyndman/1881/england/index.html
6. *Morning Post*, 14 April 1888
7. *Peterhead Sentinel and General Advertiser for Buchan District* May 1888
8. Lindset, *William Morris, His life and Work*
9. Holroyd, *Bernard Shaw: The One Volume Edition*
10. www.unionhistory.info/timeline
11. Young, *People, place and party: the social democratic federation 1884–1911*
12. *South Wales Daily News*, 9 August 1892
13. *Derbyshire Courier*, 14 July 1894
14. *Bury and Norwich Post*, 3 July 1894
15. *Leeds Times*, 7 July 1894
16. *Penny Illustrated Paper*, 7 July 1894
17. Winder, *Bloody Foreigners*
18. Hyndman, *Trade Union Unrest and the Class War*
19. Holmes, *Natural Born Rebel*

Chapter Fourteen

1. Murphy, *Shooting Victoria: Madness, Mayhem, and the Rebirth of the British Monarchy*
2. Charles Dilke (spartacus-educational.com)
3. Gosmann, *Republicanism in the Nineteenth Century* (JSTOR 1962)
4. Dilke was to be cremated himself
5. *Republicanism in the Nineteenth Century*
6. Charles Dilke (spartacus-educational.com)
7. Jenkins, *Dilke: A Victorian Tragedy*
8. Corbett, *On Crawford v. Crawford and Dilke,* 1886 (via branchcollective.org)
9. *Gloucester Citizen*, 21 February 1894
10. One Person, Many Votes: Plural Voting In The UK | A Venerable Puzzle (wordpress.com)

Chapter Fifteen

1. Twitter @RichardDawkins, 16 February 2020
2. Holt, *New Yorker*, January 17, 2005
3. Aberdeen
4. Galton, *Statistical Inquiries into the Efficacy of Prayer Fortnightly Review*, vol. 12, pp. 1872
5. Newsome, *The Victorian World Picture*
6. Webb, *The Decay of Capitalist Civilisation*
7. The British Physical Deterioration Report (1904)
8. Eugenics and Final Years – The Galton Institute website
9. bbvaopenmind.com/en/science/bioscience/the-era-of-eugenics-when-pseudoscience-became-law

Bibliography

Attwood, N, *The Prostitute's Body: Rewriting Prostitution in Victorian Britain* (Pickering and Chatto, 2019)

Bernard, S, *To Prove I'm Not Forgot* (History Press, 2013)

Besant, A, *Biographical Sketches* (Broadview, 2009)

Black, R, *Scandal, Salvation and Suffrage: The Amazing Women of the Temperance Movement* (Matador, 2015)

Blocker, J, *Alcohol and Temperance in Modern History* (ABC-CLIO, 2003)

Bonner, H, *Charles Bradlaugh: A Record of His Life and Work* (Unwin, 1895)

Bonner, H, *Penalties upon Opinion* (Watts, 1912)

Bostridge, M, *Florence Nightingale: The Woman and Her Legend* (Penguin, 2020)

Brow, K D, (ed) *The First Labour Party 1906–1914* (Routledge, 1985)

Cobbe, F P, *Life of Frances Power Cobbe* (Bentley, 1894)

Cohen, S, *That's funny you don't look anti-Semitic* (2005 via https://libcom.org)

Crawford, C, *The Women's Suffrage Movement: A Reference Guide 1866–1928* (UCL Press, 1999)

Darby, R, *George Drysdale, forgotten prophet of the sexual revolution* via www.academia.edu/12850842

Darby, R, *Sceptics and libertarians in the days of laissez-faire*: (via www.academia.edu/37741391)

Finn, M C, *After Chartism: Class and Nation in English Radical Politics* (Cambridge UP, 1993)

Gates, B, *Kindred Nature: Victorian and Edwardian Women Embrace the Living World* (Chicago UP, 1998)

Gossman, N, 'Republicanism in Nineteenth Century England', *International Review of Social History*, Vol. 7, No. 1, via JSTOR

Gregory, J, *Anna Bonus Kingsford and her Circle* (via www.academia. edu/3862213)

Guenon, R, *Theosophy, History of a Pseudo Religion* (Sophia Perennis, 2004)

Gwynn, S L, *The Life of the Rt. Hon. Sir Charles W. Dilke* (Library of Alexandria, 1917)

Hamilton, S, *Frances Power Cobbe and Victorian Feminism* (Palgrave, 2006)

Hamilton, S, *Criminals, Idiots, Women and Minors* (Broadview, 2004)

Hamilton, M, *Opposition to the Contagious Diseases Acts, 1864–1886*

Hewitt, M, *The Victorian World* (Routledge, 2012)

Holam, B, *Keir Hardie: Labour's Greatest Hero?* (Lion, 2010)

Holmes, I, *The London Burial Grounds* (1896)

Holmes, R, *Sylvia Pankhurst: Natural Born Rebel* (Bloomsbury, 2020)

Holton, S, *Free Love and Victorian Feminism: The Divers Matrimonial of Elizabeth Wolstenholme and Ben Elmy* (via JSTOR)

Holyoake, G, *Sixty Years of an Agitator's Life* (Unwin, 1893)

Howe, D, *British Workers and the Independent Labour Party* (Manchester UP, 1984)

Hyndman, H, *England for All* (Gilbert and Rivington, 1881)

Jupp, C, *Death in England* (Manchester UP, 1999)

Jütte, R, *Contraception: A History* (Polity Press, 2018)

Kent, S, *Sex and Suffrage in Britain, 1860–1914* (Princeton UP, 2014)

Kent, S, *Gender and Power in Britain 1640–1990* (Routledge, 1999)

Laqueur, T, *The Work of the Dead: A Cultural History of Mortal Remains* (Princeton UP, 2015)

MacKenzie, D, *Eugenics in Britain* (via JSTOR)

Malchow, H L, *Public Gardens and Social Action in Late Victorian London Victorian Studies* (via JSTOR)

Martin, J, *The role of women in education of the working classes – 1870–1904* (The Open University, 1992)

Mather, H, *Patron Saint of Prostitutes Josephine Butler and a Victorian Scandal* (History Press, 2014)

McAllister, A, *Picturing the Demon Drink: How Children were Shown Temperance Principles in the Band of Hope* (Visual Resources, 2012)

Mitchell, S, *Frances Power Cobbe, Victorian Feminist, Journalist and Reformer* (University of Virginia Press, 2004)

Morrison, J, *Eminent English Liberals in and out of Parliament* (Library of Alexandria, 1880)

Niblett, B, *Dare to Stand Alone: The Story of Charles Bradlaugh, Atheist and Republican* (Kramedart Press, 2011)

Bryan, P, *What would Keir Hardie Say?* (Kier Hardie Society, 2015)

Norman, R, *The Victorian Christian Socialists* (Cambridge UP, 2002)

Orens, J, *Stewart Headlam's Radical Anglicanism* (Illinois UP, 2003)

Owen, A, *The Darkened Room: Women, Power, and Spiritualism in Late Victorian England* (Chicago UP, 1989)

Pert, A, *Red Cactus; The Life of Anna Kingsford* (Books and Writers, 2006)

Phillips, M, The *Ascent of Women* (Abacus, 2004)

Potter, R, (ed) *Prudes on the Prowl: Fiction and Obscenity in England, 1850 to the Present Day* (Oxford, 2013)

Purvis, J, *Emmeline Pankhurst* (Taylor and Francis, 2003)

Rappaport, H, *Encyclopaedia of Women Social Reformers* (ABC-CIO, 2001)

Raw, L, *Striking a Light: The Bryant and May Matchwomen and their Place in History* (Bloomsbury, 2011)

Reid, F, *Keir Hardie: The Making of a Socialist* (Routledge, 1978)

Robertson, J, *Charles Bradlaugh: A Record of his Life and Work* (Unwin, 1908)

Rodlif, D, *The Maiden Tribute of Modern Babylon* (www.academia.edu/25358523)

Rosen, A, *Rise Up, Women!: The Militant Campaign of the Women's Social and Political Union* (Routledge, 2013)

Sanger, S, 'The Vision of George Drysdale', *Birth Control Review*, Aug. 1923

Schwartz L, *Freethought, Free Love and Feminism: Secularist Debates on Marriage and Sexual Morality, England c.1850–1889* (via://www.academia.edu/4403946)

Second, J, *Victorian Sensation: The Extraordinary Publication, Reception, and Secret Authorship of Vestiges of the Natural History of Creation* (University of Chicago Press, 2000)

Smith, J, *Crossing the Border of Citizenship: Helen Taylor, the Independent Radical Democrat Candidate for Camberwell North, 1885* (via Open Library of Humanities)

Spence, C, *The Heretic's Feast A History of Vegetarianism* (University Press of New England, 1996)

Stein, G, *Freethought in the United Kingdom and the Commonwealth* (Greenwood Press, 1981)

Stephens, M, *Imagine There's No Heaven: How Atheism Helped Create the Modern World* (St Martin's Press, 2014)

Swartz, L, *Infidel Feminism* (Manchester UP, 2017)

Tweedie, S, *History of the Temperance Movement in Great Britain and Ireland* (1862)

Tyson, B, *Bernard Shaw's Book Reviews* (Pennsylvania State UP, 1991)

Van Arsdel, R, '*Anna B. Kingsford, M.D.: Catholic Convert, Yea or Nay?' Victorian Review* (2001)

Van Drenth, A, *Socialist Antisemitism and its discontents in England* (1884–98)

Welshman, J, *Underclass: A history of the excluded since 1880* (Bloomsbury, 2006)

Wheeler, J M, *A Biographical Dictionary of Freethinkers* (Library of Alexandria, 2009)

Wheen, F, *Karl Marx* (Fourth Estate, 2010)

Winder, R, *Bloody Foreigners* (Little Brown, 2004)

Young, D, *People, place and party: the social democratic federation 1884–1911* (Durham University, 2003)

Websites

anglocelt.ie (Carlile)
aparcelofribbons.co.uk (Holmes)
churchtimes.co.uk (Butler)
churchtimes.co.uk (Butler)
electricscotland.com (Hardie)
embryo.asu.edu (The Embryo Project encyclopaedia)
galtoninstitute.org.uk
h2g2.com (Stead)
happycow.net (Kingsford)
heathertracey.co.uk (Cook)
henrysalt.co.uk (Kingsford)
historyofwomen.co.uk (Butler)

historyofwomen.org (birth control)
hopeuk.org (Carlile)
irishwomenshistory.org (Butler)
ivu.org (Kingsford)
leicestersecularsocierty.org.uk
marxists.org/archive (Hyndman)
mysteriousbritian.co.uk (Cook)
pasttenseblog.wordpress.com/
queerbio.com (Cobb)
salavationarmy.co.uk (Stead, Butler)
secularism.com
spartacus-educational.com
sueyounghistories.com (Bradlaugh)
tolpuddlemartyrs.org.uk (Dilke)
victorianweb.org
victorianweb.org (Kingsford)
womanandhersphere.com (Cobbe)

Index